10649514

DISCARDED
THE
UNIVERSITY OF WINNIPEG
PORTAGE & BALMORAL
WINNIPEG, MAN.   R3B 2E9
CANADA

REGIONS OF THE IMAGINATION

THE DEVELOPMENT OF BRITISH RURAL FICTION

PR
830
.P3-
K45
1988

W.J. KEITH

Regions of the Imagination

THE DEVELOPMENT OF BRITISH RURAL FICTION

UNIVERSITY OF TORONTO PRESS
Toronto Buffalo London

© University of Toronto Press 1988
Toronto Buffalo London
Printed in Canada

ISBN 0-8020-2654-0

∞

Printed on acid-free paper

Canadian Cataloguing in Publication Data

Keith, W.J. (William John), 1934–
Regions of the imagination
Includes bibliographical references and index.
ISBN 0-8020-2654-0

1. English fiction – History and criticism.
2. Pastoral fiction, English – History and criticism.
3. Country life in literature. 4. Nature in
literature. I. Title.

PR830.P3K45 1988   823   C88-094334-0

CONTENTS

PREFACE

This book, though complete in itself, is the third in a series of volumes devoted to English rural literature. The first, *The Rural Tradition* (1974), focused upon the main writers of non-fiction prose and argued that, when considered together, they formed a distinct and coherent 'line.' The second, *The Poetry of Nature* (1980), made a related point while concentrating on poems that record an interchange between man and the natural world. The present volume brings a similar viewpoint to bear upon rural fiction with special emphasis on regional presentation (novels with predominantly urban settings, however 'regional,' lie outside its scope). As in the previous books, then, I have found it essential to discuss the authors represented in terms of each other. Such writers as Walter Scott, Emily Brontë, George Eliot, Thomas Hardy, and D.H. Lawrence are generally considered within the history of English prose-fiction as a whole; when, however, they are viewed within a specifically regional context, other qualities emerge, and it is therefore desirable to examine them in relation to lesser-known figures like R.D. Blackmore, Eden Phillpotts, Sheila Kaye-Smith, Constance Holme, and Mary Webb. Once again it seems to me that a loose but palpable tradition thereby becomes visible, with the figure of Scott as dominating a presence for regionalists as that of Wordsworth in the subsequent history of 'nature-poetry.' There are, therefore, numerous cross-references between chapter and chapter, and, although individual chapters can be sampled on their own, the book is intended to be read as a whole that contains a developing argument.

The obvious problem confronting any writer on English regional fiction arises from the daunting amount of material available. Much of this is of little or no permanent interest, but its variety and bulk often lead the inquirer into extended and ultimately not very profitable questions of categorization. Should one concentrate on the wood or on the tallest or more beautiful of the trees? The alternatives are well described by Lucien Leclaire, the encyclopaedic surveyor of the field, in his 'avant-propos' to his study, *Le Roman régionaliste dans les Iles Britanniques, 1800–1950* (Paris: Société d'édition 'Les Belles Lettres,' 1954): 'L'importance des documents dont je disposais était telle que je dus envisager deux méthodes. Fallait-il apporter la majeure partie de ma documentation, et donner par là à mon travail un volume considérable? Ou bien devais-je me contenter de choisir quelques auteurs-jalons et fonder sur l'étude de leur oeuvre toutes mes conclusions?' (p 11). Leclaire himself opted for the first method, believing that the second would lead to distortion. Major authors, he argued, were more representative of themselves than of the movement to which they belonged. Perhaps so, but his following of the more intimidating path allows me to explore the second. I have therefore contented myself with a brief chapter of general introduction and have then concentrated on the more important writings in the genre. In approaching the subject, I have kept the following question in mind: if we concentrate on the more prominent and successful practitioners of regional fiction, including many who have gained an assured place within the national literature, do we find that they share some common qualities? In other words, my interest is not so much in the nature of literary regionalism itself as in writings that, without losing their intensely regional quality, are accepted as more than 'merely' regional.

This inquiry uncovered a paradox. Most writers on regional fiction have assumed, as I originally did, that the movement was firmly anchored in realistic conventions. But I soon came to realize that a considerable number of regionalists employed narrative structures borrowed from the tradition of 'romance.' In most regional work, indeed, I find a discernible and fruitful tension between these two not always compatible extremes. This tension takes many forms, however, and I have therefore resisted the temptation to establish rigid definitions of the two terms – or, indeed, of the genres of 'romance' and 'novel.' The writers themselves were clearly content with the kind of rough and ready distinction employed by Scott in his 'Essay on Romance' written for the 1824 *Encyclopaedia Britannica*. There he defined *Romance* as 'a fictitious narrative, in prose or verse; the interest of which turns upon marvellous and uncommon incidents' and *Novel* as 'a fictitious narrative, different from the Romance, because the events are accommodated to the ordinary train of human events, and the modern state of society.' Regional fiction tends to swing like a pendulum between these poles, and as a consequence the landscapes presented vary from meticulously accurate representations that can be both identified in the field and plotted on maps to the more elusive and ultimately more interesting 'regions of the imagination' that give the book its title.

Because most of the novels considered here are available in numerous editions, it seemed best to identify quotations by chapter- rather than page-number. In each instance I have followed whatever is the normal modern practice so far as chapter numbering is concerned; in some cases, earlier editions number by volume, but the interested reader should not encounter much difficulty in checking individual passages. (In the few cases where significant variants and revised texts are involved, the point is clarified in notes.)

Part of the first chapter appeared in somewhat different form in a paper given at Nipissing University College in 1983 and published in Vincent D. Sharman, ed., *Nature and the Literary Imagination* (Nipissing University College, Ontario, 1984). Chapter six contains material that originally formed part of an essay, 'A Regional Approach to Hardy's Fiction,' in Dale Kramer, ed., *Critical Approaches to Hardy's Fiction* (London: Macmillan, 1979). Parts of chapter nine first appeared in 'Another Way of Looking: Lawrence and the Rural,' in Michael Ballin, ed., *D.H. Lawrence's 'Women in Love': Contexts and Criticism* (Wilfrid Laurier University, Ontario, [1982]), and a highly concentrated version of chapter ten was published as 'John Cowper Powys and the Regional Tradition' in *Powys Notes*, 2 (Fall 1986). Otherwise, the material is published here for the first time.

In conclusion, I would like to offer special thanks to Jane and Michael Millgate for reading much of the manuscript and for saving me from a number of errors and infelicities; also to James Carley, who kindly read the Powys chapter. They are not, of course, responsible for any inadequacies that doubtless remain. And, as always, thanks to my wife Hiroko, who has been dragged 'thorough bush, thorough brier' on a number of uncomfortable rural literary pilgrimages in the years during which this book was being prepared.

W.J.K.

English Department, University College, University of Toronto

ACKNOWLEDGMENTS

This book has been published with the help of a grant from the Canadian Federation for the Humanities, using funds provided by the Social Sciences and Humanities Research Council of Canada.

For permission to quote from the writings of D.H. Lawrence, acknowledgments are made to Laurence Pollinger Limited and the Estate of Frieda Lawrence Ravagli, and to the following publishers:

Cambridge University Press (for *The Lost Girl, St. Mawr and Other Stories,* and *The White Peacock*);

Viking/Penguin (for *Collected Letters, Lady Chatterley's Lover, The Rainbow, Sons and Lovers,* and *Women in Love*);

William Heinemann (for *Phoenix* and *Phoenix II*).

For permission to quote from the writings of John Cowper Powys, acknowledgments are made to the Estate of John Cowper Powys, and to the following publishers:

The Bodley Head Ltd (for *A Glastonbury Romance* and *Owen Glendower*);

Harper and Row Inc. (for *Wolf Solent*);

Macdonald and Jane's (for *The Autobiography of John Cowper Powys, The Brazen Head, Maiden Castle, Rodmoor, Visions and Revisions*);

Pan Books [Picador] (for *After My Fashion*);

Village Press (for *Letters to C. Benson Roberts, Letters to His Brother Llewelyn, Obstinate Cymric, Porius, Rabelais, Suspended Judgments,* and *Wood and Stone*).

REGIONS OF THE IMAGINATION

ONE

Introduction

DEFINING THE REGIONAL

At first sight, the defintion of 'regionalism'and 'the regional novel' promises to be a relatively easy task. We are concerned, surely, with fiction set in a distinctive locality – one that takes on, through the power of literature, an independent imaginative existence which renders the setting at least as important as (and possibly more important than) any of the more traditional elements of narrative. No sooner have we said this, however, than a number of perplexing questions begin to arise: can a region be too large – or too small? can a novelist be master (or mistress) of more than one region? does a writer have to be born and brought up in a region in order to portray it adequately? can a single novel establish a region or must a novelist produce a series of books with a common background? is literary regionalism, in any case, a matter of background or should regional aspects be more prominent than the word 'background' generally implies? might not, indeed, the regional novel be adequately defined as fiction in which background becomes foreground – or even participant? Moreover, other words related to 'regional' but not identical with it can also raise problems: is there any precise distinction that can be drawn between 'regional' on the one hand and such adjectives as 'provincial,' 'parochial,' 'topographical,' or 'local' on the other? I hope to cast light on these and other questions in the course of this book, but some of them are so crucial that their implications must be discussed before we can proceed with any confidence to a consideration of specific regional authors.

First of all, what is a region? This is the fundamental question, and an obvious place to begin is with dictionary definition. Here, however, the *Oxford English Dictionary* proves somewhat unhelpful, though it is interesting – and surprising – to discover that the earliest use of 'regionalism' that it records occurs as late as 1881.[1] 'Region' itself has, of course, a much longer history, but the relevant definitions are disappointingly vague at the edges: 'A large tract of land; a country; a more or less defined part of the earth's surface, now esp. as distinguished by certain natural features, climatic conditions, a special fauna or flora, or the like ... An area, space or place, of more or less definite extent or character.' This vagueness ('more or less') stems no doubt from the simple but awkward fact that geographical regions bear no necessary relation to political or administrative boundaries.

This difficulty is often reflected in regional writing. The *Life of Thomas Hardy* (ostensibly by his second wife but written in the main by Hardy himself) records that the novelist originally employed the term 'Wessex' because there was no available word for the area which he recognized as forming a distinct entity but which extended over parts of at least six modern counties. Indeed, Hardy claimed that 'he had grown to forget the crossing of county boundaries within the ancient kingdom – in this respect being quite unlike the poet Barnes, who was "Dorset" emphatically.'[2] Yet William Barnes had made substantially the same point when discussing areas linked by a common dialect: 'The forms of folk speech do not change at the map boundaries of Counties, but rather at ridges of hills and streams.'[3] Exmoor, the setting of *Lorna Doone*, extends over parts of both Devon and Somerset (the county boundary, in fact, runs down the middle of Badgworthy Water), and, when the book became popular, Blackmore was plagued with letters arguing the claims of the rival counties for the distinction of providing the landscape for his romance. Similarly, Sheila Kaye-Smith's series of regional novels set in the area known geographically as 'the Weald' constantly move back and forth over the boundaries of Sussex and Kent. 'East Sussex,' she remarks significantly, 'is far more like West Kent than it is like West Sussex.'[4] 'Border-country,' as we shall see, becomes a valuable concept for many regional novelists. It is clear, then, that literary regionalism has a good deal in common with geographical regionalism but much less with its socio-political counterpart.

These three basic divisions of the subject – socio-political, geographical, and literary – are distinguished and discussed by F.W. Morgan in his pioneering article entitled 'Three Aspects of Regional Consciousness' (1939). He argues that the rise to prominence of all these was 'roughly contemporaneous' in the half-century immediately preceding his study, and that they 'have enough characteristics in common to justify the assumption that they bear some relation to each other.' Their most important feature is that 'they all show signs of a developing consciousness of the smaller units of the earth.'[5] He sees political regionalism as taking various forms ranging from what he calls the 'spiritual' (the revival of decayed and decaying languages, etc.) to the economic ('an improved means of ordering the material side of social life'),[6] and notes that geographical regionalism increasingly stresses the interaction between human activity and the local conditions of rock-formation, soil, and climate. Literary regionalism naturally contains elements common to the other two. Morgan, indeed, offers a useful tentative definition when he describes the regional novelist as one who produces 'a living picture of the unity of place and people, through work.'[7]

Before passing on to a more specific consideration of literary, and especially fictional, regionalism, it may be helpful at this point to quote a definition by H.J. Massingham, himself a rural writer but not a novelist. Regionalism, he insists,

> means all the factors of a given region, and each is woven into the other. The parts, the units, the cells, are not separable, and the region itself is what binds them together into a living whole. The region is built up out of twin irreducible essentials, its geology and the soils evolved from it in correspondence with the native types of vegetation. These in turn condition the architecture, husbandry and crafts of the region, expressed in a variety of forms that extend over their general history and prehistory but are included within a single general framework – the land and the rock. Thus a specific quality manifests itself in the complete presentation of a region, in precisely the same way as it does in a work of art. A region thus presented *is* a work of art ... [8]

For my purpose here, of course, Massingham's insistence on the essential connection between regionalism and art is crucial; furthermore, it should not be assumed that this association is determined by the preconceptions of a literary man. E.W. Gilbert, a geographer who insists that geography is one of the humanities, makes a similar point. He argues that 'the art of describing a region ... is quite as difficult as the art of describing the character of a human individual' and notes that 'the geographer often speaks of the "personality" of a region and this is exactly what the novelist has brought out so strongly.'[9] Moreover, since regional geographers have moved away from the idea of a 'natural' region, believing that 'human occupation has transformed almost every region wholly or at least in part,'[10] the novelist with his emphasis on the relation between human beings and their environment is likely to find regional differences important to his art, and by the same token can provide material which, apart from its literary merits, will prove valuable to students of the region portrayed.

Two years after Morgan's article appeared (and, one suspects, independently), Phyllis Bentley, herself an accomplished Yorkshire novelist, produced her

P.E.N. booklet, *The English Regional Novel* (1941). Her discussion is worth considering in some detail, partly because it remains to this day a useful introductory survey of its subject, partly because the very qualifications and disagreements that it provokes can lead to valuable new insights. She extends the period of intensive literary regionalism further back than Morgan ('I am inclined to believe at present that the golden age of the English regional novel is approximately 1840 to 1940'),[11] but the characteristics she identifies, though more elaborate than his, are remarkably similar. She agrees with him that regional differences become a particularly fruitful subject for writers in the nineteenth century because certain anti-regional developments (notably the extension of the road- and railway-systems and the increasing mobility achieved thereby) made the differences between region and region more evident while in the very process of minimizing or destroying them. She accounts for the regional diversity of the British Isles in terms of the numerous different racial groups that went to make up the British people and the remarkable geological-cum-geographical variants existing within so small an area. She emphasizes the importance of dialect in contributing to a sense of regional distinction, while her insistence that 'a trade in England is often conterminous with a region' (p. 38) connects with Morgan's assertion that 'the true regional novel has people at work as an essential material.'[12]

Bentley's initial definition of the regional novel seems innocuous enough: 'It is a novel which, concentrating on a particular part, a particular region, of a nation, depicts the life of that region in such a way that the reader is conscious of the characteristics which are unique to that region and differentiate it from others of the common motherland' (p. 7).' But when she goes on to elaborate upon this basic definition, her rigorous insistence on uniform criteria for establishing regional content creates difficulties. Dividing the elements of any novel into 'character,' 'plot,' 'setting,' 'narrative,' and 'theme,' she tests the extent to which each of these elements may be designated regional. Particular emphasis is placed on plots, which should 'depend on the region for their causality' (p. 21). This leads her, for instance, to claim Charlotte Brontë's *Shirley* as the 'first great English regional novel' (p. 14) rather than Emily's *Wuthering Heights*, which passes her test triumphantly so far as 'setting' is concerned but is shown to be limited in 'dialect' and 'character' (only the servant Joseph qualifies here) and fails lamentably in terms of 'plot' and 'theme.' *Shirley*, by contrast, passes in all areas except 'theme,' which is also a stumbling-block for so obvious a regionalist as Thomas Hardy. While an intimate connection between the actions of the characters and the region in which they live may reasonably be expected, to require a plot to be *uniquely* confined to a particular area is surely, except in the case of historical fiction, to ask too much. Indeed, if one were to carry this requirement to an extreme, the only novels I can think of that would qualify (besides Thomas Hughes's *The Scouring of the White Horse*, which depends on the traditional customs associated with the White Horse of Uffington, one of the few hill-figures of unquestioned antiquity in England) are several by John Cowper Powys, notably *A Glastonbury Romance*.

Certain further limitations in Bentley's assumptions about regionalism become manifest in her concluding statement about the merits of the regional novel. 'Its first great merit,' she claims, 'is, of course, its brilliant illuminations of English landscape' (p. 45). This is indisputable, though it is worth noting that the illuminations in question need not be primarily descriptive. John Cowper Powys wrote in *Visions and Revisions* (1915) of 'that tendency to "describe scenery," which is so tedious an aspect of most modern work,'[13] and the sense of the moors in *Wuthering Heights* does not come to us through formal description of landscape. This first merit, then, is acceptable only if we do not interpret it too narrowly as advocating an emphasis on descriptive realism.

The suspicion that Bentley may have assumed if not consciously intended a limiting emphasis here is strengthened by her next statement, which needs to be quoted in full:

> Its transcendent merit is that of verisimilitude. A detailed faithfulness to reality, a conscientious presentation of phenomena as they really happen in ordinary life on a clearly defined spot of real earth, a firm rejection of the vague, the high-flown and the sentimental, an equally firm contact with the real: these are the marks of the regional novel, which occupies in fiction the place of the Dutch school of painters in art. (p. 45)

Verisimilitude is, admittedly, an important aspect of most regional fiction, but it is not, I think, a necessary part. The concern for realistic portrayal dominates one strand in literary regionalism. It is conspicuous, for example, in much of George Eliot and in parts of Hardy (both employ the analogy to Dutch painting, Eliot in *Adam Bede* [ch. 17], Hardy in the subtitle of *Under the Greenwood Tree* – 'A Rural Painting of the Dutch School'); it is also crucial to Eden Phillpotts and the later Sheila Kaye-Smith. But one has only to mention the names of other novelists whose work can legitimately be included in regional fiction – Sir Walter Scott, Emily Brontë, R.D. Blackmore, Mary Webb, and John Cowper Powys himself – to realize that 'romance' and regionalism frequently go hand in hand. Phillpotts presents Dartmoor with documentary accuracy, while Blackmore transforms Exmoor into a rich imaginative world; Kaye-Smith's weald of Kent and Sussex is a transcript of reality, but Webb's Shropshire has undergone an artistic metamorphosis. This is not to say that elements of realism are absent from the work of those writers in whom 'romance' is strong – literary pilgrims would hardly flock to the so-called Doone Valley or the original of Sarn Mere if their creators had severed all contact with geographical reality – but it is important to insist that photographic realism is only one strand in regional fiction, and that verisimilitude is an inadequate and limiting criterion.

Bentley's final 'merit' also contains a realistic bias, and probably reflects the wartime conditions during which her study was written: 'Lastly, the regional novel is essentially democratic. It expresses a belief that the ordinary man and the ordinary woman are interesting and worth depicting' (p. 45). This is valuable in reiterating Morgan's concern with characters at work, and we certainly get a sense in most regional fiction of the everyday world of manual labour; one thinks of the scenes in the carpentry workshop, the dairy, and the farm kitchen in *Adam Bede*, the presentation of harvesting, milking, and swede-topping in *Tess of the d'Urbervilles*, the portrayal of working communities in Phillpotts and Kaye-Smith. Nor are these confined to the 'realistic' strand in regional writing: there are comparable scenes in Blackmore and Webb. But Bentley's 'ordinary' is in need of qualification. While it is true that regional fiction frequently concentrates on the working people of the countryside (and, indeed, extended the range of fiction in so doing), we must beware of what Glen Cavaliero has wittily described as 'literary peasant-spotting.'[14] The great houses are as much a part of their regions as the small cottages, and their inhabitants, even when not confined by local society and local boundaries, can hardly be excluded from regional fiction. Admittedly, they may lack the sharpness of regional distinction that we find in those humbler characters who are, as it were, 'bound to the soil.' None the less, Arthur Donnithorne, the young squire, is as integral to *Adam Bede* as the name character or Hetty Sorrel; while Hardy may be less successful in depicting characters like Mrs Charmond and the Stoke-d'Urbervilles than in portraying Giles Winterbourne and Tess, he recognizes their essential place in the Wessex scheme. Nor should we forget (and certainly not disqualify) the novels of Constance Holme that so often centre upon estate-management. 'Pastoral,' wrote Dr Johnson in *The Rambler*, 'admits of all ranks of persons, because persons of all ranks inhabit the country,'[15] and in this case what applies to the pastoral also applies to the regional.

But overemphasis on the 'ordinary' must be qualified in another way as well. I have already noted that regional fiction encompasses romantic as well as realistic elements, and this implies that it can include not only the ordinary but the extraordinary. Scott's Highlands and Lowlands, Blackmore's Doone Valley and Plover's Barrows Farm, Constance Holme's 'green gates of vision' alongside the workaday world of the country estates, John Cowper Powys's enchanted Maiden Castle adjoining an authentic Dorchester, all suggest that assumptions about verisimilitude and the ordinary have only a limited validity when applied to the astonishing variety possible within regional fiction.

Moreover, there is one aspect of the regional novel that Bentley curiously neglects. Though she writes briefly about the historical development of the British Isles and the racial variety of its inhabitants, she has virtually nothing to say about time and change. This is especially surprising since, after all, a region has evolved its characteristic features – which distinguish it from other areas – through the passage of time. At one extreme, there are the vast geological ages that determined the physical features of a particular countryside; at the other, the changes taking place in a decade or two, changes for which human beings are responsible and which lead to sudden prosperity or sudden decline. The former rarely appear directly, though they are related to the concern for archaeology and prehistory in the novels of Hardy, Phillpotts, and Powys. Examples of the latter include Hardy's presentation of the agricultural depression in the late nineteenth century, Constance Holme's analysis of the fate of the landed estates written, as she notes in her preface to the World's Classics edition of *The Lonely Plough*, 'at almost the last moment of the old order of things,' and Sheila Kaye-Smith's portrait of the betrayal of agriculture after the First World War in *The End of the House of Alard* and *The Ploughman's Progress*.

A common complaint against the regional novel, however, is that it tries to ignore time and change, initiating what Raymond Williams has called 'a sustaining flight to the edges of the island, to Cornwall or to Cumberland,'[16] an escapist retreat to the backwaters where the illusion of a stable regional world could still be kept up. Evidence can obviously be assembled in support of this view; Hardy's early titles, *Under the Greenwood Tree* and *Far from the Madding Crowd*, document the continuing interest in (and so, perhaps, a continuing need for) this kind of nostalgic solace. But Hardy's main concern in his Wessex novels is change (generally decline) in the agricultural world. This necessitates the contrasting of past and present that seems endemic to regional writing, and also explains why regional novelists often subsume into their profession the roles of archivist and local historian. Indeed, we may go so far as to state that, although the impulse to catch the moment before it passes away is frequent in regional writing (as it is, of course, in many other branches of literature), when we see a rural community – generally a village – caught in an artistic eternity like the proverbial fly in amber, we are in the presence of a *limited* regionalism. It is not unreasonable to assert that the best regional novels are concerned not with a static rural society but with a countryside in process.

Despite its shortcomings, Phyllis Bentley's booklet remains valuable as a pioneering survey of its subject. More detailed – indeed, exhaustive in its comprehensiveness – is Lucien Leclaire's *Le Roman régionaliste dans les Iles*

Britanniques, 1800–1950 (1954). Leclaire traces the history of regionalism as an element in British fiction and attempts to classify regional narrative into various types. For the last half of his time-span these comprise 'le régionalisme pittoresque: 1870–1895' (including Blackmore and Hardy), 'le régionalisme attendri: 1890–1914' (including Phillpotts), 'le régionalisme réaliste et natura-liste: 1900–1925' (including Kaye-Smith), and 'le régionalisme interprétatif: 1920–1939' (which brings together an unlikely company including D.H. Lawrence, Constance Holme, John Cowper Powys, and Mary Webb). His study is admirable as a reference book, but I confess to finding his categorizations no more satisfactory than Bentley's realistic bias. Despite the overlapping of dates, the categories seem too deterministically neat to fit the sense of varied possibility that we find in the literature.

My own working test for regional fiction is less systematic but ultimately, I believe, more justifiable than theirs. I accept all those novels, irrespective of their verisimilitude or romantic leanings, that present a locality distinctive in its character and related (at however great an imaginative remove) to a corresponding countryside identifiable on a map of the United Kingdom. The all-important quality is what Morgan neatly describes as 'an atmosphere which is not transferable.'[17] My criterion, then, is practical (to some extent, perhaps, personal) rather than theoretic. If the moorland of *Wuthering Heights* estab-lishes itself as a distinct area that dominates the novel – as it surely does – I accept it as regional despite the novel's poor showing on Bentley's battery of tests. *Shirley* may in fact present an authentic region, but if it does not register as such in the reader's imagination, then I find its status as a regional novel somewhat questionable. I am concerned here with novels or series of novels that succeed in creating an imaginative world which is unique in that it establishes its own 'reality' (in a sense closer to Plato than to Phyllis Bentley) but taking its origin from a recognizable stretch of countryside – the 'Hardy country,' the '*Wuthering Heights* country,' 'Eden Phillpotts's Dartmoor,' etc. In many respects, regionalism is an ordering principle, a formal device; it allows a writer to focus on a specific locality (what David Jones would call a 'known' or 'differentiated' site) and there find a manageable setting – a welcome limitation of possibility – for a vision that may well extend beyond the regional. The artistic variety that goes to the creation of such imaginative regions will form the subject of this book.

RELATED TERMINOLOGY

But several of the questions raised at the opening of this chapter remain unanswered, and it may be helpful now to narrow our focus by differentiating 'regional' from related words and then to discuss the connection between the regional novel and other fictional forms. The crucial words are 'rural,' 'provincial,' 'pastoral,' 'natural,' 'naturist,' 'local,' and 'topographical.' The first five can be treated quite briefly. 'Regional' and 'rural' are by no means synonymous. While most regions that have attracted novelists are in fact rural, Arnold Bennett's Five Towns form a notable exception, and several of the regional novelists who write about Yorkshire (including Phyllis Bentley herself) concern themselves with industrial landscapes or at least with regions where industrialism is prominent. D.H. Lawrence's mining countryside is another obvious instance. However, since my concern here is specifically rural, and because the constant combination of the two terms would prove clumsy, throughout this book the word 'regional' will be used to signify a distinctive area that is predominantly rural in character.

While 'provincial' also sometimes overlaps with 'regional,' it is a term of urban origin applying to areas – or regions – beyond the orbit of any influential centre. Unlike 'regional,' 'provincial' carries an unstated assumption that local differences are of little consequence. Although Jane Austen's novels have occasionally been described as 'regional' (W.L. Renwick makes the – to me – extraordinary statement that 'it is a commonplace of criticism that hers are regional novels as truly as Hardy's or Arnold Bennett's'),[18] they are more accurately categorized as 'provincial' – out of town. Indeed, an anonymous reviewer in *Blackwood's Edinburgh Magazine* in 1818 recognized as a 'singular merit' of her writings the fact that 'we could conceive, without the slightest strain of imagination, any one of her fictions to be realized in any town or village in England.'[19] Significantly, the centres in which society gathers – London, Bath, Lyme Regis – are given their proper names, as are the various (undifferentiated) counties, but her rural villages and country houses are imaginary as well as similar. Elizabeth Gaskell's novels, too, though frequently containing regional elements, are more correctly designated provincial, since they derive much of their interest from portraying life outside London. *Sylvia's Lovers*, however, qualifies as a genuinely regional novel, and I shall be showing how her novels further the cause of regionalism while generally avoiding the label. George Eliot, though drawing upon regional detail, also tends towards the provincial, as I shall attempt to demonstrate at the appropriate time.

'Pastoral' is another term sometimes employed – notably by Michael Squires in *The Pastoral Novel* (1974) – but it is not one that I find particularly helpful. Also urban in origin, it has the disadvantages of implying a high degree of literary artifice and convention, of equating rural settings with a golden age of idyllic retreat, and (despite Squires's attempt to link pastoral fiction to a precise geographical spot) of conjuring up a generalized countryside without regional differentiation. In my opinion, it overlaps awkwardly with both 'regional' and 'rural' and (at any rate, for my immediate purpose) is better avoided. The terms 'natural' and 'naturist' are also sometimes employed (for example, by John Alcorn in *The Nature Novel from Hardy to Lawrence* [1977] and Roger Ebbatson in *Lawrence and the Nature Tradition* [1980)]; but these relate to a philosophical and scientific understanding of 'Nature' which, though important for some writers, leads towards generalizing intellectual issues and away from the specific and individual regional concerns with which I am interested here.

'Parochial,' 'local,' and 'topographical' need more lengthy consideration. All imply particularity rather than generality; indeed, unlike 'regional' they may be said to be *too* particular. Literally (I am not concerned here with the unfortunate extension of the word which suggests narrowness and pettiness), 'parochial' implies confinement to the boundaries of a single parish. Such a small area is generally too limited to contain all the geographical peculiarities of a region (though *Wuthering Heights* must, as usual, be considered an exception). Hardy's *Under the Greenwood Tree* is a good example of a parochial novel. It is interesting to note that it eventually becomes part of a regional series, but would hardly qualify on its own as a regional work. Moreover, 'parochial' almost inevitably blends into 'local,' the only distinction being that 'local' implies a particular use of an existing model while 'parochial' can be applied (as in some of Austen's settings) to an imagined, generalized parish. Local novels have the distinction – and sometimes the disadvantage – of containing references that are immediately recognizable by residents. Here is an example pertaining to Gaskell's *Cranford*, originating in the Rev. H. Green's *History of Knutsford:*

> A woman of advanced age [in Knutsford], who was confined to her house through illness, about three years ago, asked me to lend her an amusing or cheerful book. I lent her *Cranford*, without telling her to what it was supposed to relate; she read the tale of Life in a Country Town; and when I called again, she was full of eagerness to say: – 'Why, Sir! that Cranford is all about Knutsford; my old mistress, Miss Harker, is mentioned in it; and our poor cow she did go to the field in a large flannel waistcoat, because she had burned herself in a lime-pit.'[20]

Similarly, *Scenes of Clerical Life* included so much local detail, relating to both scenery and inhabitants, that Warwickshire readers immediately identified 'Milby' as Nuneaton. And soon after R.D. Blackmore published *Perlycross*, William Corner, an ex-resident of Culmstock, Devon, wrote an article in the *Critic* identifying both the locale and the characters; Blackmore replied, denying most of the identifications of individuals, though one suspects that Corner was close to the truth.[21] The 'local' novel, then, often encompasses actual people and happenings in a fictional structure which is little more than a disguised memoir, and although only readers from the immediate area will be in a position to recognize the transcripts from actuality, outsiders are likely to assume instinctively an authentic realism within the book. While overlapping with the regional, the 'local' novel confines itself to holding the mirror up to a local nature, rarely if ever creating a superimposed imaginative realm.

A related term, more commonly applied to American than to English regional writing, is 'local colour,' which implies the extraction of unique qualities – often merely quaint or picturesque – from a local matrix. It derives, one suspects, from the practices of popular journalism. We are all aware of the kind of formula novel in which a standard plot (generally: boy meets girl; obstacles separate them; obstacles are removed; boy gets girl) is repeated time after time against different, generally exotic backgrounds – Venice, Hong Kong, the Canadian prairies, and perhaps even an English region like Cornwall or the Lake District. The differentiating qualities are naturally both obvious and superficial. The result, in Q.D. Leavis's words, is 'the kind of regional novel that gets local colour mainly in the form of dress, cooking and interior decoration, with a little judicious period idiom.'[22] In my terminology, however, this does not count as regional at all. Indeed, it is at the furthest extreme from regionalism since the background clearly has no genuine relation to the story. Fictions that qualify as authentically regional belong unquestionably to a particular place; their deeply sunk roots will not allow transplantation.

'Topographical' is, of course, similar to 'local,' and the two adjectives frequently overlap in meaning. But it is distinguished, I think, either by the undisguised use of actual place-names or by a conscious appeal to accompanying maps, whether real or fictitious. Thus Trollope, whom Phyllis Bentley credits as the first to invent 'a consistent fictitious topography' (p. 20), might be cited as a novelist who is topographical rather than local, while George Eliot tends towards the opposite end of the spectrum (her rural descriptions may well be based on actual models, but they are not intended to be unique and we do not feel the need for maps as adjuncts to her work). Here, however, more questions arise: how far does a regional novel need to be genuinely topographical? or, rather, to what extent is it an advantage for readers to be aware of an actual topography? A certain amount of topographical accuracy is, I suspect, invariably a feature of regional writing, since regional implies not only the local but the locatable. Trollope's Barsetshire may be fictitious but it is recognizably representative, and in the opening chapter of *Doctor Thorne*, where the novelist first surveys his invented country, he is careful to anchor it 'in the west of England.' A totally imaginary regionalism (Tolkien notwithstanding) would, I submit, be inconceivable.

In much regional writing we find an effect best described, perhaps, as 'double exposure.' Hardy's map of Wessex, for example, which is now firmly established as an accompaniment to any serious edition of his fiction, consists of a map of the west of England with the natural features identical but with the towns and villages, only lightly disguised in name, superimposed upon it. Much the same could be said about Mary Webb's Shropshire. Similarly, in the early fiction of D.H. Lawrence, though no maps were involved (the current Cambridge Edition contains some), the immediately local names of 'the Lawrence country' are transformed but outlying areas retain their actual names; so Eastwood becomes Bestwood in *Sons and Lovers* and Cossall becomes Cossethay in *The Rainbow*, but Nottingham, Southwell, and the Hemlock Stone appear undisguised in both novels. In Phillpotts and Kaye-Smith (and generally in Blackmore, since *Perlycross* is very much an exception), most of the larger man-made and natural features, and often even the names of farms and houses, are topographically authentic. But although this helps to convey a sense of regional particularity, it by no means guarantees it. Unless they are familiar with Sussex or Kent, casual readers of Kaye-Smith are unlikely either to know or care whether the places mentioned can be identified on a map, and if they are merely listed as names no sense of a regional identity is likely to emerge.

When we turn to related literary forms, we find a comparable overlap. The forms in question are the social novel, the historical novel, and the romance, though the first need not detain us long. There is a sense in which regional fiction is at the opposite extreme from the social novel, since the latter is inevitably committed to the typical or representative while the former deals in particulars which are not necessarily applicable outside the region. Interrelations are, of course, possible. The evidence of rural decline conspicuous in *The Mayor of Casterbridge, Tess of the d'Urbervilles*, and *Jude the Obscure*, though close to the particular realities of the west country, has a general illustrative relevance to the agricultural situation in late nineteenth-century England as a whole. On the other hand, Kaye-Smith's *The Ploughman's Progress*, though a bitter general statement about the condition of agriculture between 1924 and 1933, sufficiently reflects the local conditions of Sussex and Kent to maintain a regional authenticity while making a more broadly applicable social protest. A constant danger for regional fiction, however, is that in *confining* itself to local differences, it may distort by neglecting the broader general issues.

The connections of regional fiction with the historical novel and with the romance must be treated together, since in practice they are hardly separable. Northrop Frye proffers 'the general principle that most "historical novels" are romances.'[23] Certainly all three terms are likely to come together in any discussion of Scott's Waverley novels (or romances) and are never quite disentangled thereafter. A concern for the local past that produced the regional present becomes an important factor in most of the novelists we shall be considering in the following chapters. Scott's novels of Scotland go back beyond the Jacobite rebellions of the eighteenth century to the period of the Civil Wars in *A Legend of Montrose* to the Covenanters in *Old Mortality*, and beyond. The action of *Wuthering Heights* extends well back into the eighteenth century; *Lorna Doone* is set at the time of the Monmouth rebellion of 1685, and most of Blackmore's other novels reach back at least to the period of the Napoleonic Wars. Although *The Trumpet-Major*, set in the same period, is the only historical novel of the Wessex series, Hardy is continually harking back to the historical and even archaeological past throughout his work, and much the same can be said of Phillpotts's Dartmoor series. Mary Webb's best-known novel, *Precious Bane*, though not a historical novel in the strict sense of including historical personages, is set firmly in the past (it begins at the time of the Corn Laws of 1815), and although Constance Holme's work and the better-known novels of Kaye-Smith are roughly contemporary in setting, both record rural practices that extend far back into the national past (it is interesting to note, moreover, that Kaye-Smith's first two published novels, *The Tramping Methodist* and *Starbrace*, took place in the eighteenth century). And John Cowper Powys, while evoking a strange temporal *mélange* of past and present in his Wessex romances, delves back into the atavistic past of the race in *Owen Glendower* and *Porius*.

A surprising number of regional novelists, in fact, reveal serious historical and antiquarian interests. It is not perhaps fortuitous that the first significant publication of Sir Walter Scott (author, we remember, of a novel entitled *The Antiquary*) was *Minstrelsy of the Scottish Border* (1802–3), in which he preserved the traditional ballads and songs of the border country. He was later to perpetuate the legends and historical anecdotes of the area in a comparable way within his fictions; indeed, Hazlitt called Scott 'the amanuensis of truth and history.'[24] Hardy was dubbed 'The Historian of Wessex' by J.M. Barrie, and we remember that he contributed a paper on the archaeological finds at Max Gate to the Dorset Natural History and Antiquarian Field Club and set a whole volume (*A Group of Noble Dames*) in the Casterbridge museum. Phillpotts, Lawrence, and Powys were all, in their different ways, learned in the history and prehistory of their regions. George Eliot's preoccupations with memory and Constance Holme's with the historical traditions of her own family both attest to the supreme importance for regionalists of a concern for the processes of history.

As I have already indicated, the blurring of distinctions between regional fiction, historical fiction, and romance dates from the achievement of Scott, and this is, I think, because Scott successfully exploited the tendency of local history and memory to preserve records of the unusual and the exceptional. Such records, whether genuine history or 'airy nothing,' are immensely strengthened if they can be given 'a local habitation.' 'The *Romans* were here,' says the antiquary; 'the Romans were *here*,' says the local historian. Regionalism can sometimes combine both emphases. Certainly the association of traditional tale with a particular locality has the effect of increasing its claims to authenticity, and the regional novelist is well aware of this. At one extreme, Scott attempts to foster popular awareness of historical tradition by setting romantic adventures (Waverley's attraction to Flora McIvor, Osbaldistone's desperate quest in the Highlands) side by side with genuine historical figures and authentic locales; at the other, John Cowper Powys reproduces the details of Glastonbury and Dorchester with unparalleled accuracy but superimposes upon them such fantastic creations as Johnny Geard and Uryen Quirm. And in the middle we have Blackmore elaborating on regional legends of the Doones and making them so real to a generation of readers that local tall tale takes on the dignity of accepted popular history.

'Romance,' of course, is a form often applied dismissively as the province of the trivial and the second-rate. Writing of the Brontës, Tom Winnifrith notes how the word can so often suggest 'the deterioration of the novel seen as a means of escape from the realities of the world.'[25] He reminds us, however, that it can also lead us to comparisons with the works of Shakespeare, Spenser, and Sidney, and there is certainly no intrinsic reason why the term should imply a lack of seriousness. Moreover, the necessary conjunction of fiction and realism seems less obvious in a literary milieu containing the work of, for instance, Patrick White and Gabriel García Márquez than it did a generation ago. We now see more clearly that the patterns of romance frequently offer a structural basis for fiction, and by the same token they often need in turn a credible setting in which they may thrust down roots. Blackmore is central here. As Max Keith Sutton has documented at some length, most of his novels are modelled on displaced classical legends (the Persephone myth in *Cripps the Carrier*, for example), and one remembers at this point Hardy's famous remark in *The Woodlanders* (ch. 1) about 'dramas of a grandeur and unity truly Sophoclean' enacted in the 'sequestered spots outside the gates of the world' that constitute his Wessex. Mythic structures are never far below the surface of Powys's novel-romances, and on a decidedly more realistic level Phillpotts's characters play out the patterns of traditional story on a humble level within the localized boundaries of Dartmoor.

The superimposition of such general stories upon specific places naturally presents problems for the regional novelists – hence Phyllis Bentley's protest that so many professedly regional novels lack a uniquely regional theme. We seem back, indeed, to the dilemma of the local colourists already discussed. I submit, however, that myth and legends *can* in the course of history become rooted in particular localities, that by a literary equivalent of Darwinistic evolution they take on distinguishing characteristics determined by local conditions. Thus a number of places in England and Wales lay claim to identical Arthurian connections (the battlefields of Mount Badon and Camlann, the location of Camelot, the place where Excalibur was cast away, the site of Arthur's tomb) and such stories become part of an essentially local experience. Thanks to *Lorna Doone*, Doone Valley now appears (though it may perhaps be incorrectly located) on Ordnance Survey maps of the Devon-Somerset border; most guide-books to Hardy's Wessex identify Tess's village or Lucetta's Casterbridge house in Dorchester, and one even went so far as to specify the window of the house from which Sue jumped to escape Phillotson in *Jude the Obscure*. Here, in examples of varying importance and seriousness, we see the making of local tradition in process. And we must not fall into the error of assuming that these matters are confined to the naiveties of an unsophisticated rural fiction. More than one English public house is better known for its association with a Dickensian character than for any of its flesh-and-blood patrons. The movements of Conrad's fictional characters in his 'Eastern World' can be (and have been) topographically plotted. Joyce's inventions, Stephen Dedalus and Leopold and Molly Bloom, perpetually haunt an authentic Dublin. Literary critics neglect the significance of place in fiction at their peril. The associations of imaginary characters from the literary past with real places that can be visited in the present are universal. Through the centuries romance and reality have never been far apart. We need not therefore feel embarrassment if historical fiction, romance, and the regional novel obstinately tend to coalesce. Regionalism has always flourished on borderlands; not the least interesting of these is the disputed country that lies between realism and romance.

THE BEGINNINGS OF REGIONALISM

It is impossible to pin down the beginnings of regional fiction by reference to a specific date or a specific work. Even the writers discussed in part I of this book, whose contribution to regionalism is hardly in question, I have categorized – too cautiously, perhaps – as moving 'Towards Regionalism.' But before them, there are a number of writers and works (not necessarily novelists or novels) that made the development of regionalism possible. Before we proceed to more definite territory, then, it will be as well to indicate, if only briefly, the faint beginnings of the process.

If one turns to the work of Henry Fielding with a particular interest in localities and background description (and it is worth noting at this point that Hardy insisted on regarding Fielding 'as a local novelist'),[26] one is continually struck by the lack of specificity. In *Joseph Andrews* (1742), London is named, but all we can say about the rest of the action is that it takes place outside London. Fielding is explicit about his avoidance of place-names:

The reader must excuse me if I am not particular as to the way they took, for as we are now drawing near the seat of the Boobys, and as that is a ticklish name, which malicious persons may apply, according to their own inclinations, to several worthy country squires, a race of men whom we look upon as entirely inoffensive, and for whom we have an adequate regard, we shall lend no assistance to any such malicious purposes.   (Bk. 3, ch. 2)

Fielding was not a barrister for nothing. There is, of course, a large ingredient of flippancy in his excuse, but it points towards a real problem which later writers, deliberate in their regionalism, will encounter. Scott seems to have obscured the origin of his story in *The Bride of Lammermoor* and transferred it across half of Scotland to avoid giving offence to descendants of the family involved. The more accurate the detail, the greater the likelihood of unpleasantness. John Cowper Powys, indeed, lost all the profits from *A Glastonbury Romance* as the result of a libel action.

But Fielding's natural descriptions are equally unspecific. Here is the longest example in *Joseph Andrews:*

> ... they came to one of the beautifullest spots of ground in the universe. It was a kind of natural amphitheatre formed by the winding of a small rivulet, which was planted with thick woods, and the trees rose gradually above each other, by the natural ascent of the ground they stood on; which ascent as they hid with their boughs, they seemed to have been disposed by the design of the most skilful planter. The soil was spread with a verdure which no paint could imitate, and the whole place might have raised romantic ideas in older minds than those of Joseph and Fanny, without the assistance of love.   (Bk. 3, ch. 5)

A rivulet, wood, trees, beauty. This is as generalized as a stage-set (which the 'natural amphitheatre' suggests), the minimal background required for the human action.

Tom Jones (1749) shows a slight advance. Squire Allworthy's estate is immediately located in Somersetshire (Bk. 1, ch. 2) and the text is scattered with authentic place-names of the west country, primarily because the plot is so dependent upon escapes and pursuits that the relative locations of the main characters need to be made clear to the reader. But natural descriptions remain vague:

> ... our hero was walking in a most delicious grove, where the gentle breezes fanning the leaves, together with the sweet trilling of a murmuring stream, and the melodious notes of nightingales formed all together the most enchanting harmony. (Bk. 5, ch. 10)

And topographical description is similarly avoided:

> Jones walked forth in company with the stranger, and mounted Mazard Hill; of which they had no sooner gained the summit, than one of the most noble prospects in the world presented itself to their view, and which we would likewise present to the reader; but for two reasons. *First*, we despair of making those who have seen this prospect, admire our description. *Secondly*, we very much doubt whether those, who have not seen it, would understand it. (Bk. 9, ch. 2)

A generation later, with Smollett's *Humphry Clinker* (1771), we are in a totally different fictional world. Here, especially when the action moves into Scotland, topographical description becomes prominent and picaresque fiction blends into travel-book. From being merely background, and perfunctory background at that, local description is now offered for its own interest and its own sake. The general is giving way to the particular; one is tempted to suggest that writers of all kinds are becoming obsessed with counting the streaks of the tulip. Englishmen, certainly, are becoming more and more interested in the topographical and antiquarian details of their local countryside. Travel-books, archaeological treatises, agricultural reports, historical accounts, disquisitions on scenery, chapters on natural history become alike fashionable. The last twenty years of the eighteenth century are a time of much literary activity, and not inconspicuous within this activity is the work of such writers as Arthur Young, William Gilpin, and Gilbert White. None of these has a direct connection with regional fiction, but their indirect influence is considerable. Young's journeys presupposed an awareness of the variety of conditions affecting agricultural prosperity in different parts of the country. Gilpin's tours 'chiefly relative to picturesque beauty' taught a generation to look at the countryside with new eyes and to apply artistic terminology to natural scenery. And White not only popularized the idea of local history (comprising antiquities as well as details of flora and fauna) but insisted on the ecological uniqueness of the individual locality. It would not be inaccurate, I suggest, to categorize the descriptive passages I have quoted from Fielding as pre-Gilpin and pre-White landscapes.

Within fiction itself, description comes to the forefront in the Italianate romances of Ann Radcliffe. Of interest here is not the actual detail but the emotional impression of a specific landscape that she is able to suggest. When one comes to examine the passages in question, they quickly collapse into their basic ingredients: 'tremendous precipices,' 'headlong torrents,' 'sublime mountains,' 'majestic prospects,' 'romantic heights,' etc. Moreover, they are not only imaginative but imaginary; as is well known, at the time of her initial successes,

The Romance of the Forest (1791) and *The Mysteries of Udolpho* (1794), Radcliffe had not travelled in the countries about which she wrote. What is important for our purposes is the model that they provided for work of more genuine regional particularity. Despite the fustian quality of so many of Radcliffe's descriptions, without them the settings of Scott's *Waverley* could hardly have been produced in the form in which we know them.

But the honour of creating inspiration for Scott must be divided between Ann Radcliffe and a writer much closer to regional interests: Maria Edgeworth. Indeed, George Watson, in his introduction to the Oxford English Novels edition, goes so far as to assert that '*Castle Rackrent* (1800) is the first regional novel in English, and perhaps in all Europe.'[27] Certainly the novel – if novel it can be called – contains many elements that later come to be recognized as characteristic of regionalism. The emphasis on customs and manners (what, in her capacity as self-styled editor, she calls 'a specimen of manners and characters');[28] the presentation through colloquialism and dialect; the employment of anecdote, personal recollection, and oral tradition (all duly identified and authenticated in notes); the vivid recreation of a particular way of life; an insistence – as Watson points out – on 'something that almost deserves the pompous name of documentation':[29] all these are present in *Castle Rackrent* and render it not, I would say, a landmark of regionalism itself but a landmark on the road to regionalism.

Any distinction drawn in these matters, as I have indicated earlier, must be to some extent arbitrary. For my own part I cannot accept Watson's high claim because I believe that the ultimate requirement of regional fiction – the unmistakable presence of a specific locality – is lacking. '*Rackrent* pictures a world identified in place and time,' claims Watson,[30] but no one, surely, has ever gone to Ireland in search of 'the Rackrent country.' Although Edgeworth includes various fictitious place-names, we are never given any clues to the part of Ireland in which the novel takes place. One can only claim it as a region if one considers Ireland itself a region. There is no differentiation of this landscape from any other Irish landscape, and this is the crucial distinction that needs to be made between Edgeworth and Scott. Scott generously acknowledged his debt to *Castle Rackrent* in writing *Waverley*, but he extended Edgeworth's method and transformed her directional hints. With Scott, we can say, adopting an imagery appropriate to his work, we are crossing the border into genuinely regional writing.

PART ONE: TOWARDS REGIONALISM

TWO

Sir Walter Scott

THE ROMANCE OF PLACE

'Scott never knew the Highlands; he was always a Borderer.'[1] Robert Louis Stevenson's observation is perhaps sufficient to reassure the non-Scot that it is legitimate to consider 'the author of *Waverley*' as a regionalist as well as (or rather than) a nationalist. To the outsider, certainly, his northern locales – and I am not concerned with the others here – are initially remarkable for their common Scots flavour, but it is not long before one begins to make some discriminations between the settings. To take an extreme instance, it soon becomes clear that Scott himself is conscious of being outside his region in describing Orkney and Shetland landscapes in *The Pirate*, and further thought reveals the essential justice of Stevenson's remark. Scott, like most of the later regionalists to be discussed in this book, wrote best about the countryside which he knew best, and this may be roughly designated as the area between Edinburgh and the border with England.

This area had impressed itself upon Scott during the all-important years of his childhood. As his devotees know, from the time of his attack of infantile paralysis at the age of eighteen months, Scott was regularly sent to recuperate and strengthen his physique in the Roxburgh countryside, first to his grandparents at Sandyknowe near Smailholm, and later to his aunt at Kelso. 'Wattie,' as he was then called, was an unusually precocious child, and the experiences of this early period proved crucial to his subsequent creative development. Moreover, because of the immense influence of the Waverley novels, the interests and preoccupations which Scott blended in his fiction became central features in the evolution of literary regionalism.

The future writer could not have been presented with a more promising locale. 'All the Border Country,' Edgar Johnson has written in his biography, 'was haunted and historic ground.'² In every direction could be seen hills, settlements, ruins, houses, around which had gathered traditions and stories of the past. The small boy, at first prevented by his weak legs from moving with any ease, zealously assimilated these legends – and at Sandyknowe there were many prepared to indulge him in his local enthusiasms: 'All those about Wattie, the cow bailie and the ewe milkers, the housekeeper and the maids, were steeped in the fairy legends and historic tales of that ancient countryside, and from them he eagerly absorbed these stories of wizardry, romance and war.'³ The essential point is that the tales in question arose out of the local and visible landscape. From an early age Scott 'associated' stories with specific places. When he came to write his novels (and, for that matter, his poems) of Scotland's past, he felt the need to emphasize the settings in which the historical events took place, to provide as it were a literary equivalent for the landmarks that provoked the stories of his childhood. Most important of all, perhaps, he evolved a rich fictional formula – 'romantic' events set against 'real' landscapes – that initiated a strong tradition within the regional novel.

'Association' is in fact a key word for the understanding of Scott. This had been recognized by Coleridge when he observed: 'every old ruin, hill, river, or tree called up to his mind a host of historical or biographical associations.'⁴ It had also been recognized by Scott himself; locality, he told Anna Seward, 'recalls to us not merely the local scenery, but a thousand little nameless associations which we are unable to separate or to define.'⁵ And he elaborates upon the point in an important autobiographical fragment referring to holidays at his aunt's:

> The neighborhood of Kelso, the most beautiful, if not the most romantic village in Scotland, is eminently calculated to awaken [feeling for the beauties of the natural world]. It presents objects, not only grand in themselves, but venerable for their associations. ... The romantic feelings which I have described as predominating in my mind, naturally rested upon and associated themselves with these grand features of the landscape around me; and the historical incidents or traditional legends connected with many of them, gave to my admiration a sort of intense expression of reverence, which at times made my heart feel too big for its bosom. From this time the love of natural beauty, more especially when combined with ancient ruins, or remains of our fathers' piety or splendor, became with me an insatiable passion.⁶

One cannot but be struck in these sentences not only by the emphasis on association but by the clustering of words like 'romantic,' 'historical,' 'legends,' 'ruins,' 'landscape,' 'natural beauty.' For Scott, history and topography are inextricably connected, and the characters in his novels are constantly being impressed by the legendary and historical associations of their environment. Here, for example, is a rarely quoted passage from *The Pirate* in which Scott seems to reproduce in another region of Scotland an equivalent to his own experience at Sandyknowe. The young Mordaunt Mertoun finds himself in a lonely part of the Shetlands where the native Zetlanders recount to him 'the strange legends of Berserkers, of sea-kings, of dwarfs, giants, and sorcerers.' Scott continues:

> Often the scenes around him were assigned as the localities of wild poems, which, half-recited, half-chanted by voices as hoarse, if not so loud, as the waves over which they floated, pointed out the very bay on which they sailed as the scene of a bloody sea-fight; the scarce-seen heap of stones that bristled over the projecting cape as the dun or castle of some potent earl or noted pirate; the distant and solitary grey stone on the lonely moor as marking the grave of a hero; the wild cavern, up which the sea rolled in heavy, broad, and unbroken billows, as the dwelling of some noted sorceress. (Ch. 2)

Tradition, Scott observes in *The Bride of Lammermoor*, is 'always busy, at least in Scotland, to grace with a legendary tale a spot in itself interesting' (ch. 5). His ability to breathe life into the dry bones of historical record, to be the opposite of his own Dr Dryasdust, depends upon his locating the events of past history within landscapes that can be visited in the present. If this sounds to us an obvious procedure, it is an index to the influence which Scott's vision has had upon our basic assumptions.

But Scott's early experience of Border country pervades his writings in a more subtle way. A border is a place of drama and contrast – not only the likely scene for clashes between rivals but a locality, often emphasized by geographical features, where one way of life ends and another begins. It is, then, an ideal setting for novels of action. Many of Scott's stories, notably *The Black Dwarf*, *The Bride of Lammermoor*, and *Redgauntlet*, are literally tales of the Anglo-Scottish border that take their origin from border conflicts. Others, like *Waverley* and the central part of *Rob Roy*, exploit the contrast within Scotland between Highlands and Lowlands. Moreover, the principal habitations within the books are often deliberately poised on natural boundaries that, as it were, symbolize the conflict evident elsewhere in the individual work. Baron Bradwardine's Tully-Veolan in *Waverley*, exposed to the raids of Highland freebooters, is a case in point. So, in *The Antiquary*, is Sir Arthur Wardour's 'ancient Gothic parlour' at Knockwinnock, 'whose windows on one side looked out upon the ruthless ocean, and, on the other, upon the long straight avenue' (ch. 5). An especially prominent example is the Castle of Tullietudlem in *Old*

Mortality: 'The tower commanded two prospects, – the one richly cultivated and highly adorned; the other exhibiting the monotonous and dreary character of a wild and inhospitable moorland' (ch. 11). In *Rob Roy* Scott alludes in his introduction to 'this strong contrast betwixt the civilized and cultivated mode of life on the one side of the Highland line and the wild and lawless adventures which were habitually undertaken and achieved by one who dwelt on the opposite side of that ideal boundary'; within the text itself we are told that 'the river of Forth forms a defensible line betwixt the Highlands and Lowlands of Scotland' (ch. 28) and the 'clachan of Aberfoil' is strategically situated at this point.

But landscape is, of course, only the visible manifestation of a division that is reflected more crucially in the character, customs, and manners of the human beings who live within it. Rose Bradwardine and Flora Mclvor are probably the most obvious examples of characters set against appropriate backgrounds and emblematic of opposed ways of life. Rob Roy and Nicol Jarvie , and Redgauntlet and Josiah Geddes also belong here. Francis R. Hart has argued that this pattern reflects Scott's 'divided inheritance – son of the shrewd city solicitor, grandson of the patriarchal Border.'[7] That Scott consciously exploited the pattern can be deduced from his well-known statement – admittedly late, but surely representing the principle of composition – in his 1831 preface to *The Fortunes of Nigel:*

> Lady Mary Wortley Montague has said, with equal truth and taste, that the most romantic region of every country is that where the mountains unite themselves with the plains or lowlands. For similar reasons, it may be in like manner said that the most picturesque period of history is that when the ancient rough and wild manners of a barbarous age are just becoming innovated upon and contrasted by the illumination of increased or revived learning and the instructions of renewed or reformed religion. The strong contrast produced by the opposition of ancient manners to those which are gradually subduing them affords the lights and shadows necessary to give effect to a fictitious narrative.

Yet again we find in Scott an original presentation of an effect that becomes a common feature of subsequent regional literature – Thrushcross Grange replacing Wuthering Heights, Lorna Doone's move from the Doone Valley to Plover's Barrows Farm, Casterbridge against Egdon Heath. But what is expressed through a geographical and topographical image is frequently the result of profound historical change. Waverley, Nicol Jarvie, and Fairford and Lattimer may represent the mood of the present, but Fergus McIvor, Rob Roy, and Redgauntlet belong resolutely to the past. Scott's subject-matter inevitably turns him into a historian and antiquary.

THE POWER OF THE PAST

In the 1829 General Preface to the Waverley novels, Scott reports that an illness in later boyhood at first 'threw [him] back on the kingdom of fiction' but that 'familiar acquaintance with the spacious miracles of fiction brought with it some degree of satiety, and [he] began, by degrees, to seek in histories, memoirs, voyages and travels and the like, events nearly as wonderful as those which were the work of imagination.' So a taste for stories of wild adventure blended into one for stories of the past that carried with them the additional attraction of authenticity. This led ultimately to Scott's first important literary achievement, his compilation of ancient ballads and songs entitled *Minstrelsy of the Scottish Border* (1802–3), the very title of which is indicative of his instinct to link historical record with a particular locality. For our purposes, the circumstances of its compilation are as significant as the book itself. Scott's 'raids' into Liddesdale in the 1790s to collect the materials were journeys in time as well as space. Lockhart's account shows clearly the primitive condition of the region: 'At this time no wheeled carriage had ever been seen in the district – the first, indeed, that ever appeared there was a gig, driven by Scott himself for a part of the way, when on the last of these seven excursions.'[8] Lockhart claimed justly, as a number of modern scholars have pointed out, that the germ of most of Scott's subsequent work can be traced back to the compilation of the *Minstrelsy*. At this point Scott the antiquary was born and, as A.O.J. Cockshut has written, 'without the antiquary in him, his best novels could not have been written.'[9] Scott maintained his antiquarian interests throughout his life. Thus in the year following the publication of his novel appropriately entitled *The Antiquary* he contributed a substantial introduction to the *Border Antiquities of Scotland*.

His gathering of oral materials for *Minstrelsy of the Scottish Border* was undertaken in full awareness of the fact that the traditional songs were in danger of being lost. The recollection of this balladry, he reports, 'has, of late years, become like that of a "tale which was told." ' ... The causes of the preservation of these songs have either entirely ceased, or are gradually decaying.' At the end of the preface he laments the way in which 'the peculiar features of [Scotland's] manners and character are daily melting and dissolving into those of her sister and ally.'[10] Simultaneously, then, with the awareness of historical heritage came a concern for its preservation – a concern intimately related to contemporary political developments. And although one might at first expect that the need would be most urgent for records from the earliest periods, the acceleration of change in the previous two or three generations had rendered the preservation of more recent history equally necessary. Scott made the point eloquently in the 'postscript' to *Waverley*: 'There is no European nation which, within the course of half a century or little more, has undergone so complete a change as this kingdom of Scotland' (ch. 72).

Scott was one of the first to realize – doubtless because of his interest in ballad-collecting – the historical importance of *oral* testimony, of the preservation of eye-witness accounts taken from participants who were not in a position to present a permanent account of their experiences. Fortunately, he lived at the time of the last opportunity to record such memories of the 1745 Jacobite rebellion. Characteristically, place, history, and 'romance' united in Scott's mind. After alluding to his early recollections of Highland scenery and customs in the General Preface to the Waverley novels he continues:

> I had been a good deal in the Highlands at a time when they were much less accessible, and much less visited, than they have been of late years, and was acquainted with many of the old warriors of 1745, who were, like most veterans, easily induced to fight their battles over again for the benefit of a willing listener like myself. It naturally occurred to me that the ancient traditions and high spirit of a people who, living in a civilized age and country, retained so strong a tincture of manners belonging to an early period of society, must afford a subject favourable for romance.

The result was, of course, *Waverley,* and although subsequent novels never quite repeated the same combination of carefully researched historical reconstruction and accurately reproduced oral testimony (since his novels set in the immediate past lacked the impact of important political events and his later historical works dealt with periods beyond the reach of living recollection) the adaptation of orally transmuted anecdotes and reliance on traditional story and memoir, all linked with a particular terrain, became characteristic of his writings.

Thus the Waverley novels or romances (that Scott employs both nouns to describe his fiction has considerable significance in itself) represent attempts at cultural conservation analogous to those displayed in the *Minstrelsy.* And here I would submit that there is no more eloquent testimony to Scott's literary intentions than the opening chapter of *Old Mortality* where 'Peter Pattieson' presents an account of the descendant of the Covenanters from whom the book derives its name. The passage needs to be quoted at some length, and should be read as an 'objective correlative' to Scott's own aims. 'Old Mortality' has given up his farm and settled existence to devote his life to preserving the records of the past:

> In the language of Scripture, he left his house, his home, and his kindred, and wandered about until the day of his death, a period of nearly thirty years.
> During this long pilgrimage the pious enthusiast regulated his circuit so as annually to visit the graves of the unfortunate Covenanters who suffered by the

sword, or by the executioner, during the reigns of the last two monarchs of the Stewart line. ... Their tombs are often apart from all human habitation, in the remote moors and wilds to which the wanderers had fled for concealment. But wherever they existed, Old Mortality was sure to visit them when his annual round brought them within his reach. ...

... As the wanderer was usually to be seen bent on this pious task within the precincts of some country churchyard, or reclined on the solitary tombstone among the heath, disturbing the plover and the blackcock with the clink of his chisel and mallet, with his old white pony grazing by his side, he acquired, from his converse among the dead, the popular appellation of Old Mortality. ...

... To talk of the exploits of the Covenanters was the delight, as to repair their monuments was the business, of his life. He was profuse in the communication of all the minute information which he had collected concerning them, their wars, and their wanderings. One could almost have supposed he must have been their contemporary, and have actually beheld the passages which he related, so much had he identified his feelings and opinions with theirs, and so much had his narratives the circumstantiality of an eye-witness.

In his introduction to the novel (1830), Scott describes his own brief meeting with 'Old Mortality,' which parallels part of 'Peter Pattieson's' account. Thus out of Scott's personal experience (according to his own testimony) came an incident which he transformed into a powerful image of his own art. Like 'Old Mortality,' Scott spent a lifetime preserving and recreating the history and traditions of his nation's past; like 'Old Mortality' again, he had so steeped himself in the records of this past that his narrative took on 'the circumstantiality of an eye-witness.' Moreover, his emphasis on refurbishing the tombstones, the monuments erected at the place of death, together with the description of country churchyards and open heaths, indicates the importance of linking historical records with local settings. Although some commentators have questioned the relevance of 'Old Mortality' and the preliminary chapter, I would argue that, as a symbolic representation of Scott's deepest concerns, his is a presence that should pervade not only the novel to which he gives his name but the whole Waverley series.

MANNERS, MORES, AND FACTS

Old Mortality reminds us that, although Scott frequently wrote of exceptional leaders like the fictitious Fergus McIvor and Redgauntlet or the historical Claverhouse and Rob Roy, he is no less concerned with recreating the lives and habits of ordinary people. Too much emphasis can be placed in discussions of

Old Mortality on Scott's interpretation of the character of Claverhouse; he is equally intent on portraying the all-but-forgotten Covenanters who would otherwise lack any memorial. John Buchan is demonstrably wrong when he maintains that Scott introduced antiquarian and social detail into his fiction 'as a relief, to provide a rest for the mind in the midst of exciting action.'[11] He is interested not only in traditional tales of unique events – though these are frequently incorporated into the fictions and glossed in the copious notes added to later editions – but also in preserving a record of the everyday customs and habits of the people. And here we come upon the first of many dualities that characterize Scott's work: while part of his interest – we might call it the school-boy part – was focused on exciting stories of exceptional deeds, another part concerned itself with the more mundane, ordinary events of social history.

'Descriptions of scenery and manners' is the significant phrase used in the General Preface to the 1829 edition, and in the 'Advertisement' to *The Antiquary* (1816) he went so far as to admit: 'I have been more solicitous to describe manners minutely than to arrange ... an artificial and combined narrative.' Despite its title, this novel sets the customs of the present against the often dubious interpretations of the past. The Jonathan Oldbuck of the early chapters seems in part a parody of Scott's own antiquarian enthusiasms, and the character of greater impact and dignity is Edie Ochiltree, who is presented as 'the news-carrier, the minstrel, and sometimes the historian of the district' (ch. 4). In the introduction to *Tales of My Landlord*, Jedediah Cleishbotham is probably speaking for Scott when he praises Gandercleugh as an excellent place in which to see 'the manners and customs of various tribes and peoples,' and the inscription refers to these stories as 'tales, illustrative of ancient Scottish manners, and of the traditions of their respective districts.' (It is interesting, given our special concern here with Scott's legacy to regionalism, to note the way the importance of regional differentiation is insisted upon in the last phrase.) To this side of Scott we owe the carefully detailed vignettes often iden-tifiable by chapter-titles in *Waverley* – 'A Scottish Manor-House Sixty Years Since,' 'The Hold of a Highland Robber,' 'A Highland Feast'; the archaeological reconstruction of the wappen-schaw at the opening of *Old Mortality*; the references to representative customs ('a Scottish old-fashioned burial' [ch. 23], 'the manners of the country' [ch. 30]) in *The Bride of Lammermoor*; the care-ful account of a whale-hunt in *The Pirate*.

This use of fictional form for the popularization of social history was a fea-ture of Scott's writing recognized as early as the reviews of *Waverley*. The anonymous reviewer in the *British Critic* observed: 'We are unwilling to consider this publication in the light of a common novel ... but as a vehicle of curious accurate information upon a subject which must at all times demand our attention – the history and manners of a very large and renowned portion of the inhabitants of these islands.'[12] A basically similar position was argued to a negative end by John Wilson Croker in the *Quarterly Review*. He pronounced dogmatically that 'we have a great objection ... to historical romance, in which real and fictitious personages and actual and fabulous events are mixed together to the utter confusion of the reader and the unsettling of all accurate recollections of past transaction,' and wished that the author had written a history of the Jacobite uprising of 1745 instead of a novel.[13] Croker here initiates an argument that reverberates down to our own time. I make no claims to adjudicate this controversy here, but it needs to be borne in mind when we encounter the criticism, persistent in treatments of regional writing, that a novel illustrating the mode of living of a particular area at a particular moment in time is somehow inferior to more imaginative, 'creative' fiction. In many instances a form of imagination is equally present in efforts at historical reconstruction.

That there are artistic problems involved in the blending of 'prosaic' fact and 'romantic' fiction cannot be gainsaid. Most readers of Scott have probably experienced the strange shifting of gears that often interrupts the flow of the narrative. Sometimes, for example, he openly introduces into his text discussions of the accuracy and representativeness of his portraits, as in the following passage relating to Dandie Dinmont in *Guy Mannering*:

> The present store-farmers of the south of Scotland are a much more refined race than their fathers, and the manners I am now to describe have either altogether disappeared, or are greatly modified. Without losing the rural simplicity of manners, they now cultivate arts unknown to the former generation, not only in the progressive improvements of their possessions, but in all the comforts of life. Their houses are more commodious, their habits of life regulated so as better to keep pace with those of the civilized world. (Ch. 24)

Encountering this passage out of context, the reader could be forgiven for presuming it to originate in a work of non-fiction. Scott is intent on producing straightforward historical commentary (*in* context, of course, its prelude to an account of the irrepressible Dinmont constitutes a tonal *tour de force*). Another, shorter example is the following comment on Mrs Wilson, housekeeper at Milnwood in *Old Mortality*: 'Such were the manners of a certain class of domestics, once common in Scotland, and perhaps still to be found in some old manor-houses in its remote counties' (ch. 5). Comparable passages are not uncommon within the text of the novels; more often, however, they occur in the notes, introductions, and appendices that have cluttered Scott's fiction since the time of the 1829 collected and annotated edition.

Scott's decision to encase his narratives in introductions and notes which, as it were, ground his romances in fact –whether historical or topographical or both – had profound consequences for the development of regional literature. It was, of course, a feature of the times. One gets something of the same effect in Wordsworth's poetry, where the details and glosses to modern editions, based mainly on the Isabella Fenwick notes, lay considerable stress on topographical details, both explanatory references to places mentioned in the texts and information concerning the places in which the poems were written. Moreover, we can surely discern the combined influence of Scott and Wordsworth on both the prefaces and the notes to Hardy's Wessex novels, though these are decidedly less detailed. The development of the process, with popular response to the fictions forcing the novelists to comment on their use of actual localities, seems remarkably similar in both cases. With Scott, however, the matter was magnified by popular interest in originals for the characters as well as in geographical equivalents for the settings. As soon as *Waverley* appeared, Scott records that 'the good people of Edinburgh are busied in ... finding out originals for the portraits it contains,'[14] and in 1817, in the *Quarterly* review of *Guy Mannering*, asserts that 'there is scarcely a dale in the pastoral districts of the southern counties but arrogates to itself the possession of the original Dandie Dinmont.'[15] Moreover, the first edition (considerably expanded three years later) of Robert Chambers's *Illustrations of the Author of Waverley* appeared as early as 1822, offering identifications of characters and settings in the early novels.[16]

Topographical identifications were even more popular than those of characters. For a generation, tours of the more dramatic parts of the British Isles in search of what William Gilpin christened 'picturesque beauty' had been fashionable (Wordsworth had been following Gilpin's lead in his Wye tour that brought him to the area around Tintern Abbey). At the opening of *Guy Mannering*, the name character is on a British tour, and the popularity of the Waverley novels extended this interest. Scott's note in *Rob Roy* directed to 'the reader whose curiosity may lead him to visit the scenes of these remote adventures' is symptomatic. The exploitation of Scott's novels by advocates of the Scottish tourist trade goes back to Scott's own time and, like Hardy after him, he could do no more than add a tinge of detached irony to an enforced acquiescence. His note concerning the location of Baron Bradwardine's residence in *Waverley* is characteristic:

There is no particular mansion described under the name of Tully-Veolan; but the peculiarities of the description occur in various old Scottish seats. The house of Warrender upon Bruntisford Links, and that of old Ravelston ... have both contributed several hints to the description in the text. The House of Dean, near Edinburgh, also has some points of resemblance with Tully-Veolan. The author has, however, been informed, that the house of Grandtully resembles that of the Baron of Bradwardine still more than any of the above. (Ch. 8)

The sly humour behind that last sentence was surely an inspiration to Hardy when he wrote the 1912 addition to his preface to *The Woodlanders:*

To oblige readers I once spent several hours on a bicycle with a friend in a serious attempt to discover [the exact locality of Little Hintock] but the search ended in failure; though tourists assure me positively that they have found it without trouble, and that it answers in every particular to the description given in this volume.

None the less, Scott was accustomed to make geographical excursions while writing his novels with the object of refreshing his impressions of the background. Edgar Johnson notes, for instance, a visit to 'the Lennox and Drumlanrig' while preparing *Rob Roy* and another to Lanarkshire as late as the writing of *Castle Dangerous*.[17] Once again one is reminded of Hardy's customary practice.

The relationship between fact and fiction in Scott is decidedly complicated – part, like the prolonged secrecy over the authorship of the novels, of his delight in mystification. F.A. Pottle, indeed, has gone so far as to maintain that one reason for the vividness and fascination of Scott's supposedly factual notes is that 'they were often half-fiction.'[18] But by the same token his fictions are often half-true. His legacy to subsequent novelists is immense, and it is nowhere more noticeable than in the domain of regional fiction. Subsequent regionalists tend to emphasize one or other of the extremes that Scott combined with such apparent ease; some stress representative manners to such an extent that the narrative declines into illustrative documentary, while others spin impossible tall tales against beguilingly credible backgrounds. Scott's practice, indeed, becomes a yardstick against which the achievements of his successors can be usefully measured. But his own method fluctuated and developed in the course of his career as a writer of prose fiction. We must now turn to a consideration of the technical means by which Scott communicates his sense of locality.

SCOTT AND LOCALITY

When Waverley at last crosses the 'stupendous barrier' (ch. 7) that separates the Lowlands and Tully-Veolan from the Highlands and the haunts of Donald Bean Lean and Fergus McIvor, it might fairly be claimed that he moves out of the world of Maria Edgeworth into that of Ann Radcliffe. Although the narrator, reflecting Waverley's own attitude, refers to 'Italian forms of landscape' and 'the picturesque' while describing the peasant inhabitants of the village, and finds the solitude and repose of the Baron's park 'almost romantic' (ch. 8), the overall impression of Tully-Veolan suggests historical fidelity and representativeness – a stylized genre-painting, perhaps, but restrained and accurate. As we have seen, topographers are able to name various houses, some or all of which contributed details to the fictional estate. It is a composite, to be sure, but the description rings true; as readers we accept it within a verifiable locality.

But the romantic Highland landscapes are beyond the reach of maps. If we believe them at all, they provide no more than a dream-landscape, and sometimes, as in the notorious 'Highland Minstrelsy' chapter, the backdrop for an operatic aria. We move, with Waverley, into a different stylistic convention and a correspondingly different literary environment:

> It was towards evening as they entered one of the tremendous passes which afford communication between the high and low country. The path, which was extremely steep and rugged, winded up a chasm between two tremendous rocks, following the passage which a foaming stream, that brawled far below, appeared to have worn for itself in the course of ages. A few slanting beams of the sun, which was now setting, reached the water in its darksome bed, and showed it partially, chafed by a hundred rocks, and broken by a hundred falls. The descent from the path to the stream was a mere precipice, with here and there a projecting fragment of granite or a scathed tree which had warped its twisted roots into the fissures of the rock. On the right hand, the mountain rose above the path with almost equal inaccessibility. (Ch. 16)

There is a great deal of attempted visual detail here (Marcia Allentuck has called it 'one of the finest descriptions reminiscent of Rosa's canvases'),[19] but what is conveyed is a mood rather than a landscape. The rhetoric – the repeated 'tremendous,' words like 'chasm,' 'foaming stream,' 'darksome bed,' 'precipice' – is essentially Radcliffe's. This is a generalized sublimity. Our attention is directed not to an actual Highland setting but to the conventions of Italianate Gothic. Scott is here, of course, reproducing the landscape as the susceptible Waverley responds to it, and it is hardly surprising that, by the end of the chapter, Waverley has given himself up to 'the full romance of his situation' and Scott interprets: 'What a variety of incidents for the exercise of a romantic imagination, and all enhanced by the solemn feeling of uncertainty, at least, if not of danger!' True, Scott pricks the bubble of romantic exaltation by reminding us that the cause of Waverley's journey was ' – the Baron's milch cows!' but we are certainly invited to respond, at least in part, to the 'romance' of his adventure.

Waverley is then transported across a lake to the robber's cave and he 'prepared himself to meet a stern, gigantic, ferocious figure, such as Salvator would have chosen to be the central object of a group of banditti' (ch. 17). Donald Bean Lean, we learn immediately, 'was the very reverse of all these.' Scott again pricks the bubble, much in the same way that Radcliffe (eventually) explains her mysteries by naturalistic means, and there follows a genre-painting offered as a picture of manners among the Highland outlaws. But it exists on a level of reality distinct from that of Tully-Veolan.

By the time Waverley reaches the next stage in his initiation, Fergus McIvor's house at Glennaquoich, the Gothic effects are intensified. Scott clearly intends the scene of Flora McIvor's harp-playing in a carefully stage-managed highland valley to balance Rose Bradwardine's lowland garden, but the effect, though powerful, is also crude. Again the vocabulary of Radcliffe is conspicuous: 'the wild, bleak and narrow valley,' 'a crag of huge size,' another 'chasm,' rocks showing 'their grey and shaggy crests,' 'a romantic waterfall,' Waverley's 'sensation of horror' (ch. 22). Flora herself is likened to 'one of those lovely forms which decorate the landscapes of Poussin,' and *chiaroscuro* effects derived via Radcliffe from the Italian painters abound.

Curiously enough, although the text emphasizes the romantic elements in the scene – Waverley is specifically likened to a 'knight of romance' and the glen 'seemed to open into the land of romance' – Scott tries desperately in one of his topographical notes to locate the scene on a map of Scotland. This note demands full quotation because in it we see two of Scott's aims in the novel clashing head-on:

The description of the waterfall mentioned in this chapter is taken from that of Ledeard, at the farm so called on the northern side of Lochard, and near the head of the lake, four or five miles from Aberfoyle. It is upon a small scale, but otherwise one of the most exquisite cascades it is possible to behold. The appearance of Flora with the harp, as described, has been justly censured as too theatrical and affected for the lady-like simplicity of her character. But something may be allowed to her French education, in which point and striking effect always make a considerable object.

The light-hearted, bantering tone of the last two sentences betrays Scott's awareness of a fundamental strain in the chapter as a whole. By the time he came to add the note, he surely realized that the style of the description precluded any prosaic identification. The world of romance cannot so easily be imposed upon the real world of maps and tourists. Here, indeed, is another instance of the kind of pressure from the literary pilgrims that we find in the later introductions and notes of Hardy. What began as an imaginative landscape is in the process of blending into the conventions of regional description.

Scott's second novel, *Guy Mannering*, while repeating and thus establishing a number of conventions that form the staple of his novels about Scotland's past, introduces some new elements. First, and this is important within a context of literary regionalism, it is a novel set in the past but lacking any connection with a known historical event, and no authentic character like Bonnie Prince Charlie or Claverhouse or Rob Roy appears within it. Moreover, the setting is Galloway in south-west Scotland, and this is not a part of the country that Scott knew well. Edgar Johnson records a visit in 1793 only, and it seems clear that Scott relied for most of his local detail on his friend Joseph Train.

This being so, we might expect the descriptions to continue in the generalized, 'picturesque' manner of *Waverley*. In fact, however, Scott makes a considerable advance in this novel towards topographical realism. The account of Ellangowan Castle, for example, might be expected to contain decided Radcliffian elements, but the effect is surprisingly restrained. Guy Mannering

> now perceived that the ruins of Ellangowan Castle were situated upon a promontory, or projection of rock, which formed one side of a small and placid bay on the sea-shore. The modern mansion was placed lower, though clearly adjoining, and the ground behind it descended to the sea by a small swelling green bank, divided into levels of natural terraces, on which grew some old trees, and terminating upon the white sand. The other side of the bay, opposite to the old castle, was a sloping and varied promontory, covered chiefly with copsewood, which on that favoured coast grows almost within water-mark. A fisherman's cottage peeped from among the trees. Even at this dead hour of night there were lights moving upon the shore, probably occasioned by the unloading of a smuggling lugger from the Isle of Man, which was lying in the bay.   (Ch. 2)

There is a controlled, documentary quality about this. No attempt is made to heighten our emotions, despite the available associations of rocks, castle, night-setting, and smuggling. The eye is fixed upon the object ('A fisherman's cottage peeped from among the trees'), and we are given the bare details only. The morning scene offered in the following chapter is similarly factual and direct.

Indeed, the language of Gothic fiction and references to Italian painters are in this novel deliberately limited to the letters of Julia Mannering, and Scott creates an eloquent contrast between her response and that of his narrator. Westmorland, she tells her friend Matilda, 'is the country of romance. The scenery is such as nature brings together in her sublimest moods – sounding cataracts – hills which rear their scathed heads to the sky – lakes that, winding up the shadowy valleys, lead at every turn to yet more romantic recesses – rocks which catch the clouds of Heaven. All the wilderness of Salvator here, and there the fairy scenes of Claude' (ch. 17). Both here and in Brown/Bertram's apostrophe to the remains of Hadrian's Wall (ch. 22) we find the elevated sensibility that in *Waverley* had characterized the narrator while setting up, as it were, the objects of his hero's romantic response. And even in the Hadrian's Wall scene, as Jane Millgate has recently noted, Bertram is realistic enough to get hungry![20]

James Reed has observed that, 'when landscape and character are divorced, Scott becomes no more than a tourist, a painter of brilliant scenery. ... Much has been written about his powers as a "descriptive writer", but for him, the event, not the panorama, was what counted.'[21] As he develops as a novelist, I suggest, landscape and character, which began as discrete entities, become increasingly unified. In *Old Mortality*, for example, the moor across which Morton is led before the battle of Drumclog might be thought of as a natural candidate for an exercise in the romantic sublime, but in Scott's mature treatment the effect is closer to Hardy's evocation of Egdon:

> This desolate region seemed to extend farther than the eye could reach, without grandeur, without even the dignity of mountain wilderness, yet striking, from the huge proportion which it seemed to bear to such more favoured spots of the country as were adapted to cultivation, and fitted for the support of man; and thereby impressing irresistibly the mind of the spectator with a sense of the omnipotence of Nature, and the comparative indifference of the boasted means of amelioration which man is capable of opposing to the disadvantages of climate and soil. (Ch. 15)

Despite the reference to a spectator, this passage is concerned not with the picturesque attitude of the tourist, but with the problems of the local inhabitants for ever combating 'the disadvantages of climate and soil.' This is essentially a regionalist view, and it is one that predominates in Scott's most characteristic work. It is only in the closing chapters of *Old Mortality*, where the realism of the Covenanters' struggles is replaced by the romance of Burley's hideaway in the Black Linn of Linklater (ch. 43), that he reverts to the Radcliffian mode.

In his later work, Scott becomes increasingly interested in the effects that can be produced by juxtaposing the conflicting responses of his characters to the landscapes through which they pass. The central contrast between the backward-looking Rob Roy and the progressive Nicol Jarvie is expressed by means of their response to their environment. Rob Roy waxes sentimental: '"The heather that I have trod upon when living, must bloom ower me when I am dead; my heart would sink, and my arm would shrink and wither like fern in the frost, were I to lose sight of my native hills"' (ch. 35). Jarvie, on the other hand, is fully prepared to drain a beautiful lake in the interests of commercial profit (ch. 36). A similar effect is achieved in *A Legend of Montrose* where the narrative action begins in the second chapter with a description of a 'romantic' scene, but 'those who journey in days of doubt and dread pay little attention to picturesque scenery.' Later we are confronted with 'one of the grandest scenes which nature affords' (ch. 11), but Scott offers a contrast between what Dalgetty 'might have' observed or admired and his actual interest in finding a place to rest and eat. In these effects Scott has completely integrated his landscapes with his characters.

But perhaps *The Bride of Lammermoor* is the Scott novel that had the greatest impact upon subsequent regional literature. Though set at a crucial point in Scottish history, just before the Union of 1707,[22] it is not directly associated with any specific historical events and, like *Guy Mannering*, contains no authentic historical characters. The origins of the story, which Scott has radically altered and the details of which are in any case disputed, belong to ancient history and legend. To complicate matters still further, Scott transferred the story from its place of origin in Wigtonshire to the Lammermuir Hills closer to his own locality, and so was able to link the tale with the traditional legends and superstitions from Thomas the Rhymer onwards that pervade his own border-country.

The result is complex. Despite the persistent identification of Wolf's Crag with Fast Castle on the coast between Dunbar and Berwick, the discrepancy between the story's legendary origins and the area to which Scott transplants it discourages any detailed local connections. Even as enthusiastic a topographer as W.S. Crockett considered all topographical identification for the novel 'hopeless and unprofitable guess-work.'[23] The fictional landscapes, comprising Ravenswood Castle, Wolf's Hope and the ruined tower, the Mermaiden's Fountain and the Kelpie's Flow, are all vividly realized, but they belong to the world of imagination rather than to any cartographical terrain. By the same token, although the succession of Sir William Ashton to the estates of the Master of Ravenswood after 1689 reflects a genuine movement of history, the novel has none of the historical texture that we find in *Waverley* or *Old Mortality* or *The Heart of Midlothian*. As Hart has remarked, 'its imaginative grounding in Gothic vision and folk or primitive fatalism makes it seem more remote from historical reality than almost any other of the novels.'[24]

None the less, *The Bride of Lammermoor* contains the regional essentials of romance. Caleb Balderstone's famous 'raid' on Wolf's Hope to provide provisions for his master's guests represents the last gasp of feudal privilege in answer to the Protestant challenge of *Realpolitik*. Lucy Ashton's 'romantic disposition, delighting in tales of love and wonder' (ch. 30) links her with the doomed past of Ravenswood and makes credible the contact between her father the Lord Keeper and Alice Gourlay, 'the very empress of old women, and queen of gossips, so far as legendary lore is concerned' (ch. 3). We see here an achieved

THE
UNIVERSITY OF WINNIPEG
PORTAGE & BALMORAL
WINNIPEG MAN. R3B 2E9
CANADA
DISCARDED

coexistence within a single novel of characters as temperamentally opposed and generically contrasting as, let us say, Heathcliff and Nelly Dean in *Wuthering Heights* or Carver Doone and Reuben Huckaback in *Lorna Doone*. In this novel Scott, who had so successfully demonstrated the artistic possibilities of presenting credible characters against appropriate and authentic backgrounds, also proved a pioneer in the kind of local romance that creates a region of the imagination existing in the mind as a separate fictive realm, a world in which ancient prophecies are vindicated and the story itself, like that of Heathcliff and Catherine in Emily Brontë's novel or the Doones in Blackmore's novel or Gideon Sarn in *Precious Bane*, becomes a part of the network of legends out of which it sprang.

In pointing out the structural and thematic resemblances between Scott's novel and *Tess of the d'Urbervilles*, Jane Millgate has written: 'If *The Bride of Lammermoor* provided Hardy with a romance paradigm, it did so in specifically regional terms. For Hardy, as for so many nineteenth-century writers, the Waverley novels made Scott the great representative of the regional artist, his achievement at the beginning of the century constituting both precedent and challenge for any potential follower.'[25] For some Scott set an example for historical reconstruction; his own region of the imagination, after all, was Scotland's past, and his 'contemporary' novel is significantly entitled *The Antiquary*. This trait in Scott was decidedly influential – in various forms it is reflected in Blackmore, Hardy, and Phillpotts, extending as far, I suspect, as John Cowper Powys. But, as Millgate insists, a more pervasive influence affected the whole regional movement. Such characters as Fergus McIvor, Rob Roy, Ravenswood are inseparable from their landscapes; we cannot think of Dandie Dinmont or the black dwarf or Redgauntlet except against a particular background. After Scott the perfunctory settings in most eighteenth-century fiction are unthinkable. He offered his own people a record of their own history and traditions, but to subsequent fiction, especially rural fiction, he gave an awakened sense of the spirit of place.[26]

THREE

Emily Brontë

THE LEGACY OF SCOTT: ROMANCE AND REALISM

That Scott was a profound influence on all the Brontës is generally agreed, though individual scholars differ dramatically about the precise form that this influence took. The facts are not in dispute. We know that their aunt gave them a New Year's present of *Tales of a Grandfather* in 1828, and, as Winifred Gérin has written, 'by 1834, when Charlotte told Ellen Nussey that "all novels after Scott's are worthless," they had evidently read the lot.'[1] Furthermore, we are also told that they had access to a set of Scott's novels at Keighley.[2] It is doubtful if the juvenile romances of Gondal and Angria could have been written without Scott's example, and details in the novels are continually recalling precedents in Scott. Even the complicated story around the pseudonyms of Acton, Ellis, and Currer Bell may well owe something to the obstinate anonymity of 'the author of *Waverley*.'

Wuthering Heights reveals the connection at least as readily as any other Brontë novel. Its setting 'sixty years since' is an obvious similarity, and the contrast between a cultivated existence in the valleys and a more rugged and primitive life on the hills – a contrast in which the landscape reflects complementary manners and mores – is strikingly close to the conventions of Scott's 'border-country.' There are, to be sure, certain geographical likenesses between the Yorkshire moors and the Highlands of Scotland that might naturally provoke connections, but this should not detract from Scott's importance in showing how such landscapes could be successfully incorporated into fiction. The same could be said about the early introduction of both Scott and the Brontës to balladry and local tales. Gérin points out that Tabitha Ackroyd, the Brontës' servant, was 'a local woman, well versed in the lore of the countryside,' that 'her tales of bygone times were a fu[r]ther stimulus to the imagination,' and that the children were 'brought up in the aural tradition of sung ballads, thanks to Tabby, irrespective of their readings in Percy's *Reliques*, and Scott's *Border Minstrelsy*.'[3] The comparison with Scott at Sandyknowe is clear enough, but Scott's practical example, his proof that such material could be transformed into original literature, must have been invaluable.

Other connections, perhaps less persuasive in themselves, become increasingly impressive as the evidence multiplies. Nelly Dean and Joseph have both been seen as deriving from the Scott tradition of independent and garrulous servants (Joseph's position in a 'line' stemming from Andrew Fairservice in *Rob Roy* and Caleb Balderstone in *The Bride of Lammermoor* is, I think, especially clear). Heathcliff himself has a complicated literary ancestry, including Milton's Satan and numerous Byronic heroes, but one of the more evident strands of literary kinship links him with Ravenswood. As Q.D. Leavis has remarked, 'the tone of *Wuthering Heights* is at times that of Scott, and the doomed Ravenswood is laid under contribution not only for the pattern of Heathcliff's name but for his nature and circumstances.'[4] Further, I suspect that the experiences of Lockwood during the night spent at Wuthering Heights in the third chapter owe something to Lovel's night in the Green Chamber in *The Antiquary*, while Florence Swithin Day, in a booklet that often pushes its source-hunting to grotesque lengths, remarks shrewdly that Emily Brontë's story 'is really a "Tale of My Landlord".'[5] More recently, Ian Jack has compared the opening description of Wuthering Heights to the approach to Tully-Veolan in *Waverley*.[6]

But the most important, if mystifying, legacy that Scott bequeathed to Emily Brontë was a fondness for combining romantic and realistic elements in his plots, and this is a subject that concerns us here because the landscape of the novel reflects the same blend. It *is*, I am convinced, a blend, though some of the more doctrinaire commentators insist on one element at the expense of the other. In *The Anatomy of Criticism* Northrop Frye classifies the novel unequivocally as a 'romance,' while to Arnold Kettle it is just as unequivocally 'not a romance.'[7] Q.D. Leavis sees it as 'in the Scott tradition, a historical and not a contemporary novel'; for Kettle once again '*Wuthering Heights* is about England in 1847.'[8] Barbara Hardy insists that it is 'inappropriate to ask questions about its social relevance'; Terry Eagleton, on the other hand, finds 'the crux of *Wuthering Heights* to be a social one' with Heathcliff representing 'the victory of capitalist property-dealing over the traditional yeoman economy of the Earnshaws.'[9]

Either/or or both/and? One of the most remarkable qualities of Emily Brontë's novel is its capacity to absorb and reflect the varying – often, indeed, contradictory – attitudes that are brought within its orbit. And I suggest that a study of the novel from a regional viewpoint can help to explain this puzzling characteristic. Perhaps nowhere else is the impact of regionalism more evident than in the differing responses to *Wuthering Heights* from the date of its first publication to the present time. To us 'the Brontë country' is a familiar idea, but to Emily Brontë's contemporaries it was almost totally unknown. Elizabeth Gaskell quotes a description of Haworth in a Keighley newspaper of 1840 (only seven years before the novel was published, from a town only three miles away) as 'situated among the bogs and mountains, and, until very lately, supposed to be in a state of semi-barbarism.'[10] It is hardly surprising, then, that an anonymous reviewer in the *Examiner* (January 1848) described Emily Brontë's characters as 'savages ruder than those who lived before the days of Homer' and observed that 'it is with difficulty that we can prevail upon ourselves to believe in the appearance of such a phenomenon [as Heathcliff], so near our own dwellings as the summit of a Lancashire or Yorkshire moor.'[11]

Charlotte Brontë seems to have had this reviewer's reaction in mind when she wrote her 'Editor's Preface to the New Edition of *Wuthering Heights*.' Because the attitude is so alien to our own response, it is worthwhile quoting her comments at some length:

> I have just read over *Wuthering Heights* and, for the first time, have ... gained a definite notion of how it appears to other people – to strangers who knew nothing of the author; who are unacquainted with the locality where the scenes of the story are laid; to whom the inhabitants, the customs, the natural characteristics of the outlying hills and hamlets in the West-Riding of Yorkshire are things alien and unfamiliar.
>
> To all such *Wuthering Heights* must appear a rude and strange production. The wild moors of the north of England can for them have no interest; the language, the manners, the very dwellings and household customs of the scattered inhabitants of those districts, must be to such readers in a great measure unintelligible, and – where intelligible – repulsive. ... [Such readers] will hardly know what to make of the rough, strong utterance, the harshly manifested passions, the unbridled aversions, and headlong partialities of unlettered moorland hinds and rugged moorland squires ...

The growth of regional awareness, of an interest in local differences, has doubtless been stimulated by *Wuthering Heights* – to such an extent, indeed, that it may well be difficult for us to understand the kind of reaction that Charlotte describes. We can now consult numerous historical and sociological studies that confirm the validity of Emily's presentation. Gaskell did much to educate the Brontës' reading public on this matter at the opening of her *Life of*

Charlotte Brontë. By Swinburne's time, the manners recorded in the novel no longer seemed unintelligible; one of his Westmorland correspondents reported that she 'had known wilder instances of lawless and law-defying passion and tyranny, far more horrible than any cruelty of Heathcliff's, in her own neighbourhood.'[12] In our own century, Arnold Kettle can assert that the Earnshaws and Lintons 'live not in a never-never land but in Yorkshire,' V.S. Pritchett can describe the novel as 'the most realistic statement about the Yorkshire people of the isolated moorland and dales that I have ever read,' and we are unlikely to question their statements.[13]

None the less, those who insist upon the romantic elements in the novel must not be ignored. There *is* a suggestion of the supernatural if not the diabolical about Heathcliff; it *is* possible, within the imaginative ethos of the novel, that Catherine's ghost haunts the moors outside Wuthering Heights. The story of Heathcliff – the uncertainty of his origins, the violence of his passions, his almost necrophilic obsession with Catherine's grave, the mystery of his last days and death – harks back to the melodramatic puppets of Gondal and Angria, and beyond them to Gothic fiction and romantic tales of horror. The moors decidedly belong to Yorkshire, but I am forced to insist that, *pace* Kettle, they also belong, if not to a 'never-never land,' at least to a region of the imagination. When Cathy and Heathcliff escape from Wuthering Heights on to the moors, they move out of a realistic ambience into another dimension, another fictional realm. Emily Brontë's presentation of the landscape of her novel is not inconsistent; rather, it shifts and adapts itself to the varying, fluctuating needs of the story. The regional elements may not be absolutely central to her work, but they are of undeniable importance in providing an anchor connecting her imaginative flights to a solid, realistic basis. For this reason, an examination of her carefully organized locality merits detailed attention.

GIMMERTON AND 'THE MOORS'

'No work of literature was ever more inseparably identified with a definite spot on the earth's surface than *Wuthering Heights* ... yet it is a drama of elemental conflict and suffering that might have been played out on any stage.'[14] Ernest A. Baker here puts his finger on the difficulty of discussing the novel in regional terms. That the book evokes a strong sense of locality few readers would be prepared to deny;[15] the firm impression of Haworth and 'the Brontë country' in the public mind is sufficient to establish this, over and above the 'feel' of a particular terrain that dominates the novel. 'Its every fibre,' wrote Lord David Cecil, 'smells of the Northern soil where it had its root.'[16] But it is by no means easy to demonstrate that fact by reference to the words on the page.

Here an initial distinction needs to be made, I think, between geographical and communal realism. The emphasis in *Wuthering Heights* is on physical rather than social locality. Everyone recalls Wuthering Heights and Thrushcross Grange, but few are likely to remember for very long that the two dominant residences in the book lie within the parish of Gimmerton. Despite references to 'neighbours' (ch. 6) and 'the Gimmerton band' (ch. 7), we have little sense of a local community of which the main characters form a part, and this is explained to some extent by the fact that Gimmerton itself is a straggling village lacking a physical centre, 'a parish where two or three miles was the ordinary distance between cottage and cottage' (ch. 9). The isolation is evident later, when Nelly Dean mentions 'a rough sand-pillar, with the letters W.H. cut on its north side, on the east, G., and on the south-west, T.G. It serves as guide-post to the Grange, and Heights, and village' (ch. 11). Of local inhabitants we hear regularly of Dr Kenneth, from time to time of a curate and a lawyer, once of 'Dame Archer' (presumably a midwife); otherwise there are occasional vague references to neighbours, tenants, and labourers, and that is all. Gimmerton Church would seem to imply a congregation, but by the last page of the novel the one building that might be expected to provide a local centre is in decay. The reader is in a comparable position to Cathy Linton, who at the age of thirteen 'had not once been beyond the range of the park by herself' and of whom we are told that 'Gimmerton was an unsubstantial name in her ears' (ch. 18). This is a story, then, not about a distinctive and cohesive community but of scattered settlements surrounded – even dwarfed – by the untamed moorland.

Geographical references are hardly more frequent. There are none of the lists of places and natural objects that become so familiar in George Eliot and Hardy and Eden Phillpotts and Sheila Kaye-Smith. Besides Peniston Crags (a focal point in the landscape not unlike the Devil's Chair in Mary Webb's *The Golden Arrow*), we find scattered references to Gimmerton Sough (or brook), Blackhorse marsh (comparable to the Wizard's Slough in *Lorna Doone*), the Lees and 't' Nab.' Otherwise the phrase that recurs is simply 'the moors.' And outside reference is confined to Lockwood's unspecified 'sea-coast' in the first chapter, Mr Earnshaw's visit to Liverpool where he finds the young Heathcliff, a passing allusion to 'the next town' (ch. 10), and a few casual references to London (chs. 17 and 31). Again, that is all. When characters move out of the orbit of Wuthering Heights and Thrushcross Grange they move into a void – and this is as true of Isabella and Lockwood as of the ever-mysterious Heathcliff. Gimmerton is certainly a place apart. To Lockwood, who claims to be 'of the busy world' (ch. 25), it is 'completely removed from the stir of society' (ch. 1), and Heathcliff describes him at Thrushcross as 'banished from the world' (ch. 31). Clearly, there is no question of Gimmerton's being presented as in some way a microcosm representative of a larger reality. The world of *Wuthering Heights* is not only isolated but different.

It is hardly surprising, then, that the novel doesn't respond to Phyllis Bentley's formal requirements for regional fiction. She states herself that only setting and one character ('the horrid old manservant Joseph')[17] are truly regional, and many other aspects that we might recognize as regional characteristics are conspicuous by their absence. Although John Cowper Powys is justified in laying emphasis on 'the long, bitter, tragic, human association of persons who have lived for generations on the same spot,'[18] there is little sense – despite the prominence of the opening date, '1801' – of a historic or prehistoric past in the book itself. Two casual references to 'elf-bolts' (flint arrowheads, ch. 12) are all that we hear of the prehistory of the area, and although this can be explained by the fact that the Haworth moors are not rich in ancient monuments, it distinguishes the landscape dramatically from Hardy's Wessex or Phillpotts's Dartmoor – and even, to some extent, from Scott's Scotland (certainly the area around Haworth cannot compare with Scotland in terms of the history of the immediate past). The moors are not so much prehistoric as primordial. They do, however, give rise to a local folklore, and this aspect of the region we shall find crucial a little later in the discussion. Nor is work a prominent aspect of the novel. We know that work is done at Wuthering Heights, but only rarely do we see characters such as Joseph or Hareton actually engaged in rural labour. A character may be sent out to bring home the sheep or to attend to the day-to-day routines of the farm, but we never see one of those scenes of agricultural activity that are customary in, among others, George Eliot and Hardy.

Above all – and here Emily Brontë is at her furthest remove from Scott – we find none of the minute description of local scenery that we might well assume, with Phyllis Bentley, to be a *sine qua non* of the regional novel. Emily Brontë employs a standard regional formula, however, in first presenting the locality through the eyes of Lockwood, an outsider. Certainly he describes Wuthering Heights itself in considerable detail, and through him we derive a good deal of information about the ways of life of the area; but he has little or nothing to say about the natural world outside – mainly because he never ventures into it. More than one commentator has remarked that the route between Wuthering Heights and Thrushcross Grange is both well marked and clear in our minds but that the landscape beyond is a blank, and part of the reason is that Lockwood confines himself to the path. The moors themselves are the preserve of Catherine and Heathcliff – a private realm from which even Nelly Dean is generally excluded.

There is no doubt, of course, that Emily Brontë herself knew the moors intimately. Indeed, since she was in Charlotte's words 'a native and nursling of the moors' ('Editor's Preface'), it may not have occurred to her to describe what was the encompassing environment of everyday life. Country-dwellers in general often find difficulty in realizing that what is familiar to them needs to be explained to their readers; Edward Thomas, for example, noted that a countryside is rarely appreciated until it has been tamed.[19] The moors here are untamed, and the natives such as Zillah merely accept them for what they are. Catherine and Heathcliff (along with their creator) reveal their 'Romantic' sensibilities in responding to the attractions of desolate scenes and the combination of solitude and liberty to be found in the wilderness. They 'feel' them, but they keep their feelings to themselves; there is no impulse to describe them for the benefit of others. Indeed, the landscape is often a correlative (though hardly an *objective* correlative) of the characters themselves, especially Heathcliff. Charlotte Brontë was hardly exaggerating when she observed to W.S. Williams: 'some of his spirit seems breathed through the whole narrative in which he figures: it haunts every moor and glen, and beckons in every fir-tree of the Heights.'[20] Moreover, it is part of Emily's artistry that she uses the landscape to reflect the attitudes of her characters. It has no fixed 'meaning,' not even a fixed appearance – as Lockwood observes, 'in winter, nothing more dreary, in summer, nothing more divine, than these glens shut in by hills' (ch. 32). Q.D. Leavis rightly denies 'a mystique to the moor' and admirably sums up its creative function: 'It is not even powerful over man's destiny like Egdon Heath. The moor is a way of pointing a distinction.'[21]

REGIONAL AND ELEMENTAL

The regional quality of *Wuthering Heights* is stamped upon the very texture of the book. It is there in the assured way of life that Lockwood misunderstands or approaches with condescension. Nelly Dean's obstinate insistence on serving dinner country-style at noon rather than at five (ch. 2) is one example, stated but never explained. Lockwood's failure to realize that farm-duties take precedence over the claims of an uninvited guest at the time of a snow blizzard is another (one thinks of Mary Crawford's puzzlement in *Mansfield Park* when she cannot get a farm-cart to transport her harp at the height of harvest). The bluff north-country directness the tone of which Lockwood can never quite interpret is particularly noticeable, and Lockwood's function within the story is, at least in part, to emphasize through his own rather pallid urbanity the unabashed vigour of Yorkshire rural ways.

Nowhere is the sanctioned local custom more subtly presented than in the character of Nelly Dean, and I find Phyllis Bentley's already mentioned acceptance of only one truly regional character in the book (Joseph) extraordinarily – and uncharacteristically – imperceptive. Joseph is dramatically and vividly portrayed, and he provides an alternative viewpoint on the whole action which, albeit extreme, can be too easily simplified and dismissed by twentieth-century readers. Furthermore, his dialect, reproduced in its full vigour and angularity, forces us to experience as well as observe the local flavour of the district; the hardness of the local speech represents the hardness of the local culture. But Joseph is a supernumerary with little or no importance to the main action, however much he contributes to the all-important atmosphere. Only seen from the outside, he is perilously close to being no more than a chorus character. Nelly, on the other hand, is the representative voice of local sanity. She embodies the regional viewpoint, reflects the values of whatever community exists in Gimmerton, and provides a moral and pragmatic norm against which the challenging, perhaps transcending values of Catherine and Heathcliff can be measured.

Not the least important result of viewing *Wuthering Heights* from a regional point of view is the opportunity offered of seeing Nelly in better focus. She is easily misread, and I am referring here not merely to the silly North American fashion of trying to cast her in the role of villain.[22] All Nelly's characteristics – her bluntness, her bossiness, her firm application of simple moral rules of conduct, her ways of dealing with children, her perilous balance between loyalty to her employer and a canny concern for her own interest, her garrulity, her no-nonsense directness – all these mark her as a regional personality, a characteristic product of the Yorkshire moors. Hers, in Mark Schorer's words, is 'the perdurable voice of the country.'[23] She functions, of course, as a total contrast to Lockwood: female instead of male, native instead of outsider, speaker instead of writer, rustic instead of urban-sophisticated – but her most important contribution is the suffusing of the story with a regional attitude. She it is who initiates the process of transforming the story of Wuthering Heights, of Catherine and Heathcliff, into a local legend. She belongs, indeed, to that select, irrepressible literary company that includes the Nurse in *Romeo and Juliet* and Mrs Poyser in *Adam Bede*. I am not arguing that we are expected to embrace her position without qualification; on the contrary, I believe that Catherine and Heathcliff transcend – at least in imaginative terms – the moral position that she represents. But in recognizing this, we do not have to 'reject' her position, to stigmatize it as narrow or inadequate. I agree with those commentators who see her as 'the voice of normal human limitation,' her judgment 'a relevant though not a final comment.'[24] Without it, we would be unable to measure the unique quality of Catherine and Heathcliff's relationship.

And here, I suggest, we are close to the particular function of the regional qualities in this novel, a function we shall not encounter again until we come to consider the work of John Cowper Powys. In order to render credible the transcendent realm to which Catherine and Heathcliff aspire, Emily Brontë knew that she must create a vividly realized regional setting from which it could be distinguished. Walter E. Anderson has remarked that Emily Brontë 'invites us to release her principal subject from ordinary limits and values and to focus on a transcendental realm.'[25] Precisely, but this can only happen if the 'ordinary limits and values' are firmly etched in. Just as Nelly provides a solidity that enables us to accept what might otherwise seem incredible behaviour in her charges, so the moors function as a remarkable catalyst for our acceptance of the transformation. Because the landscape is made real to us, including the rural elements that make up what Kettle calls 'the concrete, local particularity of the book,'[26] we are predisposed to accept the 'romantic' figures that move against it. One reason why Heathcliff is more impressive than the Byronic heroes from whom he derives is that a suitable landscape (of heath and cliff) has been provided for him.

My reference to the landscape associations of Heathcliff's name is not a mere rhetorical flourish. Throughout the text the characters who yearn towards a metaphysical realm are clothed in decidedly physical imagery. Anderson notes that 'Heathcliff is like the moor itself,' and remarks later: 'Their furious passion is like a tempest on the moors.'[27] At this point we come to understand why the normal process of landscape-description is of no use to Emily Brontë. She needs, rather, to fuse her chief characters with the elemental qualities of the landscape. So the contrast between Heathcliff and Edgar Linton is said to resemble 'what you see in exchanging a black, hilly, coal country, for a beautiful fertile valley' (ch. 8); the words are Nelly's, and she mistakes Catherine's preference, but the description of men in terms of landscape reflects a habitual process in the novel. When Catherine tries to differentiate her feelings for Edgar Linton and Heathcliff, she is similarly forced back upon natural imagery: 'My love for Linton is like the foliage in the woods. Time will change it, I'm well aware, as winter changes the trees – my love for Heathcliff resembles the eternal rocks beneath' (ch. 9). And when, a little later, she tries to explain Heathcliff to Isabella, she describes him as 'an unreclaimed person, without refinement – without *cultivation; an arid wilderness of furze and whinstone'* (ch. 10; my italics).

The very names help. All sorts of explanations have been offered for the origin of Heatcliff – from Scott's *The Black Dwarf* (where there is a character called Earnescliffe), for example, or from the slight alteration of local names. It is even possible to see a literary analogy, a combination of Macbeth's blasted heath with King Lear's cliff, while the association of 'heath' and 'heathen' so close to the surface of Hardy's Egdon may also be important. But the combination of natural vegetation ('heath' is a flower as well as the environment in which it often grows) and 'the eternal rocks beneath' is surely primary. One finds it implicit, though doubtless unrecognized by the speaker, in Lockwood's final paragraph about 'the moths fluttering among the heath' and 'the sleepers in that quiet earth.' Nor must we forget the title of the novel.

'Wuthering,' as Lockwood is careful to explain in the first chapter, has bleak meteorological connotations which link the house to the elements. 'Heights,' moreover, has an abstract as well as a geographical meaning; Heathcliff and Catherine, we may say, achieve heights beyond the imaginative capacity of the educated Lockwood or the regional Nelly Dean – even, perhaps, of ourselves as readers.

No wonder Catherine and Heathcliff 'haunt' the moors at the close of the book. Anderson's insistence on 'the reader's final impression that these lovers do not rest quietly in the grave but walk together as spirits on the Heights'[28] seems to me indisputable. But this is not to say that the fiction ends on the level of a conventional ghost story. Commentators do an injustice to Emily Brontë's effect if they fail to come to terms with the unequivocally regional evidence at the end of the book. This evidence rests not merely on the exaggerated fears of a small sheep-boy ('as a little boy blubbers,' Tom Winnifrith remarks unfairly).[29] Nelly Dean takes care to insist that 'the country folks, if you ask them, would swear on their bible that [Heathcliff] *walks.*' And the boy's testimony is borne out by his sheep, who refuse to pass 't' Nab' where Catherine and Heathcliff are said to haunt. True, Nelly Dean herself has taken over the scepticism of her employers; to her the boy's claims are explained by 'the nonsense he had heard his parents and companions repeat,' but the important point, surely, is that Catherine and Heathcliff have become the stuff of local legend. They end as *genii loci,* spirits of the (regional) place. The bare moors are now inhabited; they belong, as it were, to story. Paradoxically, by escaping from the limitations of the regional, Catherine and Heathcliff have become absorbed by the regional. We remember Catherine's dream in which 'heaven did not seem to be [her] home' and she was flung out 'into the middle of the heath on the top of Wuthering Heights; where [she] woke sobbing with joy' (ch. 9). We first hear of the two going for a 'scamper on the moors' (ch. 3), and at the end that is where we leave them, gathered into the artifice of eternity but (more important) reunited for ever on the untamed moors where the heath grows out of eternal rock.

FOUR

Urbanism, Realism, and Region

CHARLOTTE BRONTË AND 'SHIRLEY'

Formally, Charlotte Brontë's *Shirley* (1849) conforms to all the main specifications for a regional novel. Set in 'a certain favoured district in the West Riding of Yorkshire' (ch. 1) during the machine-breaking disturbances of 1811–12, it is from the opening page sharply defined in both place and time. Its background is the newly established woollen mills that were changing the face of the local countryside. The emphasis falls upon social and economic problems stemming from the workers' fears of redundancy and unemployment on account of the development of ever more complex machinery; furthermore, the uncertain markets at the time of the Napoleonic Wars exacerbated what was already a sensitive situation. As Elizabeth Gaskell documented in her *Life of Charlotte Brontë*, the accounts of an attack on Hollow's Mill and the attempted assassination of Robert Moore can be paralleled in the local history of the area. 'Yorkshire' as both noun and adjective reverberates throughout the book. The famous three curates in the opening chapter, as more than one critic has pointed out, underline the regional differentiation by being themselves from other regions. Kathleen Tillotson, indeed, has described the book as 'defiantly regional' when quoting the significant passage which indefatigably narrows down and localizes a specific phenomenon: 'A yell followed this demonstration – a rioters' yell – a north-of-England – a Yorkshire – a West-Riding – a West-Riding-clothing-district-of-Yorkshire rioters' yell' (ch. 19).[1]

Clearly, we are in a very different world from *Wuthering Heights;* geographical resemblances there may be, but the tones of the two novels can never be reconciled with each other. From the start, Charlotte Brontë insists upon the realistic elements in her story: 'Something real, cool, and solid, lies before you; something unromantic as Monday morning' (ch. 1). And the contrast between romantic imaginings on the one hand and the basic facts of 'real life' on the other are continually alluded to. Caroline Helstone at eighteen is at the stage when 'Elf-land lies behind us, the shores of Reality rise in front' (ch. 7); a little later, she is forced to return 'from an enchanted region to the real world' (ch. 10). Shirley Keeldar confesses to Helstone, 'I like that romantic Hollow, with all my heart,' only to be met with the query: 'Romantic – with a mill in it?' (ch. 11). Yet despite the assurances borne out by the narrative voice that we must face up to reality and eschew vain dreams, the plot, with its conventional complications of pairs of lovers and especially Caroline's unlikely reunion with her long-lost mother, has palpable connections with 'romance.' Here, however, the claims of romance and reality provoke not so much a fruitful tension as an irritating discrepancy. Artistically, the reader is likely to feel uncomfortably torn between the conflicting demands of the somewhat inflated love-plot and the historical, almost sociological setting and theme. In *Shirley* there exists none of the transcending passion that can, in Wordsworthian phrase, reconcile discordant elements in the imaginative world of *Wuthering Heights*.

For students of regional fiction, however, *Shirley* is of particular interest *because* of the difficulty Charlotte Brontë encounters in trying to link plot and theme. This is a difficulty that haunts regional writing: how to develop a plot that is substantial and capable of maintaining interest without detracting from the authenticity and importance of the locale. One of the problems arises from the fact that her region is more distinctive in social and economic terms than in topographical ones. We are far more conscious here than in *Wuthering Heights* of a specific community with an economic *raison d'être*. Although the emphasis falls upon the mill-owners and the classes with which they mingle, the local gentry and clergy, we see enough of the mill-hands to gain an impression of a corporate community. By the same token, however, we have little sense of a recognizable physical area. We hear about Stilboro' Moor, where Moore's machinery is smashed and his men bound in a ditch, but we do not see it in our mind's eye as we see the moors in *Wuthering Heights*. This is partly because the characters are rarely responsive to their surroundings in any noticeable way. At the beginning of the second chapter, when Malone walks in the darkness to Hollow's Mill, we are told specifically that he 'was not a man given to close observation of Nature; ... he could walk miles on the most varying April day, and never see the beautiful dallying of earth and heaven.' And although the narrator proceeds (like Scott in *A Legend of Montrose*) to tell us what the character fails to see, it lacks an immediate urgency. Moore, of course, is 'not ... a native, nor for any length of time a resident of the neighbourhood' (ch. 2); for him the countryside is a place to be developed rather than cherished. Caroline's love for the locality takes second place to her love for Moore, and although

Shirley is supposed to be based on Emily Brontë, we are shown her independence and courage rather than her impassioned rapport with the moorland ('I *like* that romantic Hollow' [my italics] is hardly what we would expect from the author of *Wuthering Heights*).

Charlotte's main emphasis, however, is on the radical changes that had taken place in a particular spot during a single lifetime. This is, as we have seen, a concern central to Scott and not without its importance in *Wuthering Heights*. Q.D. Leavis has shown the significance of Emily Brontë's setting her novel 'at a time when the old rough farming culture based on a naturally patriarchal family life, was to be challenged, tamed and routed by social and cultural changes that were to produce the Victorian class consciousness and "unnatural" ideal of gentility.'[2] This is only one of a number of thematic strands in *Wuthering Heights*, but *Shirley* is dominated by the subject of change. Implicit throughout the book (the riot, after all, originates in a fear of impending change, and conversations continually revert to discussions about the nature of progress), it is especially evident at the close. On the last page, indeed, a new character is introduced, the narrator's housekeeper – almost certainly based, like Nelly Dean, on Tabby Ackroyd – who has known the area from birth and looks back nostalgically to the days of her childhood:

'Aye!' said she; 'this world has queer changes. I can remember the old mill being built – the very first it was in all the district; and then, I can remember it being pulled down, and going with my lake-lasses (companions) to see the foundation-stone of the new one laid. ... But I can tell of it different again; when there was neither mill, nor cot, nor hall, except Fieldhead, within two miles of it. I can tell, one summer evening, fifty years syne, my mother coming running in just at the edge of the dark, almost fleyed out of her wits, saying she had seen a fairish (fairy) in Fieldhead Meadow; and that was the last fairish that ever was seen on this country side (though they've been heard within these forty years). A lonesome spot it was – and a bonnie spot – full of oak trees and nut trees. It is altered now.'

The action of the novel focuses upon the central but crucial part of this history, before Robert Moore's most ambitious day-dreams have become 'embodied in substantial stone and brick and ashes' (ch. 37). It is not surprising that Phyllis Bentley should hail *Shirley* as a major work in regional fiction; in attempting to preserve a portion of the local historical record, Charlotte Brontë is adding her contribution to the documentary aspect of the regional movement. As literary historians, we can see it as the first fully realized expression of an important tradition in English fiction culminating in the first chapter of D.H. Lawrence's *The Rainbow* (though lacking Lawrence's creative energy). None the less, we should also recognize that, important as Charlotte Brontë's contribution may be, it is only one strand in the larger web that produces the English regional novel.

ELIZABETH GASKELL

In my introductory chapter, I suggested that *Cranford* was best classified as a 'local' rather than a 'regional' novel. Yet with the exception of *Sylvia's Lovers*, *Cranford* is the most obvious candidate in Elizabeth Gaskell's fiction for consideration here. The fact is that Gaskell's significance in the development of regionalism is indirect; few novelists were better equipped by upbringing and temperament to exploit the possibilities of regional fiction, and so obvious is the impulse to regionalism just beneath the surface of her work that it is tempting to conclude that she consciously avoided the regional mode. Indeed, it is her failure – or deliberate refusal – to become an important regional novelist that makes her case of particular interest.

At the beginning of her career as a writer, Gaskell possessed all the qualities requisite for regional fiction. First and foremost was an appreciation of the essential connection between man and his natural environment that she evidently derived from Wordsworth. The accessibility of the Lake District was, in part, a happy accident of her biography, but the obvious use of Wordsworthian techniques suggests a deeper rapport. The opening of 'The Moorland Cottage' – 'if you take the turn to the left … ' – is clearly derived from 'Michael,' and J.G. Sharps has noted that 'Martha Preston,' an early short story later rewritten under the significant title 'Half a Lifetime Ago,' seems likely to have been based on 'a local Loughrigg tale, the bare bones of which were most probably true.'[3] Whether or not it was so based, the important point is that Gaskell leaves the impression that this is a tale that took place at a particular time in a particular locality. The interaction of human story and natural setting, fiction arising out of local historical record, is at the root of her art.

Second, her employment of dialect in *Mary Barton* shows that she was scrupulous in presenting as accurate a representation as possible of local speech. Here she both followed and extended the example of Scott, whom she is known to have read with admiration. She was prepared to set dialect-speaking characters at the centre of her fiction and to treat them with seriousness and dignity. Her painstaking compromise between exact but puzzling phonetic reproduction and a notation that would prove not merely acceptable but congenial to her readers shows the importance which she set on the most obvious example of regional differentiation, and it was to prove essential to the success of *Sylvia's Lovers* where she was recreating a region and a speech with which she was not intimately familiar.

Above all, however, she possessed an eagerness to record the customs and manners of specific places and times, to preserve local stories and memories that were in danger of being forgotten. In this connection, the following extract from a letter written to James Crossley in May 1858 is especially revealing:

A friend of mine is amplifying some lectures he delivered at Knutsford during this last winter in the History of that dear little town, and a circle of country about 20 miles around. He has discovered very curious family traditions and old facts; and he wants to make his book as perfect as possible, and I would gladly do what I can to help him, remembering what Southey says of how good & well it would be if every Parish priest would write down what he hears and learns about his own Parish, as traits of customs & manners & character might thus be preserved as Memoires pour servir.[4]

Here, one might say, is a concise manifesto for the regional viewpoint. It is a passage that makes us think back to Scott ('customs & manners & character') and forward to Hardy ('very curious family traditions and old facts'), and bears witness to the constant preoccupation in regional writing with change and the need to preserve memories of past ways of life.

The reference to Southey in the letter just quoted recalls the opening of 'The Last Generation in England' (1849), her first treatment of the material that would develop four years later into *Cranford*. The article begins with a reference to Southey's recommendation which, she reports,

created a wish in me to put on record some of the details of country town life, either observed by myself, or handed down to me by older relations; for even in small towns, scarcely removed from villages, the phases of society are rapidly changing; and much will appear strange, which yet occurred only in the generation immediately preceding ours.[5]

Later, the old ladies in the as yet unnamed town are described as 'living hoards of family tradition and old custom.'[6] Many of the anecdotes first recounted here are subsequently incorporated into *Cranford*, and it is clear that they derive from Gaskell's own favourite locality of Knutsford, Cheshire.

Although she lived most of her life in Manchester, Knutsford – 'dear old Knutsford,' as she called it – remained in Arthur Pollard's words, 'to the end of her life the home of her spirit.'[7] There she had grown up, and there she would return regularly for periods of refreshment and solace. Thus it is not surprising to find her, throughout her writing career, continually veering between 'the world of Manchester' and 'the world of Cranford.' I use the phrases from Edgar Wright's chapter-titles in his pioneering study, *Mrs Gaskell: The Basis for*

Reassessment, because his balancing of a geographical locality with a fictional creation seems especially appropriate. Cranford is not Knutsford, but a particular, highly selective view of Knutsford. It is also, despite its local allusions and authentic anecdotes, something of a dream-world. Most of the writing of *Cranford* was done in Manchester, and the opening chapters specifically presuppose a London readership; the place may be said to represent an attractive rural backwater that Gaskell could visit in imagination while surrounded by the stresses of the industrial city which appears in the novel itself as 'the great neighbouring commercial town of Drumble, distant only twenty miles on a railroad' (ch. 1).

Modern readers, inaccurately but understandably, tend to think of Cranford as a village society surviving, in a charming if sad state of impoverished decline, from the world of Jane Austen – as something comparable with Mary Russell Mitford's Three Mile Cross. Although Gaskell calls it a small town, the impression is of a much smaller rural unit. This is a result of her extreme selectivity. Knutsford as a whole was decidedly larger and more 'modern.' Humphrey Repton may have been exaggerating at the other end of the scale when he wrote of 'a large manufacturing town, like Knutsford,'[8] but there can be little doubt that, in portraying Cranford, Gaskell was adapting her memories of the Knutsford of earlier days and so creating an imaginary world that could function as the antithesis to the Manchester in which she was required to live and work. Antitheses, indeed, seem to have been necessary as a stimulus to her art; we find not only geographical polarities – Cranford and Drumble, North and South – but extreme contrasts of character – Philip Hepburn and Charlie Kinraid in *Sylvia's Lovers*, Mollie Gibson and Cynthia Kirkpatrick in *Wives and Daughters*. There is nothing simplistic about these general dichotomies, but behind them is frequently the basic opposition of rural/agricultural versus urban/industrial values and ways of life.

Indeed, it would not perhaps be going too far to define the 'Cranford world' as any rural community that represented an antithesis to Manchester and/or London – and here the distinction from a specifically regional concern begins to make itself felt. Manchester alias Drumble appears in *North and South* as Milton-Northern, 'the manufacturing town in Darkshire' (ch. 4), and although the rural equivalent to Darkshire is never named (one immediately thinks of George Eliot's 'Loamshire' to be invented four years later), the unregional generality is evident. Gaskell's rural locales (more often suggested than minutely described) have a family resemblance derived from her Knutsford memories, and although they are well known to students of her fiction they need to be rehearsed here. 'The Last Generation in England' (1849), as I have noted, was an anticipation of *Cranford* offered in non-fiction terms, but the name of the town is left blank. 'Mr. Harrison's Confessions,' a novella contributed to the *Ladies' Companion* in 1851, is set in a place called Duncombe that seems to be Cranford in everything but name. Two short stories, 'The Squire's Story' (1853) and 'A Dark Night's Work' (1863), are based on incidents recorded in Knutsford history but transferred to imaginary localities, Barford in Derbyshire and Hamley respectively. *Cousin Phillis* (1865), like one of the scenes in *Cranford* itself, is based on Sandlebridge Farm a few miles outside Knutsford, which appears in the first paragraph as 'the county-town of Eltham.' And in her last book, *Wives and Daughters* (1866), Hollingford is in many of its details recognizably Knutsford once again.[9]

But the influence of Knutsford/Cranford can be detected much further afield. Thus, although *My Lady Ludlow* is set in Warwickshire, the name-character is known to be based on the same original as the Honourable Mrs Jamieson in *Cranford*, and Edgar Wright has described it as showing 'what may be called the Cranford ethos.' Wright has also argued that 'The Moorland Cottage,' though ostensibly a Lake District story, is in fact 'the first of her stories to be given a Cranford setting' and notes that the Helstone of *North and South*, however geographically distant, 'has the makings of a Cranford corner.'[10] J.G. Sharps has added 'Morton Hall' and 'My French Master' (both 1853) to the list. He argues that in the former, 'old stories and Knutsford memories seem to have been used to fill up volume-space' and identifies the narrator as 'a typically Cranfordian lady' who conveys 'anti-Drumble attitudes'; of the latter he remarks that 'the idyllic description of country life in the first chapter recalls Knutsford during Mrs Gaskell's childhood.'[11]

It seems clear, then, that Gaskell had the opportunity of creating a specific region that could have become a unifying focus in her fiction. Indeed, Knutsford and the 'circle of country about 20 miles round' mentioned in the letter to Crossley might well have been converted into a fictional region eligible for the title of 'Elizabeth Gaskell country.' But it is equally clear that, by giving different names to the various manifestations of Knutsford in her books, she *avoided* the creation of an interconnected region. That, perhaps, is to put the matter too strongly. She had no obvious model for a series of interlinked regional fictions. John Galt had made some experiments in that direction, but there is no evidence that Gaskell had read him; Trollope was developing his Barsetshire while she was writing (and we know that in 1860 she wished *Framley Parsonage* would go on for ever), but we have no reason to assume that a similar Knutsford/Cranford series ever occurred to her.

Besides, although any such speculations can be no more than tentative, we can offer various reasons why a regional scheme might not have fulfilled her intentions. The idea of a comprehensive treatment of the area, drawing on historical traditions as well as contemporary observation, seems (from a post-Hardy viewpoint) attractive. But once the selective – and highly popular –

presentation of *Cranford* (the society of Amazons, etc.) had been established, there would have been difficulties in converting it into a credible regional centre. It is possible, too, that after the controversy over *The Life of Charlotte Brontë* and her own part in the argument over the authorship of George Eliot's Warwickshire novels (Gaskell was for a time taken in by the 'Liggins' claimant) she would have been reluctant to risk local protests about identifications. Her daughters were certainly sensitive on this issue after her death, acknowledging identifiable places but resisting attempts to equate characters with local inhabitants.

Two other possible reasons suggest themselves. First, Gaskell seems to have been split between a liking for true anecdotes and the plain presentation of manners and customs on the one hand, and a tendency to fall back on melodramatic incident to resolve her plots on the other. *Cranford*, *Cousin Phillis*, and *Wives and Daughters* are closer to regional realism; *My Lady Ludlow* and *Sylvia's Lovers*, though for the most part in the same mode, are interspersed with dramatic scenes of action and crisis. Many of her lesser works – like Sheila Kaye-Smith's after her – have an almost obsessive interest in violence and sensation. This is Gaskell's version of the problem that Charlotte Brontë encountered in *Shirley*: the difficulty of reconciling the realistic and romantic sides of regional tradition. George Eliot expressed it well when she described her as 'constantly misled by a love of sharp contrasts – of "dramatic effects"' and added that she was never content with 'the subdued colouring, the half-tones of real life.'[12] Finally, there is Gaskell's acute sense (in which she resembles Eliot) of Duty. In the Preface to *Mary Barton* she reports that her initial – perhaps instinctive – idea for a work of fiction involved a setting that was rural in place and a century old in time. But her sympathy for those 'who elbowed [her] daily in the busy streets of the town in which [she] resided' caused her to turn to a contemporary and urban setting. We feel a similar pull between inclination and duty in *Ruth* and *North and South*. Later in life she felt that she had paid her debt to society, and *Cousin Phillis* and *Wives and Daughters* both return to the kind of setting and subject she found most congenial – Edgar Wright calls them 'a reaffirmation of the Cranford world.'[13] None the less, the continuing tension – parallel to the division between Manchester and Cranford – militated against a consistent regional emphasis.

Yet even if *Cranford* and the related stories ultimately evade the regional category, two of Gaskell's works show distinct regional concerns. Her most obvious contribution to the genre is *Sylvia's Lovers* (1863), and there is a certain irony in the fact that the novel is set in Whitby (Monkshaven), a Yorkshire coastal town that she knew only through a brief visit just before she began writing. Most of the qualities that we have seen emerging as desirable and accepted ingredients of regional writing are present here. It resembles

Waverley in being set about sixty years in the past, and the choice of period may well reflect the influence of *Adam Bede* (1859), a book Gaskell is known to have admired. The emphasis at the opening is on the locality (the first chapter is entitled simply 'Monkshaven'), and Gaskell begins with a precise and informative statement which suggests that she is writing local history rather than fiction:

> On the north-eastern shores of England there is a town called Monkshaven, containing at the present day about fifteen thousand inhabitants. There were, however, but half the number at the end of the last century, and it was at that period that the events narrated in the following pages occurred.

One of the central incidents is indeed adapted from local history: a riotous attack on the headquarters of the pressgang that took place in Whitby in 1793. Moreover, setting and plot are combined in the dominating figure of Charlie Kinraid, the 'Specksioneer' or whale-ship harpooner, since Gaskell stresses the fact that everyone in the town 'depended on the whale fishery' (ch. 1). Winifred Gérin, indeed, has pointed out that whale-fishing, farming, and trading were the three main industries of Whitby, and that through Kinraid, the Robsons of Hatersbank Farm, and Philip Hepburn and his employers the Foster brothers, Gaskell integrates them all into her plot.

The main lines of the narrative – Sylvia Robson torn between the rugged passion of Kinraid and the pallid devotion of Hepburn – have often prompted commentators to find connections with *Wuthering Heights,* though Gaskell's references to that novel are restrained.[14] It would also be possible to establish similarities with *Shirley.* Perhaps we are concerned here with basic themes well integrated with specific regional backgrounds. More to the point, however, a recent student of Gaskell's work has referred to 'the Brontëesque geography' of *Sylvia's Lovers* – ' "moorland," "purple crags," "waste desolation" and "small brooks that force their way from the heights down to the sea".'[15] Again, the contrast between the mercantile ordinariness of Hepburn and the active romance of Kinraid recalls the 'social' movement that Scott explored on a vast historical scale; this, too, becomes a staple of regional fiction from Nicol Jarvie in the presence of Rob Roy to Reuben Huckaback opposed to the Doones in R.D. Blackmore's 'romance.' Other significant regional elements include a careful reproduction of the local dialect, detailed descriptions of scenery, and illustrative incidents from humble life (all of which troubled the original reviewers reluctant to admit the claims of regional or provincial fiction). The emphasis on rural change is also conspicuous; 'Monkshaven is altered now into a rising bathing-place,' we are told in the concluding section (ch. 45).

Finally, I would point to the way in which Gaskell blends her story into local legend. Just as she begins with a historical statement, so she ends in tones that anticipate Hardy in his role as parish historian:

> But the memory of man fades away. A few old people can still tell you the tradition of the man who died in a cottage somewhere about this spot, died of starvation while his wife lived in hard-hearted plenty not two good stone-throws away. This is the form into which popular feeling, and ignorance of the real facts moulded the story. (Ch. 45)

We have encountered a similar phenomenon in *Wuthering Heights* ('the country folks, if you ask them, would swear on their bible that he *walks*') and we shall meet comparable instances in, for example, Hardy and Mary Webb's *Precious Bane*. *Sylvia's Lovers*, then, is in the mainstream of English regionalism, and no less so for combining romantic subject-matter with a concern for historical authenticity.

The other Gaskell work with strong regional implications is one that we might not naturally think of in this connection: *The Life of Charlotte Brontë*. But the opening sentence of the first paragraph reads as follows: 'The Leeds and Bradford railway runs along a deep valley of the Aire; a slow and sluggish stream, compared to the neighbouring river of Wharfe.' It does not require excessive imagination to see this as the opening of a regional novel (it bears, indeed, a striking resemblance to the first sentence of *The Rainbow*). And the whole of the first two chapters etches in the topographical and historical background of Haworth in a way that has become familiar to later generations for whom regional fiction is an accepted category. There is an additional resemblance, however. One of Gaskell's unconscious anticipations of the later regional novel is her use of an outsider as narrator. We find this in *Cranford* (where Mary Smith, though a native, is no longer resident but visits the town periodically – like her creator – and reports on the latest regional developments). It is true also of *My Lady Ludlow*, where Margaret Dawson is a visitor to Conington, and *Cousin Phillis*, where Paul Manning observes Hope Farm and its inhabitants with the detachment of a remote relative. Here in *The Life of Charlotte Brontë* Gaskell and her husband are the outsider-travellers who usher us into the ethos of Haworth and the surrounding countryside (see ch. 2). She is thus reflecting her lifelong insistence on the intimate connection between human beings and their local environment. Charlotte Brontë and her family are not to be understood until the area of Haworth and instances of its effect on the character of the local population have been described at length. *The Life of Charlotte Brontë* has more than once been called a novelist's biography; I would go further and see it as the biography of a writer who employed the more specific approaches of regional fiction.

GEORGE ELIOT

A human life, I think, should be well rooted in some spot of a native land, where it may get the love of tender kinship for the face of the earth, for the labours men go forth to, for the sounds and accents that haunt it, for whatever will give that early home a familiar unmistakable difference amidst the further widening of knowledge: a spot where the definiteness of early memories may be inwrought with affection, and kindly acquaintance with all neighbours, even to the dogs and donkeys, may spread not by sentimental effect and reflection, but as a sweet habit of the blood. (*Daniel Deronda*, bk. 1, ch. 3)

No passage, perhaps, could sum up George Eliot's attitude to human beings and their environment better than this. It contains so much that is central to her view of the good life – honest labour, the widening of experience, the importance of memory, love of one's neighbours – and all this not consciously willed but manifesting itself naturally in what her later namesake would describe as a unified sensibility. Yet if we read this sentence in the context of a concern for literary regionalism, we immediately detect a distancing generality. There is, to be sure, stress laid on 'unmistakable difference' but more significant is the unspecified 'face of the earth' and '*some* spot of a native land,' which seems to imply *any* spot where the rural has not been totally obliterated or the landscape changed so radically (as with the metamorphosis of Lantern Yard at the close of *Silas Marner*) that no connecting link of memory is possible.

Although much has been written about George Eliot's relation to regionalism, and despite the fact that she has been hailed as a vital inspiration to later regional writing, this sense of a non-regional generality recurs as we examine her work in greater detail. *Scenes of Clerical Life* (1858) offers a definite sense of community, and an interconnectedness of both people and story – the very feature we found absent in the work of Elizabeth Gaskell. Indeed, George Eliot may well have made her greatest contribution to the encouragement of regional fiction by demonstrating that a single area could be the setting for a number of stories all derived (or purporting to derive) from local history – not important historical events as in the Scott of *Waverley*, but the humbler annals of the poor and the ordinary as in the Scott of *The Heart of Midlothian*. Once again Scott seems to have been a dominant influence on a regionally oriented writer; he was her father's favourite author, she is said to have begun reading *Waverley* at the age of eight, and Gordon S. Haight assures us that she had read 'most of Scott' by the age of fourteen.[16] Henry Auster has shrewdly noted her good fortune, similar to Scott's, in 'having a father who was well acquainted with all ranks of his neighbours';[17] writing of Maggie Tulliver in *The Mill on the Floss*, she refers to 'all the favourite nooks about home, which seemed to have done their part in nurturing and cherishing her' (pt. 4, ch. 3), and Scott's novels are significantly mentioned in the same paragraph. Clearly, what she derived from him was not his 'romance' but a concern for preserving a record of the manners and local history of a vanished or fast vanishing past.

But although an idea of a region is implicit in *Scenes of Clerical Life*, it is hardly developed. We are aware of Shepperton and Cheveril Manor and Milby and Paddiford as congeries of people rather than as places with distinctive geographical features. The locality of the book was identified soon after publication only because its inhabitants were identified first. As we read, we tend to think of Shepperton as any rural village, Milby as any provincial Midland town. And this is at one with Eliot's emphasis on an essentially representative realism; as narrator, she insists that these are the kind of people we may meet with every day, and by the same token they could reside anywhere.

In *Adam Bede* we are offered far more illustrative detail, though this detail seems to exist primarily in the interests of realistic truth rather than for the sake of regional depiction. The scope is inevitably broader in the full-length novel; we see agricultural life, the craftsman's workshop, people at work in the fields, the woods, the farm-dairy. And Eliot's theme requires that the area (region?) in which the novel takes place is etched in more deliberately:

> that rich undulating district of Loamshire to which Hayslope belonged, lies close to a grim outskirt of Stonyshire, overlooked by the barren hills as a pretty blooming sister may sometimes be seen linked in the arm of a rugged, tall, swarthy brother; and in two or three hours' ride the traveller may exchange a bleak treeless region, intersected by lines of cold grey stone, for one where his road wound under the shelter of woods, or up the swelling hills, muffled with hedgerows and long meadowgrass and thick corn; and where at every turn he came upon some fine old country-seat nestled in the valley or crowning the slope, some homestead with its long length of barn and its cluster of golden ricks, some grey steeple looking out from a pretty confusion of trees and thatch and dark-red tiles.   (Ch. 2)

This is our introduction to the locality in which most of the action of the narrative will be played. Later, of course, we will gain considerably more information about the village and its immediate neighbourhood, but even so we never come to anything as regionally specific as Hardy's Wessex or Phillpotts's Dartmoor. It is not merely that generalizing features dominate ('*some* fine old country-seat,' '*some* homestead,' '*some* grey steeple'); the essentially emblematic names – 'Hayslope,' 'Loamshire,' 'Stonyshire' (the last two carrying faint suggestions of a Scott 'border') – belong to a totally different category from Blackmore's or Phillpotts's *actual* names and Hardy's convincing imitations of actual names ('Mellstock,' 'Weatherbury,' 'Egdon,' 'Casterbridge'). George Eliot is obviously aiming for a symbolic effect here. 'Hayslope' conjures up a vision of the restful and idyllic, while 'Loamshire' and 'Stonyshire' are unashamedly artificial; we would never expect to find them on any map. (An additional reason for this is that Eliot often combined locations – for example, mixing elements from Arbury, near Nuneaton, and Ellastone, near Cheadle, in *Adam Bede*.)

At the same time, it would be idle to deny that a distinct sense of an area that has great potentiality as a region is derived from these early books. And despite the element of retrospective idealization present in both works, the character of this political region promises to be decidedly complex. In *Scenes of Clerical Life* the emphasis is frequently on the drab and uninteresting. So the immediate environs of Shepperton are presented as follows: ' … a flat, ugly district, this; depressing enough to look at even on the brightest day. The roads are bleak with coal-dust, the brick houses dingy with smoke' ('Amos Barton,'ch. 2). Milby, similarly, is 'a dingy town, surrounded by flat fields, lopped elms, and sprawling manufacturing villages, which crept on and on with their weaving shops, till they threatened to graft themselves on the town' ('Janet's Repentance.' ch. 2). The central 'scene,' 'Mr Gilfil's Love Story,' is set in the pleasanter surroundings of moneyed privilege, and Gilfil can take Caterina to recuperate at Foxholm, 'a village that straggled at its ease among pastures and meadows,' where her window can look out on to 'a farm homestead, with its little cluster of beehive ricks, and placid groups of cows, and cheerful sounds of healthy labour' (ch. 20). George Eliot, one realizes, is feeling her way towards a regional landscape that can contain a dialectic.

In *Adam Bede* 'Loamshire' and 'Stonyshire' imply a similar juxtaposition, but the circumstances of the story take it in a different direction. While there are early references to 'the canals, an' th' aqueducs, an' th' coal-pit engines, and Arkwright's mills at Cromford' (ch. 1), and Dinah Morris feels an obligation to serve at Snowfield, 'where the trees are few, so that a child might count them, and there's very hard living for the poor in the winter' (ch. 3), the industrial landscape of Stonyshire exists only as a dark shadow on the extreme edge of the novel. None the less, although it is relatively crude as yet, we are not far from the presentation of a midland region where the rural and industrial exist side by side, or even (Paddiford, we learn in 'Janet's Repentance,' has a colliery) above and below. We get a faint, barely perceptible foretaste here – geographically, to some extent ideologically, but not yet diagrammatically – of the D.H. Lawrence country (see p. 145 below).

The Mill on the Floss also anticipates Lawrence, notably in the emphasis on Maggie Tulliver's inevitably 'widening circle,' which is an evident model for the situation of Ursula Brangwen. Ultimately, we detect a move here from the regional towards the moral/universal. At first sight, however, this seems the most consciously regional of Eliot's novels. Its opening paragraph, indeed the whole of the opening chapter, not only focuses on the local landscape but does so in terms that suggest the dominant preoccupations of the book. 'A wide plain, where the broadening Floss hurries on between its green banks to the sea, and the loving tide, rushing to meet it, checks its passage with an impetuous embrace.' The seeds of the whole novel are to be found in the opening sentence. We think of Maggie 'borne along by the tide,' her impetuosity and her need to love, and we may detect a curious attempt on Eliot's part to present a heroine who has been formed by the area in which she was born. We notice, too, the immediate insistence on the image of water which haunts the book. The town of St Ogg's is obsessed with its history of recurrent flood, and Mrs Tulliver lives in constant fear that Maggie will 'tumble in and be drownded some day' (bk. 1, ch. 2). The possibility of death by water hangs over the whole novel, and it is strange to remember that literary critics, only a generation or so ago, could argue about the arbitrary nature of the final climax; if we respond to the references throughout the book, we might well feel that it has been too obviously prepared for.

At the same time, there is a curious vagueness about the background, a vagueness that can be explained by reference to Eliot's biography. As with *Adam Bede,* her memories went back to Arbury and Griff for details of the rural life and even for such specific details as the Red Deeps. But no landscape of her youth could provide an adequate locale for the inevitable flood scene. We know, indeed, that she had begun the novel without any definite notion of where it was to be set. She even made a foray into what was later to become known as the Hardy country in an endeavour to see whether the area around Weymouth would prove suitable. Later she found what she was looking for in the Gainsborough district of Lincolnshire, with which she was by no means familiar. Some commentators would argue that such details are irrelevant to an appreciation of the complete novel; ideally, perhaps, they should be, but Eliot's shift from Warwickshire to Lincolnshire helps to explain an uncertainty that, for all its unquestioned merits, exists at the heart of the book. We learn little about the human environs of Dorlcote Mill; it is only on the last page of the book that we are told explicitly that Dorlcote is the name of the local village and not just of the mill itself. While there is a palpable if unspecific sense of region in the book, there is little sense of community. The emphasis is on family connections, Dodsons and Tullivers, rather than the society of neighbours.

An undergraduate once remarked to me, during the course of seminar discussion, that we don't learn about what a miller does in this book. The observation occurred during a comparison of *The Mill on the Floss* with Hardy's *The Mayor of Casterbridge,* and a consideration of the two novels from a regional point of view is decidedly instructive. Mr Tulliver, like Henchard, is a bluff, straightforward countryman whose intrinsic stubbornness brings about his downfall, and both men fail to move with the times in periods of dramatic change. But, while we see Tulliver in the mill and Henchard in the cornyard, Tulliver remains an individual who exists, as it were, in separation from his work, whereas it is impossible to isolate Henchard from the complex agricultural world of which he forms a part. Tulliver's story is, of course, secondary to Maggie's, but he embodies the background from which she comes, and the intellectual narrowness from which she tries to escape. Once again, however, we note the representative function that is always so important in Eliot's work and is continually pulling against her regional concerns.

The same can be seen in the presentation of Maggie herself. She is, essentially, a provincial figure torn between the desire to remain in the confined world of Dorlcote and the impulse to move into a larger world outside. Her decisions are invariably misguided, but they are explained by the limitations of her upbringing, by what she *is*. Her first attempt to run away to the gipsies is clearly a child's romantic and uninformed dream, but her attraction to Stephen Guest is a recognizably related impulse. Part of the literary controversy about Stephen derives from the inevitable split between Maggie's impressions of him and those of the reader. It is easy for us to 'place' his superficial attraction, to recognize him as shallow and inadequate. That Maggie, from her provincial viewpoint, should be dazzled by his apparent brilliance, by all the superficial urban elegance that he represents, may be disappointing, but it is hardly surprising. I insist upon the point because this section of the novel at one and the same time demonstrates the importance of the provincial/metropolitan split and reveals the limitations, for Eliot's purpose, of a fully regional commitment. Maggie Tulliver, like Lawrence's Ursula Brangwen, stands not merely for the young women of the midland counties but for a whole generation coming to recognize the narrowness of their traditional lives yet unable to make the transition to a newer, fascinating, but rootless urban world.

In *The Mill on the Floss* the dichotomies are between agriculture and commerce, between the nuclear family and the larger imperatives of group and class, between traditional rural values and the patterns of an urbanized, increasingly centralized culture and way of life. If reference to industry is muted here, the novel still has a contribution to make to the great Victorian theme of rural versus industrial that is the focus of this chapter. I have had occasion to make several comparisons between Eliot's works and those of Lawrence, and this is because in Lawrence this debate gets its profoundest and most searching treatment in English literature. Regional fiction had much to contribute to this debate, but it had other aspects that could not readily be assimilated into the particular tradition that Eliot and Lawrence dominate.

Maggie's sense of 'romance' is, as it were, her weakness; Ursula overcomes this tendency, but Lawrence shows us the price she pays. Most later regionalist writing, with the singular exception of Hardy's, catered for readers for whom the price was too much. The impulse towards 'romance,' towards a recreation in literary terms of the imaginative qualities that seemed doomed in the late Victorian world, remained strong. At its simplest it provided little more than escape, but in its subtler manifestations it offered an alternative fictional vision that, while it could hardly provide a balancing importance, is too substantial to be ignored. In writers like R.D. Blackmore, regionalism flourished and represented not only a protest against an ever-growing centralism but a literary haven where the forms and structures of 'romance' could still survive.

PART TWO: THE FLOWERING OF REGIONALISM

FIVE

R.D. Blackmore

BLACKMORE, REGIONALISM, AND HISTORICAL ROMANCE

R.D. Blackmore can be claimed as the first unequivocally (if not exclusively) regional English novelist, not only because he produced in *Lorna Doone* one of the classics of the genre but because the vast majority of his fiction has an emphatic (if often only superficial) connection with a particular setting. Since much of his work is little known, it will be worthwhile to list his regional fiction with their complete titles:

Cradock Nowell: A Tale of the New Forest (1866)
Lorna Doone: A Romance of Exmoor (1869)
The Maid of Sker (1872)
Alice Lorraine: A Tale of the South Downs (1875)
Cripps the Carrier: A Woodland Tale (1876)
Mary Anerley: A Yorkshire Tale (1880)
Christowell: A Dartmoor Tale (1881)
Springhaven: A Tale of the Great War (1887)
Kit and Kitty: A Story of West Middlesex (1894)
Perlycross: A Tale of the Western Hills (1894)
Slain by the Doones (1895); short stories, published in England in 1896 as
    Tales from the Telling House
Dariel: A Romance of Surrey (1897)

In terms of regional setting, most of these speak for themselves. The exceptions are *The Maid of Sker*, which divides its attention between the south coast of Glamorgan and the north coast of Devon; *Cripps the Carrier*, which is set in the area of Oxford; and *Springhaven*, which belongs to the Sussex coast. It should be added that *Alice Lorraine* takes in the Kentish hop-fields as well as Sussex, while the 'Western Hills' of *Perlycross* are the Blackdown Hills of south Devon.

Slain by the Doones is a collection of four short stories, three set in Devonshire and one in Wales. With the exception of the last-mentioned story and *Mary Anerley*, where he admitted to have 'wandered a little too far North,'[1] Blackmore confines himself to southern England, but the range there is vast. Max Keith Sutton has noted that the novels 'celebrate rural life in every southern shire from Kent to Devon, except Dorset.'[2] Since Blackmore's novel-writing career frames that of Thomas Hardy, the exception was wise – and almost certainly deliberate.

But this range of regional interest recalls one of the questions posed in my introductory chapter: can a regional novelist be master of more than one region? At first sight, it would seem that Blackmore could be cited as evidence for a positive answer. A closer look at his novels suggests, however, that the apparent regional diversity is in fact deceiving. It would be fair, I think, to list *Lorna Doone, The Maid of Sker, Christowell,* and *Perlycross* as the four novels in which the reader's awareness of setting is most intense – and these are all set in the west country. Only in these do we experience the landscape as a notable presence rather than as a convenient backdrop, and even among these in *Lorna Doone* alone can it be described as integral to the story. Too often in Blackmore there is the sense that a plot of intrigue and unlikely adventure has been imposed arbitrarily on a particular locality.

Alice Lorraine, for example, is described as 'A Tale of the South Downs' and is made to take place in the Sussex village of Steyning, but there is no necessary connection between plot and setting. The book contains surprisingly little description or evocation of the Sussex downland, and although a number of authentic place-names are employed they remain no more than names. There is nothing regional about the astrologer's mysterious box which sets off the plot nor about Hilary Lorraine's adventures and misadventures in the Peninsular War which take up a significant proportion of the pages. Indeed, the element in the plot that most deserves the adjective 'regional' is a supposedly local prophecy put into the mouth of a rustic 'sibyl' called Nanny Stilgoe (ch. 25) – and this seems to derive not from any authentic Sussex legend but from *The Bride of Lammermoor. Cradock Nowell* is a more complex instance. The book contains a strong sense of forest-country in general, yet specific references to the New Forest itself are confined once again to the peppering of the text with real place-names. Local connections are tenuous and verge on the playful: a murder takes place in the forest during a hunting expedition and one of the characters – not connected with the crime – is called Rufus! The absurd plot ('absurd' is a recurrent epithet in Blackmore criticism where his plots are concerned) could have taken place anywhere; regional aspects are limited to peripheral allusion. All in all, one is disturbed but not surprised to find

Blackmore admitting to his publisher Alexander Macmillan in the course of writing the novel: 'I have been there [the New Forest], but not enough to escape the chance of a solecism.'[3] Blackmore's regionalism is not yet firmly based.

At this point, however, it is necessary to insist that Blackmore did not begin his career with the idea of becoming a regional novelist, and may indeed never have thought of himself as such. At least five fictional modes can be discerned within his narratives: sensationalist melodrama, pastoral romance, regional (or rural) idyll, historical fiction, displaced myth. There is a considerable amount of overlap, of course, and *Lorna Doone* contains elements of all five. Sutton has rightly stressed the influence of both Bulwer-Lytton and the early Wilkie Collins upon his work.[4] The murders, abductions, and disappearances that are such prominent features of his stories doubtless derive from the popular successes of these writers. But Blackmore was also an enthusiastic classicist – he was more proud of his translation of Virgil's *Georgics* (1871) than of any of his novels – and his rustic scenes are always likely to revert to traditional pastoral themes and motifs. These are most evident in *Cradock Nowell*, which establishes its pastoral connections via references to Theocritus and *As You Like It*, and in *Cripps the Carrier* and *Kit and Kitty*, with their evocations of woodland and orchard; it is also worth noting that the original title-page of *Lorna Doone* bore an epigraph from Theocritus's eighth idyll.

Blackmore disapproved of the social and political developments of his own time, and his forays into historical fiction often result in his best work. *Lorna Doone* is not only the first of his historical romances but the one set furthest back in time. His favourite period is that of the Napoleonic wars, and many novels reach their climax at or just after a historical event. Thus *The Maid of Sker* culminates at the Battle of the Nile, while *Mary Anerley* and *Springhaven* (in which both Nelson and Napoleon appear) include Trafalgar; *Alice Lorraine*, as already indicated, includes a section on the Peninsular War, and *Christowell* takes its origin in an incident from the same period. I shall be discussing Blackmore's relation to Scott in more detail later; here it will suffice to point out that for Blackmore (as, indeed, for Hardy) the Napoleonic period represented – chronologically and symbolically – what might be called an English equivalent to Scott's preoccupation with the Jacobite rebellions.

Here the constant interrelation between regionalism, history, and romance is once again conspicuous. But in Blackmore it takes its place within a broader framework: a deliberate juxtaposition of the exotic and the dangerous with the familiar and the peaceful. 'Romance' for Blackmore can only exist in contrast to the ordinary and habitual. This is most readily discernible (because of their crudity) in his first and last novels. *Clara Vaughan* (1864) offers no claims to the status of regional fiction, though much of it takes place in Gloucestershire and Devon, but the plot depends upon the unlikely impact of a Corsican vendetta on the generally peaceful lives of English gentry and yeomen. *Dariel,* though described as 'A Romance of Surrey,' achieves its incredible climax when a bluff, honest, and not very successful Surrey farmer (known to his friends as 'Farmer George') wins his exotic bride by intervening in tribal rivalries among the Lesghians of the Caucasus. These are the extremes, but we see a similar kind of effect in the more successful books. The 'romance' of the Doones is contrasted with the solid, unromantic qualities of John Ridd (in regional terms, the Doone Valley contrasts with Plover's Barrows Farm like the Highlands and Lowlands in Scott or Wuthering Heights and Thrushcross Grange in Emily Brontë); the melodramatic and sensationalist elements in *The Maid of Sker* are narrated through the salty down-to-earth realism of David Llewellyn. And in all the stories set at the time of the Napoleonic Wars, the peace of the English villagers is contrasted with the action-packed fights by land and sea in which some of the more adventurous take part.

Beneath the basic romance-pattern, however, lies another, deeper dimension of displaced myth. On closer examination, most of Blackmore's melodramatic plots, which seem so grotesque if judged from the standpoint of conventional Victorian realism, are found to parallel stories from classical legend. Clara Vaughan, for example, in her single-minded determination to avenge her father's murder, shares many of the qualities of Electra; and the story of Adrastus the son of Gordius lies palpably though a little less obviously beneath the plot of *Cradock Nowell.* Persephone, however, is Blackmore's favourite mythic figure, and the story of her death and rebirth is echoed not only at the climax of *Lorna Doone,* but in *Cripps the Carrier* (where the squire's daughter disappears and is thought to have been killed but is ultimately restored to her father) and in *Kit and Kitty* (where the narrator's wife is kidnapped but eventually rescued).[5] This mythic dimension does not, of course, excuse the absurdities, since Blackmore's attempt to transplant the stories into a different genre must often be judged clumsy and unsuccessful. I mention it here because we need to be aware of the other elements that coexist in his regional narratives (the grafting of traditional myth upon regional specificity is later achieved successfully by John Cowper Powys).

Blackmore made an uncertain start as a novelist; it is instructive to watch him finding his true *métier* in the regionalism of *Lorna Doone,* though disappointing that he failed to establish himself thereafter in the form to which he was best fitted. *Clara Vaughan,* understandably in a first novel, is decidedly imitative; it provides the strong plot (the heroine steadfastly investigating and solving the mystery of her father's murder) that seemed likely to win popularity in the early 1860s. But critics are agreed that its most successful scenes are those involving John Huxtable, the giant but gentle wrestling yeoman-farmer of

Tossil's Barton in Devonshire. Blackmore himself admits in a letter: 'The Devonshire scenes are ... taken from the pith of Devonshire life, in wh. I am thoroughly inborn & ingrained.'⁶ Huxtable is, of course, a prototype of 'girt Jan Ridd,' but the differences in terms of narrative technique are considerable. Like *Lorna Doone, Clara Vaughan* is a first-person novel; but Huxtable and Tossil's Barton are portrayed from the outside by a heroine who is a stranger to the county and a member (though impoverished) of a higher class. The description of Heddon's Mouth Cleave (bk. 1, ch. 16) is impressive, but the self-conscious response of Clara as sophisticated outsider renders it ultimately less memorable than Exmoor as seen through the eyes of a native. And John Huxtable himself, though presented warmly and even unforgettably, is an essentially comic character whose rustic quaintness has a quality of vivid Dickensian caricature; he lacks the depth and solidity that Blackmore eventually discovers in John Ridd.

In setting his second novel, *Cradock Nowell,* in a particular locality, Blackmore appears to be moving with deliberation towards a regional concern. Indeed, specific reference is made in an early chapter (bk. 1, ch. 3) to 'John Huxtable, of Tossil's Barton, in the county of Devon,' whose 'native grain and staple' are compared to those of Rev. John Rosedew. For a moment it appears as if a regional preoccupation is going to develop alongside an interrelation of characters and places, but nothing comes of this. The plot, as I have already noted, bears no necessary relation to the New Forest, and the name of the protagonist was in fact borrowed from a monument in the church at Newton Nottage, Glamorganshire, which Blackmore had noticed as a child. But there are two significant developments in *Cradock Nowell.* One is the employment of the omniscient author convention through which Blackmore's reactionary (or, to be fairer, Tory Radical) sentiments come through loud and clear; this conservativism becomes a feature of later novels, but is more successful when integrated into a suitable first-person narrator such as John Ridd, or David Llewellyn in *The Maid of Sker.* The other is the memorable description of the great storm of October 1859. Perhaps because of his activities as a fruit-grower, Blackmore is particularly sensitive to extremes of weather, and meteorological particularities often strengthen his later regional scenes; examples include another great storm which historically hit Widecombe-in-the-Moor in 1638 and which Blackmore transfers in *Christowell* to another part of Dartmoor in the 1840s, the sandstorm in *The Maid of Sker,* and the unusually heavy winters that are so important to the plots of *Lorna Doone, Cripps the Carrier,* and *Kit and Kitty.*

The difference between Blackmore's first two novels, *Clara Vaughan* and *Cradock Nowell,* and his third, *Lorna Doone,* is staggering. He seems to move from the tentatively experimental to the confidently achieved without any pause. Oddly enough, however, there is no record to suggest that Blackmore himself was aware of his great leap forward. If he had known how successful his romance would be, he writes dryly, he would have taken more pains with it. At other times he claims that it is by no means his favourite among the novels. And some of his later admirers, notably Eden Phillpotts, have complained that the success of Lorna Doone has exalted it improperly above his other work.[7] I must therefore state my own conviction that in this novel alone Blackmore manifested the full extent of his powers, and that the superiority of the book is explained by its greater regional particularity and by the way Blackmore draws the story out of the landscape rather than imposing an independent plot upon it. But that raises the vexed question of the Doones, which needs to be discussed in some detail.

BLACKMORE, THE DOONES, AND SCOTT

Despite Blackmore's own disclaimers (to be considered later), Lorna Doone, with its seventeenth-century setting and the account of the Battle of Sedgemoor, has obvious claims to be considered within the tradition of the historical novel. At the same time, it centres upon the story of the Doones of Badgworthy, and the historicity of the Doones is in dispute.[8] Are the stories of the Doones historical, legendary, or invented 'romance'? Or (what is not quite the same question), did Blackmore consider them historical, legendary, or 'romantic'? The problem is complicated enough in itself, but it is rendered even more so by the proliferation of a more recent phenomenon that can reasonably be described as a 'Doone cult,' spurred by the popularity of Lorna Doone and in many respects dependent upon it. The subject cannot be avoided because, despite the arguments of some commentators, it is an essential part of the literary experience of the text. This interest in the historicity of the Doones that the novel has provoked is an indirect but equivocal tribute to the sense of reality that pervades it. So much sounds authentic that we expect the Doones to be part of the historical reality. But what are the facts?

First, there is no solid evidence for the historical existence of the Doones. They appear in no contemporary records, and the 'proofs' that have from time to time been offered (a gun inscribed with the Doone name, a Doone diary destroyed by fire between a published account of its existence in 1901 – conveniently just after Blackmore's death – and any attempt to test its authenticity) fail to stand up to unprejudiced examination. One is forced back upon the notoriously unreliable testimony of legendary story. But here, for our purposes, is some solid literary evidence. Blackmore doubtless elaborated, as every writer of fiction is privileged to do, but he certainly did not invent the whole idea of the robbers of Badgworthy. And there is equally no doubt that Blackmore himself accepted without question the historical existence of the

Doones; it is possible, of course, that he was mistaken, but the fact that Blackmore believed that he was basing his romance on a historical foundation is beyond dispute. He is not deliberately misleading his readers when, for instance, after relating a traditional story about the Doones he adds a footnote: 'This vile deed was done, beyond all doubt' (ch. 5).

Legends grow and adapt themselves like living organisms. The Doone stories eventually evolve into a consistent (unlikely but not absolutely impossible) narrative set in the seventeenth century. As the result of a family feud within a Scots clan, the Stewarts, a banished claimant to the property of Doune Castle is said to have taken refuge with his followers in the remote recesses of Exmoor, living by means of terrorism resulting in plunder and later through blackmail exaction in the tradition of the Highland caterans. Specific stories of these raids are recorded from various parts of the moor. Some versions claim that the bandits were defeated (as in *Lorna Doone*) towards the end of the seventeenth century, others that the Doones left when a settlement was reached with later members of the Stewart family. Oral testimony to such stories is supposed to have extended back to the late seventeenth century itself, but this is doubtful. They seem to have been first gathered together in manuscript form by two antiquaries in the 1830s. References to the stories begin to appear in print in the 1850s in guide-books and essays relating to mid-nineteenth-century tourism; in a review article, 'Wanderings on Exmoor' in *Fraser's Magazine* (October 1857), for instance, the Doones are described as 'infamous in Moorland story.'[9] They enter fiction in a clumsily written serialized romance, 'The Doones of Exmoor,' which appeared in the *Leisure Hour* in 1863. Both these predate *Lorna Doone*, and both relate the story of the Doones murdering a child while a servant hides in an oven and of Tom Faggus's escape from his enemies when his horse leaps over Barnstaple Bridge *(Lorna Doone*, chs. 69 and 75). The main narrative in 'The Doones of Exmoor' is retold by Blackmore in 'Frida; or, the Lover's Leap,' one of the stories in *Slain by the Doones*.[10]

Blackmore himself stated that he had learned some of the stories from his grandfather, who was rector of Oare in the last decade of the eighteenth century. In the original preface to the novel, moreover, he insisted that 'any son of Exmoor, chancing upon this volume, cannot fail to bring to mind the nurse-tales of his childhood – the savage deeds of the outlaw Doones in the depth of Badgworthy Forest, the beauty of the hapless maid brought up in the midst of them, the plain John Ridd's Herculean power, and (memory's too congenial food) the exploits of Tom Faggus.' It is possible, of course, that this is just a sophisticated extension of Blackmore's story-telling, but if so he risked a contemporary challenge. But he is also known to have travelled in the area just before writing the novel and to have taken notes about Doone stories from local inhabitants at Oare, Withypool, and Porlock. Throughout his life he was interested in Doone material and continually denied inventing the historical basis of his 'romance.'[11]

We can state with confidence, then, that Blackmore's story is an elaboration and ordering of legends already widespread on Exmoor. But it seems likely that there was another element which went into the making of *Lorna Doone* and has attracted surprisingly little attention. This is the influence of Scott's Waverley romances. It must be admitted, however, that hard evidence for Blackmore's familiarity with Scott's world is relatively sparse. Amy Robsart, from *Kenilworth*, is mentioned in *Cradock Nowell*, where Amy Rosedew is probably christened in reference to her. This is of interest because it establishes a connection with the one Scott novel containing reference to Devon; as F.J. Snell has pointed out, Lidcote, just north of Charles where Blackmore's uncle lived, is mentioned in the twelfth chapter of *Kenilworth*.[12] And in *Alice Lorraine* the heroine delights in the literature of her contemporaries, 'above all others, the "Wizard of the North," whose lays of romance and legend were a spur that raised the clear spirit of Alice' (ch. 57). Such references suggest an awareness of Scott's writings in both prose and verse, but specific allusion is disappointingly scarce.

Similarly, close familiarity with Scott cannot be proven from available biographical sources; but internal evidence from the novels themselves tells a very different story. Blackmore's tales of ordinary people caught up in 'romantic' adventures; the creation of fiction out of local legend and historic record; a fondness for what John Buchan, writing of Scott, called 'a specialization in localities':[13] all these suggest a disciple of 'the author of *Waverley*.' Indeed, when Robert Gordon writes, 'there is in most of Scott's novels [the] sense of a conflict between past and present, ancient lawlessness and established law, passionate nostalgia and historical fact,'[14] the similarities are such that the sentence would apply perfectly to Blackmore with the single change of the proper noun. Numerous characters and incidents in Blackmore's fiction seem to derive from Scott. John Huxtable in *Clara Vaughan* inevitably reminds us of Dandie Dinmont in *Guy Mannering*, and the dazed state of Clara Vaughan's mother after the murder of her husband bears some resemblance to the climactic scene of violence in *The Bride of Lammermoor*. *Alice Lorraine* contains echoes of the same novels in the initial talk of astrology and the use of a sibyl's folk-prophecy, while David Llewellyn's adventures on both sides of the Bristol Channel in *The Maid of Sker* are reminiscent of the Solway Forth setting of *Redgauntlet*. Indeed, Blackmore may be generally indebted to Scott for his frequent use of 'border country,' which gets a clear presentation in *Christowell*:

The line of the land is definite here, as the boundary of a parish is. In many other parts it is not so, and the moor slopes off into farmland, but here, like the fosse in an old encampment, the scarp of the moor is manifest. Over this, that well-known stream, the Christow, takes a rampant leap, abandoning craggy and boggy cradle, desolate nurture, and rudiments of granite, for a country of comparative ease where it learns the meaning of meadow.   (Vol. 1, ch. 4)

Blackmore's use of dialect is also in the Scott tradition, and many of his 'absurd plots' have a distinct flavour of the narrative contrivances of, say, *The Antiquary*. While these arguments may not appear particularly compelling when discussed individually, cumulatively they take on considerable force.

In the previous paragraph I deliberately avoided reference to *Lorna Doone*, but the resemblances there are especially strong. The Doones are perhaps the closest one could produce, credibly, to an English version of the Highland bands, and they include both the 'romantic' and violent qualities which Scott presents in Fergus McIvor's Jacobites, the followers of *Rob Roy*, and the bloodthirsty MacGregors in *A Legend of Montrose*. Lorna's bower is less theatrical than Flora McIvor's in *Waverley*, but the elements of unabashed romance are common to both; similarly, while the Doone Valley displays less of the Radcliffian sublime than the Black Linn of Linklater in which Burley hides at the close of *Old Mortality*, they share a number of similar features. The Catholic-Protestant split is another connection, and the funeral of Sir Ensor Doone may owe something to that of the Countess of Glenallan in *The Antiquary*. John Ridd's unwilling presence in the Monmouth rebellion, while different from Waverley's implication in the '45, has comparable links with religious conflict. Again, John Fry is in that long line of comic but resourceful servants that include Cuddie Headrigg in *Old Mortality* and Andrew Fairservice in *Rob Roy*, Reuben Huckaback is a decidedly Scott-like mercantile character, and one wonders whether the death of Carver Doone in the Wizard's Slough was inspired by the disappearance of Ravenswood in the Kelpie's Flow at the close of *The Bride of Lammermoor*. The whole connection between Blackmore's world and Scott's is, of course, pointed up by the explicit Scottish connection integral to the Doone story and is strengthened in Blackmore's version by the brief appearance of Alan Brandir of Loch Awe (ch. 21).

I have no wish, however, to exalt these resemblances to Scott at the expense of the differences. Blackmore, as I have already noted, opposed the classification of *Lorna Doone* as a historical novel. He makes the point forcefully in the original preface:

This work is called a 'romance,' because the incidents, characters, time and scenery are alike romantic. And in shaping this old tale, the Writer neither dares, nor desires, to claim for it the dignity, or cumber it with the difficulty of an historic novel.

This is at first surprising, not only because the pattern of the hero's participation in great events bears so close a resemblance to the situation of Waverley, but because *Lorna Doone* follows the classic pattern of historical fiction in having important historical figures, in this case James II and Judge Jeffreys, make brief appearances among otherwise fictional characters. None the less, Blackmore does not attempt, as Scott does, to offer a meditation on historical process. The Monmouth rebellion is an incident in the plot rather than a crucial historical event. John Ridd undergoes no education into the social and political movements that constitute history. 'I have nought to do with great history,' he admits at one point (ch. 24). Above all, while Scott certainly blends realism and romance, it is part of his purpose to present the inadequacy of romance when in conflict with the harsh realities of politics and modern living. Blackmore's purpose, in contrast, is to sustain the claims of romance. He presents Lorna Doone positively, whereas Flora McIvor must be rejected. Unlike Waverley, John Ridd need never be disenchanted. Blackmore's realism focuses on the details of everyday life at a particular time and place, and as a consequence the regional takes precedence over the historical. Hugh Walpole was therefore correct, I think, when he argued that *Lorna Doone* 'is not a good historical novel,'[15] though wrong when he apparently assumed that this is what it claims to be. But the regional elements in the romance deserve a section to themselves.

THE ACHIEVEMENT OF 'LORNA DOONE'

Like many examples of successful regional fiction, *Lorna Doone* is essentially a novel of contrasts. In geographical terms, the domesticated lowlands (including Plover's Barrows Farm) are set against the wild moorland (including the Doone Valley) in ways which recall the Waverley novels and especially *Wuthering Heights*. Socially, the rural yeoman's world is juxtaposed on the one hand with the primitive organization of the Doones and on the other with the polished life of London and the Court. Other oppositions include the religious tension between Catholics and Protestants, the linguistic differences between standard English and local dialect, and of course the rival literary modes of realism and romance. The two central figures, John Ridd and Lorna Doone, themselves embody all these contrasts, and their marriage at the close of the novel represents not only a personal union but the resolution of all the conflicting elements that make up both plot and theme.

Not the least remarkable effect in the romance is the way in which a temporal remoteness is linked with an extraordinary spatial immediacy. This is no traditional case of 'sixty years since.' In terms of its period setting, the book resembles *The Fortunes of Nigel* (since both take place almost two hundred years earlier than the time of publication) rather than *Waverley* or *Wuthering*

Heights. But we are rarely conscious of so great a lapse of time in the experience of reading the novel. The seventeenth century of Exmoor is less distant from us than that of London because Exmoor itself has changed less, and the book takes on a period quality only when John Ridd ventures beyond the immediate vicinity of his home. For the most part the action takes place in a credible but rarely specified past. This is partly because Blackmore has a curious ability to blend his own memories with John Ridd's (their experiences at Blundell's School, for instance) and partly because of the timeless effect implicit in the use of local sayings and proverbs, and especially of real names – not merely existing place-names (Tiverton, Dulverton, Oare, and the like) but historical proper names from local records (the Ridds, Snowes, and De Whichehalses).

But the major contrast, of course, is between the violence of the Doones and the peaceful everyday activities of the Exmoor farmers. The former dominates the plot, but the latter contribute a great deal not only to the 'feel' of the romance but also to its artistic success. Too much emphasis on the Doone outrages would turn the whole book in the direction of melodrama; it could so easily take its place with the 'absurd plots' of Blackmore's other novels, but we are prepared to grant a willing suspension of disbelief in this case because the evocation of rural life in a significant proportion of the book is fully convincing. The lyrical passages that describe the passing of the seasons, the activity of harvest, the rigours of the harsh winter, and the impact of the great thaw are as important to the total effect of the novel as the scenes of action and excitement. The regionalist emphasis on work is also prominent. We are continually reminded of rustic activities such as 'bird-catching, or the tracking of hares in the snow, or the training of a sheep-dog' (ch. 6). Important revelations take place in the dairy or during pig-feeding, and John Ridd's display of strength in digging the sheep out of the snow (ch. 42) or breaking the rock in the gold-mine (ch. 58) is as memorable as his wrestling successes or his fights with the Doones.

At one point John Ridd observes: 'I have little more to tell, because everything went quietly, as the world for the most part does with us' (ch. 12), a remark that surprises us if we pause to think about it, given the attacks by and on the Doones and all the romantic excitement that runs through the narrative. We accept it, however, in terms of the regular patterns and habitual procedures of the farm. It underlines the fact that, when he climbs the waterslide, John Ridd moves from one imaginative world into another. This is essentially a symbolic journey: on one level, he leaves the 'real world' for a world of romance, while on another the adventure can be seen as a rite of passage from the simplicities of childhood to the complexities of adult life. Of all Blackmore's novels, *Lorna Doone* is most obviously set in border-country, happily symbolized by the boundary between Devonshire and Somerset that, in John Ridd's day as well as in Blackmore's and our own, follows the course of Badgworthy Water. It is an artificial administrative boundary that Blackmore employs and accentuates here for his particular purposes, though for the most part the divisions within the novel are governed by the geographical contours of the region.

At this point, however, a stylistic contrast is involved. Much has been written in praise of Blackmore's descriptive powers, but the varieties of description within the book, paralleling the split between realism and romance, are rarely noted. So far as the rest of Exmoor is concerned, Blackmore's topographical accuracy is remarkable. W.H. Dunn has remarked that 'to follow the narrative of Lorna Doone ... on a map of Devonshire and Somerset is to have an experience of participation in the events,'[16] and this is perhaps the first English regional novel about which the remark could be made. From the third chapter, in which John Fry and the young John Ridd ride from Tiverton to Oare via Dulverton and the track skirting Dunkery Beacon, we are offered an authentic geographical area that can be plotted on a map and readily followed 'in the field.' Superficially, the moorland may remind us of the setting of *Wuthering Heights*, but the topography of Emily Brontë's novel has none of Blackmore's verisimilitude. Gimmerton is imaginary, and we are not given clues to encourage us to locate it within an actual Yorkshire. Blackmore's specificity is unrivalled before the work of Hardy, and even Hardy presents his towns and villages under slightly disguised names; not until Eden Phillpotts presents Dartmoor with an equal fidelity to names, places, and distances do we encounter a fictional story so thoroughly rooted in an actual landscape.

Yet, as many 'literary pilgrims' have learned to their disappointment, the clues fail when we try to apply the same realistic criteria to Blackmore's description of the Doone Valley. The directions and distances become blurred; the distinguishing features are not identifiable. Topographers still argue about the respective claims of Hoccombe Goyal, Lank Combe, and even Weir Water Valley as the original site for the Doones' retreat. They range from literalists who assume without question that Blackmore merely described an existing place as it once was to more imaginative readers who have granted the novelist his right to alter and recompose his scene according to the demands of his narrative. Literary critics have tended to pooh-pooh the whole controversy and remain exaltedly aloof, but in so doing they run the risk of missing one of the subtleties of Blackmore's art. The assumption of the topographers that the standards of verisimilitude present in other parts of the novel should apply equally to the Doone Valley sections is readily understandable, but a literary appreciation of the forms and conventions with which Blackmore is working can resolve the difficulty. I suggest that he makes a definite distinction between the two imaginative realms presented in the novel by deliberately varying his descriptive methods. Personally, I find the accounts of entering the Doone

Valley, whether through the so-called Doone-Gate or up the water-slide, equally unimaginable in visual terms. Blackmore invites us to read these scenes in a different way, accepting an impressionistic awareness of difficulties and danger rather than a clear picture of an identifiable locale. The Doone Valley exists, as it were, in another dimension, in a romance world acceptable to the imagination but beyond the limits of geography.

There is a sense, then, in which it is a separate world on its own, containing its own contrasts that are literary and imaginative rather than topographical. For the most part we are invited to associate it with beetling cliffs and powerful torrents, but other passages give a different impression. When Mrs Ridd first visits the valley on her 'rash visit,' she sees something much closer to a pastoral retreat: 'Down in the quiet valley there, away from noise, and violence, and brawl, save that of the rivulet, any man would have deemed them homes of simple mind and innocence' (ch. 4). And Lorna herself presents it as 'a beauteous valley, sheltered from the cold of winter, and the power of the summer sun, untroubled also by the storms and mists that veil the mountains' (ch. 20). The valley is offered in these contrasting terms, of course, because it must represent a suitable locale both for Lorna herself and for the bloodthirsty Doones. This is essentially a symbolic landscape; reality breaks in upon it later, to be sure, but it is worth pointing out that the accounts of the great snowfall and the subsequent floods coincide with the entry of representatives of the 'real world,' John Ridd and the militia, into the valley. In the earlier scenes, where John Ridd is a boy seeking marvels and adventure, Lorna's bower is an extension of herself, a pleasant retreat within the 'realm of violence' (ch. 20) and it partakes of all the literary and mythical archetypes of the paradisal world. By contrast, the Wizard's Slough – another locality that eludes the topographers – is similarly offered in symbolic terms as a descent into the underworld on two levels: a dark industrial world for the troglodytic miners, a death-place for the demonic Carver Doone.

So much for contrasts within the Doone Valley. There are, however, similar contrasts in the cultivated valleys as well. The habitual round of life may be peaceful, but it is continually punctuated with reminders of violence that have no connection with the Doones. We recall the body of a sheepstealer hanging in chains by the trackway (ch. 3), the highwayman adventures of Tom Faggus (offered in romantic fashion but curiously balancing the plunderous forays of the Doones), John Ridd himself as champion wrestler as well as loyal churchwarden, and the cruel, inhuman deception played on Simon Carfax. Above all, of course, there are the scenes of carnage at Sedgemoor, which prove in earnest the remark lightly made in an earlier chapters that 'the principal business of good Christians is, beyond all controversy, to fight with one another' (ch. 2); against this the violence of the Doones no longer seems exceptional.

I lay stress on the complexities within the romance framework because *Lorna Doone* has been read too often in the past as a straightforward adventure story that need not be taken too seriously. It is, however, an intricate and sophisticated exercise in regional romance, and I have not yet drawn attention to the most important literary effect in the whole novel – the narration of the story through the mouth of John Ridd himself. It is by this means that the romance, itself an elaboration of local folk-tale, is firmly rooted in the landscape of Exmoor. Not only is the tale told by a native, but it comes to us in the idiomatic rhythms of the west country. The story is, in Ridd's phrase, 'all in speech.' From the forthright opening sentences we feel ourselves in the presence of a dominating but reliable authority:

> If anybody cares to read a simple tale told simply, I, John Ridd, of the parish of Oare, in the county of Somerset, yeoman and churchwarden, have seen and had a share in some doings of this neighbourhood, which I will try to set down in order, God sparing my life and memory. ... I write for the clearing of our parish from ill-fame and calumny.

In fact, as I have tried to indicate, this is in no way 'a simple tale told simply,' but Ridd is so integral a part of his locality that we seem to be hearing the voice of the Exmoor countryside itself. Blackmore has found the perfect angle of narration for his story. More than the landscape description (which, in any case, is *his* landscape description), Ridd's voice helps to bind the Dooneland romance with the down-to-earth west-country realism. The authenticity of Ridd's idiom is essential for the success of the whole.

A countryman's voice, frequently employing local words and sayings (though not reproducing the full dialect – after all, he had gone to 'the very best school in the West of England' [ch. 28]), John Ridd's not only communicates the story but presents so many of the attitudes and prejudices of the rural yeoman. Once again Blackmore blends with the narrator and thus finds a credible spokesman for his own 'old-fashioned' opinions. Ridd is an old man looking back to his younger days, 'and good times they were, too, full of a warmth and fine hearth-comfort, which now are dying out' (ch. 3), and he expresses all the qualities of stubborn countrymen from staunch patriotism ('I am a thorough-going Church-and-State man, and Royalist' [ch. 5]) to unthinking xenophobia ('how perverse those foreign people are' [ch. 56]). Above all, he continually evinces a deep love for the local countryside. Of London he writes: 'it was not worth seeing, but a very hideous and dirty place, not at all like Exmoor ... whenever I wandered in the streets, what with the noise the people made, the number of the coaches, the running of the footmen, the swaggering of great courtiers, and thrusting aside of every body, many and many a time I longed to be back among the sheep again, for fear of losing temper' (ch. 24). And his return home is all the more moving: 'But how shall I tell you the things I felt, and the swelling of my heart within me, as I drew nearer, and more near, to the place of all I loved and owned, to the haunt of every warm remembrance, the nest of all the fledgeling hopes – in a word, to home?' (ch. 27)

The romantic form of *Lorna Doone* makes possible a structural symmetry that would seem out of place in a work fully committed to realism. The parallelism by contrast of John Ridd and Carver Doone is an obvious instance, and their encounter in the penultimate chapter balances Ridd's fight with Snell in the second. Ruth Huckaback saves Lorna the way Ridd once saved Ruth. Lorna Doone loses her mother and John Ridd his father on the same day. Such effects, beautifully integrated into Blackmore's design, set *Lorna Doone* artistically in a different class from the rest of his work. There are some interesting effects in the other novels. *Mary Anerley* includes the local half-historic, half-mythic figure of Robin Lyth, a sailor-smuggler immortalized in a place-name near Flamborough Head; but he never comes alive as Tom Faggus does, and Blackmore eventually makes him the conventional lost son of a respectable local magnate. The opening chapters of *Perlycross* offer a definite sense of corporate village life, and the novel is localized by the introduction of stories and characters derived by Blackmore from his father's recollections of Culmstock. Most notably, *The Maid of Sker* is of interest to students of the novel by virtue of Blackmore's bold device of telling his story through the salty narrative voice of the rapscallion Davey Llewellyn. In addition, the regions of the Glamorganshire coast and the area of north Devon near Barnstaple are finely drawn, and the story of Parson Chowne (based on Rev. John Froude) and the 'naked people' is derived from local lore. But, though the best parts of such books are those in which regional difference is conveyed most vividly, they remain interludes within adventure stories that play all too blatantly upon the conventions and stereotypes of romance. In *Lorna Doone* alone can Blackmore be accepted as a talented romancer and a regionalist of genius.[17]

SIX

Thomas Hardy

HARDY AND THE IDEA OF A REGION

If there is an immediacy and a complexity in Hardy's Wessex that we do not find in earlier (or, indeed, in much of the later) regional fiction, the reason is not far to seek: Hardy knew his region from the inside, with the intimacy and acuity of the intelligent but humbly born countryman. This enabled him to provide what he calls 'the deeper reality underlying the scenic,'[1] a dimension that lesser regionalists were unable to achieve. Brought up in Dorset when the traditional ways, though threatened, were still strong, he could claim, more than most regional writers, that 'absorption' in locality that F. W. Morgan considered so vital.[2] He had no need, as Scott or George Eliot had, to make an effort of research and imagination to 'explain' ordinary ways of life to a sophisticated, detached, for the most part urban audience. By the time he came to write his major novels, he had worked his way up through the gradations of country society to an experience of London and the literary world, but he retained his rural knowledge and many of his rural assumptions. 'My feeling for this country,' he told William Archer in 1904, 'is that of the countryman born and bred.'[3] The difference between himself and most writers of regional fiction is not dissimilar to that between Wordsworth and John Clare in rural poetry: where Wordsworth was obliged to look down (like Eliot's horse-riding traveller in the second chapter of *Adam Bede* or the stage-coach observer at the opening of *Felix Holt*), Hardy, like Clare, could feel the pressures of rural life upon his pulses – hence the curious double focus, the ability to be at one moment fastidiously aloof and at the next intimately involved, that is so characteristic a quality of his fiction.

A complicating irony in this situation is that, presumably from a sense of insecurity in the fashionable world of London society which he felt the professional need to cultivate, Hardy took pains in his lifetime to play down his less 'respectable' rural connections. As is now well documented, he attempted to control the known facts of his early life by ghost-writing his official biography and organizing its publication after his death as the work of his second wife. This enabled him, until recent researchers laboriously supplemented his account from independent sources, to elevate his parents' social position and to ignore some of his relatives. As Robert Gittings has noted, 'labourers, cobblers, bricklayers, carpenters, farm servants, journeyman joiners, butlers have no place in Hardy's memoirs, though he was related to all of these.'[4] His sensitivity about the speaking of dialect in his parents' home is another example of his insecurity, which reads unpleasantly to modern ears. These human failings in a great writer would be inappropriate to repeat here if it were not for the fact that they relate to the subject of regionalism in two important respects: first, they unfortunately disguise Hardy's unique qualifications for an authoritative presentation of the region that he made his own; second, they demonstrate in his personal life the impact of national, non-regional pressures on local regional lives that was to become the central concern of his fiction.

It has been claimed that 'Hardy's Wessex is rather the Wessex of his father's day,'[5] but in fact his early memories linked him with an agricultural world that had passed into history long before the time of his death. The Life, even in its orginally published form, offers numerous instances. Though the Stinsford choir, reproduced so lovingly in Under the Greenwood Tree, had been disbanded 'when he was about a year old' (Life, p. 17), he could remember other vestiges of an older rural England. On the darker side, these include two public executions, seeing a man in the stocks at Puddletown, and knowing a shepherd-boy who later died of starvation;[6] more positively, he was present at one of the last harvest-homes 'at which the old traditional ballads were sung,' played the fiddle at rural weddings and festivities, and was sufficiently a part of the traditional folk-culture to perform innocent practical jokes with his mother, and to witness an apparition in the company of his father that in earlier days would have taken its place in local ghost-lore (Life, pp. 24–28 passim and p. 501). Thus Hardy had personal experience both of traditional rural life and of the modern patterns that had taken its place, and in this respect he was in a unique position to portray the development of his own region through the most crucial period in its history.

Moreover, the pattern of his own maturation is profoundly characteristic; in shape it bears a striking resemblance to the 'widening circles' visible in the lives of Eliot' s Maggie Tulliver and Lawrence's Ursula Brangwen (not to mention the comparable shape of Lawrence's own life). This pattern is important because it had considerable influence over his ultimate literary presentation of his native region. At the age of sixteen he was apprenticed to an architect and church-restorer in Dorchester and continued in this situation for almost five years. Since he still lived with his parents at Higher Bockhampton, the alteration in his circumstances is likely to seem minimal to the modern reader, but an acute paragraph in the *Life* sets this phase of his biography into true perspective:

> Owing to the accident of his being an architect's pupil in a country-town of assizes and aldermen, which had advanced to railways and telegraphs and daily London papers; yet not living there, but walking in every day from a world of shepherds and ploughmen in a hamlet three miles off, where modern improvements were still regarded as wonders, he saw rustic and borough doings in a juxtaposition peculiarly close. (*Life*, p. 36)

Hardy was fascinated by this strange juxtaposition of different time-scales and different social worlds – what he was later to describe in *Far from the Madding Crowd* as 'the rustic's *Now*' which is at the same time 'the citizen's *Then*' (ch. 22) – and although his earlier work concentrated on the traditional past (in the same chapter Weatherbury is described as 'immutable,' whereas the bulk of Hardy's fiction is devoted to the effects of inexorable change), his work as a whole continually returns to the paradoxes and complexities created by the variety and fluidity of nineteenth-century rural England.

In 1862 Hardy moved to an architect's office in London, so within a few years he had moved from an isolated rural backwater to what was then the unchallenged centre of the English-speaking world. Once again his horizons were extended and he came under the influence of the most up-to-date and sophisticated cosmopolitan attitudes and beliefs. It is hardly surprising, then, that the sense of being caught between two worlds was strong in him, or that when, returning to Dorchester in 1867, he began wondering 'how to achieve some tangible result from his desultory yet strenuous labours at literature,' he should lay stress on the fact that 'he knew fairly well both West-country life in its less explored recesses and the life of an isolated student cast upon the billows of London' (*Life*, pp. 57–8). Apparently, his first, no-longer-extant novel, *The Poor Man and the Lady*, examined this dichotomy, and it is interesting to note that, initially, he seems to have considered tackling a large social canvas that would include both extremes (one thinks of Clym Yeobright torn between Paris and Egdon in *The Return of the Native*). Later, after a number of experimental and false starts, he was to concentrate on 'West-country life in its less explored recesses' as the area that he clearly knew best. Years later, in 1922, he was to express the basic regional attitude: 'I am convinced that it is better for a writer to know a little bit of the world remarkably well than to know a great part of the world remarkably little.'[7] Moreover, he took the tension between the long-established rural ways and the new urban challenges as his overriding theme. Hence the remarkable device in his fiction of a stranger or alien visitant invading and frequently dislocating the traditional ways of life of sheltered (but not necessarily innocent) Wessex. Hardy's novels, far from being confined to a regional locale, record the increasing confrontation of local and cosmopolitan, and derive much of their impact from the resultant clash.

Hardy was never more shrewd in his artistic decisions than in this insistence upon relating his 'circumscribed scene' to the larger world. The chief case to be made against regionalism is that its undue emphasis upon the uniquely local can lead all too easily to a limiting distortion. If a regional presentation confines itself to those aspects which distinguish it from other regions, no representative statement is possible. He who knows only his region, we might say, knows little of that. Raymond Williams has argued the point most cogently: 'At its weakest, in what should be seen as a defensive reflex, the "regional" novel, in excluding all but its region, excluded not only other places but these deep social and human forces [i.e., the new social mobility and the ideas and education of an extending culture] which were explicitly active within it.'[8] But Hardy, as Williams points out, refuses to limit himself in this way. Indeed, it is part of his strength (part, moreover, of his invaluable contribution to Victorian fiction) that he placed at the centre of his novels the very factors that the average regional novelist tended too often to ignore. Hardy's Wessex ('a modern Wessex of railways, the penny post, mowing and reaping machines,' as he calls it in the preface to *Far from the Madding Crowd*, which I shall be discussing in detail in the next section) is by no means protected from outside pressures.

Against Williams, however, I would argue that this development does not make Hardy's novels any the less regional. By according the relation between regional and universal so important a place in his fiction, he was drawing attention to one of the most significant trends of the age. In so doing, he could hardly be retreating to a rural backwater and avoiding the challenge of the main stream; on the contrary, he was bringing the regional dilemma to the forefront of the contemporary consciousness. I shall be demonstrating later that Hardy's novels are primarily about the impact of non-regional upon regional, and that since this was a crucial part of the Victorian regional experience, it is a legitimate (indeed, essential) preoccupation. Since the regional question is actively debated within the novels themselves, we might say that in Hardy's fiction the subject becomes fully integrated with its dialectic.

Besides, Hardy (conscious perhaps of a kind of taint by association from the limitations of other regionalists) discusses the local-versus-universal problem in his 'General Preface to the Novels and Poems.'[9] There he responded forcefully to the view that 'novels that evolve their action on a circumscribed scene ... cannot be so inclusive in their exhibition of human nature as novels wherein the scenes cover large extents of country.' Insisting that he consciously chose 'the geographical limits of [his] stage' and observing that its extent was not much smaller than that available to the writers of ancient Greece, he argues that 'the domestic emotions have throbbed in Wessex nooks with as much intensity as in the palaces of Europe,' that his Wessex characters were 'beings in whose hearts and minds that which is apparently local should be really universal.' The famous passage from The Woodlanders in which Little Hintock is described as 'one of those sequestered spots outside the gates of the world' yet also a setting for 'dramas of a grandeur and unity truly Sophoclean' (ch. 1) presents the regional/universal interconnection in a nutshell. Similarly, in The Return of the Native, Clym Yeobright is a poignant example of the way local and universal elements clash within the compass of a single life. He too thinks of Egdon as a 'sequestered spot' (bk. 3, ch. 4) but finds that it shares 'the chafing of social necessities' with the larger world he thought he had renounced. All this is not, of course, a specific defence of regionalism, but it shows that Hardy is intent upon freeing himself from the possible limitations of the regional viewpoint without sacrificing any of its advantages.

One possible way of distinguishing a regional novelist from his merely local or provincial counterpart is to note how the former writes of a specific locality but for as wide an audience as possible (most of whom exist outside it) while the latter may be seen as writing primarily for the inhabitants of the area itself. It would be wrong, I think, to look down on the provincial writer (Hardy himself considered 'provincialism of feeling' invaluable [Life, p. 151]), but he is obviously limited in scope. Too often, localism of any kind becomes a mere tactic for evasion, a means of avoiding contact with the broader, more dominant issues of the time. Hardy was clearly conscious of the problem. Thus, although he admired William Barnes, the Dorset dialect poet, he considered that 'his place-attachment was strong almost to a fault'[10]– and one can see how studiously the novelist avoided the danger himself. Viewing Wessex from a more detached perspective than Barnes, Hardy never failed to see the macrocosm beyond the microcosm. Above all, his cosmopolitan experience enabled him to appreciate the ultimate (yet perhaps redeeming) irony concerning regionalism: that, although the sense of particularity is emphasized by reference to the local, only a cosmopolitan, with the generalizing experience that renders comparison possible, is in a position to recognize the regional when it is encountered.

THE CREATION OF WESSEX

With the exception of Trollope (who had different, non-regional intentions),

Hardy was the first English novelist to postulate a series of novels all focusing upon a particular locality. He tells us in the 1895 preface to *Far from the Madding Crowd* that it was in the chapters of that novel,

> as they appeared month by month in a popular magazine [the *Cornhill*], that I first ventured to adopt the word 'Wessex' from the pages of early English history, and give it a fictitious significance as the existing name of the district once included in that extinct kingdom. The series of novels I projected being mainly of the kind called local, they seemed to require a territorial definition of some sort to lend unity to their scene. Finding that the area of a single county did not afford a canvas large enough for this purpose, and that there were objections to an invented name, I disinterred the old one.

As Ian Gregor has pointed out, in one of the best critical studies of *Far from the Madding Crowd*, this is 'very much a remark of hindsight.'[11] Most discussions of the topic concentrate on the implications of the decision for Hardy's career as a novelist. Here I wish to inject into this debate a parallel consideration of its implications for regional fiction in general.

The first point deserving consideration is the revival of the term 'Wessex'.[12] Hardy does not elaborate upon the 'objections to the invented name' but he would seem to have been dissatisfied with Trollope's imaginary, unlocated 'Barsetshire' and Eliot's excessively allegorical 'Loamshire' and 'Stonyshire.' 'Wessex' was an ideal term ready for his use. Not only did it sound authentic, on the analogy with Essex, Sussex, and Middlesex, but its past existence gave an ambiguous, quasi-historical justification to Hardy's procedure. Later in the same preface he describes the area as 'a partly real, partly dream-country.' 'Wessex,' the name of an ancient kingdom that had once existed but did so no longer, offered him precisely the combination of local connection and imaginative freedom that he needed. Whether he chose the term for this purpose or discovered its appropriateness after he had made the decision to employ it is, however, a question that can never be authoritatively answered.

The revisions made by Hardy when his novels were republished, especially those for the collected editions of 1895–6 and 1912 (significantly entitled the 'Wessex Novels Edition' and the 'Wessex Edition' respectively), disguise the somewhat haphazard process by which the individual books were integrated into a regional series. *Desperate Remedies* and *Under the Greenwood Tree*, which both preceded *Far from the Madding Crowd*, were therefore completed before the Wessex series had been initiated. The former does not contain the word even in the revised texts, which include vague references to 'a western county' and 'the south of England' (ch. 1), etc., though other now familiar Hardy place-names (Casterbridge, Budmouth, Corvsgate) replace earlier inventions

(Froominster, Creston, Humdon). The references to 'Wessex' in *Under the Greenwood Tree* were first introduced in 1896, but other names that were eventually to establish themselves in the Wessex scheme appear in the pre-Wessex first edition of 1872 (Casterbridge, Budmouth, Yalbury, Mellstock itself).

From *Far from the Madding Crowd* onwards, such references become more confident and more consistent, and the cumulative associations of names begin to form a notable part of Hardy's fictional technique. After the publication of *The Return of the Native* (1878), for example, he had only to drop the name 'Egdon' (in *The Mayor of Casterbridge, Tess of the d'Urbervilles*, 'The Withered Arm,' etc.) for the whole atmospheric character of the famous first chapter to be evoked. None the less, the task of rendering the whole imaginative area topographically consistent was a major undertaking, and although this was for the most part achieved, it is still possible to find minor discrepancies in the revised texts. So successful has Hardy's creation become, however, that it is now difficult to credit the statement offered in the *Life* (p. 77) that 'Hardy's wilful purpose in his early novels until *Far from the Madding Crowd* appeared, if not later, [had] been to mystify the reader as to their locality.'

When Hardy states that his projected series 'seemed to require a territorial definition of some sort to lend unity to their scene,' his stress is upon the fictional possibilities of a region rather than upon the regional possibilities of fiction. Each, however, tends to foster the other. F.W. Morgan, writing of Hardy's Wessex from the viewpoint of regional sociology, observes: 'The scenery varies from the clay lowland of the Vale of Blackmore to the chalk uplands of the centre and coastal regions and the heath country of the south east. But there was a unity in diversity, for the different geographical traits were complementary to each other with their different products from meadow, arable, chalk pasture, woodland, or heath.'[13] Hardy presents what John Holloway, in a fine phrase, calls 'the varied integration of a region,'[14] and the importance of his seeing his chosen region not only in picturesque terms but in economic ones cannot be overestimated. To make the point baldly, a dairy-farmer needed not only green meadows for his herd but a regular water-supply, a labour force of dairymen and milkmaids, and accessible markets for his produce. Similarly, Hardy's concern for the 'local' can only be achieved with reference to a wider area, upon which the local depends and of which it is an essential part. He is committed, then, not to a single (and simple) 'local area' but to a number of interlocking local areas, and the regional background in this way reflects the interlocking relationships of his human characters. Hardy was the first writer in English to present this broader regional concept, and its influence may be clearly noted in the later regional concerns of lesser writers like Phillpotts and Kaye-Smith.

Hardy's Wessex, then, is wide enough to include broad varieties of terrain and social life yet is none the less 'a circumscribed scene' that can be held in the mind as a unit. Casterbridge is as much a part of it as Egdon; indeed, these two can be seen as the extreme poles of Hardy's world. Egdon is the primitive, untamed world of nature that dwarfs the human beings who attempt to earn a living upon it. Casterbridge, on the other hand, is the human centre: county town, market town, administrative and agricultural focal point. Between these extremes, of course, are a series of localities differentiated by their geographical and geological qualities which in turn determine the agricultural life that is possible within them. These include the mellow orchard-vale of *The Woodlanders*, the village solitudes of Mellstock and Marygreen, and on its outer fringes the romantic ruggedness of 'Off Wessex' portrayed in *A Pair of Blue Eyes* and the primitive society of the Isle of Slingers that forms the background to *The Well-Beloved*. Each, of course, has its own 'local' atmospheric quality, and each has devoloped in a different way and can therefore boast a distinctive history and store of tradition. Nor is it exclusively 'rural'; the pressures of the non-regional and even anti-regional are represented by the 'military-station' at Melchester, the university city of Christminster, elegant Bath, and the fashionable resorts of Budmouth and Sandbourne. I would insist that these places are as much parts of Wessex as Blackmore Vale or the Hintocks or Egdon Heath itself, since it is part of the social history of the nineteenth century that town and country were no longer separate or separable. Wessex, we might say, contains almost all possible varieties of English scene within its boundaries while at the same time retaining – albeit a little desperately – its authentic regional status.

The foregoing discussion may well give the impression that Hardy belongs unquestionably to the 'realistic' tradition of regional writing, with an emphasis on accuracy and verisimilitude. Certainly, Hardy prided himself on his fidelity to the facts of social history. 'At the dates represented in the various narrations,' he insists in the General Preface, 'things were like that in Wessex,' and his meticulous preservation of rural information and events, from newspaper clippings and other sources, in his 'Facts' notebook is evidence of his concern for truth and exactitude. On the other hand, of course, Wessex is offered as a 'partly real, partly dream-country' and Hardy never underestimated the imaginative aspect of the novelist's art. For all his concern with topographical accuracy, he disguised that same accuracy by assigning fictitious names to his towns and villages, despite the fact that their position on maps reproducing the outline of south-west England rendered them easily identifiable. His own Wessex map contains the warning: 'It is to be understood that this is an imaginative Wessex only, & that the places described under the names given are not portraits of any real places, but visionary places which may approximate to the real places more or less.'[15] It is a characteristically evasive statement, but it allows Hardy to view his region as both a historic and social entity and as an imaginative realm. It is precisely this doubleness in Hardy that causes certain readers to have doubts about his qualifications as a regionalist. Just as Raymond Williams sees his preoccupation with change and the impact of the non-regional as separating him from traditional regionalism, so others see his imaginative qualities as similarly suspect. Writing in a tribute to the work of Eden Phillpotts, Waveney Girvan asserts: 'Hardy is much less the regional novelist than Phillpotts ... the Dorset of Thomas Hardy and the Dorset I know are not, or are only occasionally, the same place. Hardy etherealizes and gives a picture, to my mind at least, of a romanticized, rarefied Dorset.'[16] Here once again we encounter the realistic bias present in so many assumptions concerning literary regionalism. Hardy, however, was shrewdly aware of the problem and elaborated upon it in an important but little-known passage in his essay 'The Profitable Reading of Fiction' which relates to the local/universal problem already discussed:

> To distinguish truths which are temporary from truths which are eternal, the accidental from the essential, accuracies as to custom and ceremony from accuracies as to the perennial procedure of humanity, is of vital importance in our attempts to read for something more than amusement. There are certain novels, both among the works of living and the works of deceased writers, which give convincing proof of much exceptional fidelity, and yet they do not rank as great productions, for what they are faithful in is life garniture and not life.[17]

Hardy's capacity to heighten his effects is seen in particularly dramatic terms in *The Return of the Native*. Egdon itself, of course, is an example of Hardy's improving on the topographical original, since he both combined a number of small heaths in the area and considerably extended their boundaries. As Denys Kaye-Robinson reports, '"Egdon" was never the huge, wild moor that he depicted.'[18] But the physical transformation is exceeded by its imaginative counterpart. The opening chapter, in which it is presented without any human connections, is too famous to need discussion here. Its impact is best conveyed by the scene a little later in the novel in which the song-party take their leave from Damon Wildeve and 'The Quiet Woman':

> Wildeve attended them to the door, beyond which the deep-dyed upward stretch of heath stood awaiting them, an amplitude of darkness reigning from their feet almost to the zenith, where a definite form first became visible in the lowering forehead of Rainbarrow. Diving into the dense obscurity in a line headed by Sam the turf-cutter, they pursued their trackless way home. (Bk. 1, ch. 5)

From such passages we derive our sense of Egdon as not so much a local terrain as an archetypal condition. Hardy continually uses a realistic detail to suggest larger issues. The Guy Fawkes bonfire kindled above 'the ashes of the original British pyre' (bk. 1, ch. 3) becomes an emblem of tradition and continuity; Diggory Venn the reddleman suggests visually the 'dyed barbarians' of Egdon's past (bk. 6, ch. 1). Even Hardy's allusions to Greek tragedy, sometimes dismissed as an autodidact's self-conscious parade of learning, serve the purpose of setting the regional story in a larger human and mythic context. And inner and outer landscapes continually merge as the image of the November flames is internalized into the fiery passions of Eustacia and Wildeve.

The Mayor of Casterbridge also offers convenient illustrations of Hardy's heightening techniques. It does not initially *feel* like a regional novel; the emphasis is too much on the people, their inter-relationships, and the concatenation of events that brings about Henchard's fall. But if we look further, another aspect emerges – a contrast between the old regional Caster-bridge (to which Henchard belongs) and the more 'respectable' market town (for whom Farfrae is representative). Casterbridge/Dorchester is presented with reasonable fidelity in its topographical and historical detail, but it also functions as an objective reflection of Henchard himself. He meets his estranged wife in the Ring associated with the violence of ancient executions and prize-fights; he saves Lucetta and Elizabeth-Jane from a bull, and two chapters earlier we have been reminded of the 'large square called Bull Stake' with the surviving stone post 'to which the oxen had formerly been tied for baiting with dogs to make them tender before they were killed in the adjoining shambles' (ch. 27). In modern-day Casterbridge, the regional has been pushed to the outskirts, notably to Mixen Lane where it is capable of bursting out into contemporary violence, as in the skimmity-ride. It will be seen that Hardy's employment of regional detail invariably transcends its realistic effects.[19]

Hardy's Wessex, then, is a highly complex creation. It refuses to simplify the regional situation, and can as a result become almost bewildering in its variety. This leads to conflicting generalizations when certain particulars are empha-sized at the expense of others. Hardy's relation with the past is an especially perilous subject. Because he dwelt so lovingly on historic and even prehistoric details, some see him as wholly preoccupied with a vanished world. Thus, despite Hardy's own insistence on the presentation of 'a modern Wessex,' Thom Gunn asserts that his 'mastering obsession, in his prose as well as in his poetry, was a regret for the past.'[20] Others resort to paradox. So A.J. Guerard writes: 'He was both attracted and repelled by the stabilities of his native region.'[21] Impressive, albeit selective, evidence could be assembled for all these positions, and they are not perhaps as irrevocably opposed as they may seem at first sight. Because Hardy was aware, like Scott, of the accelerating speed of change in his world, he was similarly intent upon preserving a record of the past. Because he knew that tension and conflict are the staples of fiction, he knew that the anomalous juxtaposition of curious survivals and breathtaking changes provided promising material for his novels. Although the conservative and progressive positions may often be found side by side in Hardy's work (see, for example, his essay 'The Dorsetshire Labourer'), it is convenient here to discuss his analysis of past and contemporary Wessex separately; I shall therefore consider in the next section his presentation of the past with particular reference to his short stories and then go on to discuss his portrayal of a changing Wessex in his major fiction.

'HISTORIAN OF WESSEX'

'Hardy has more in common with Scott than with any other British novelist.'[22] Lord David Cecil's statement may be a little extreme, given the continuing influence of Scott that I have been tracing in this book, but there is no doubt that an intimate connection exists between the Waverley novels and Hardy's work. Indeed, when Scott was less highly regarded than he is today, this connection was an embarrassment to some critics, and as recently as 1974 Lennart Björk made the quaint remark that his 'somewhat extravagant praise of Scott ... has caused some suspicions about Hardy's literary taste.'[23] More recently, however, the debt has been taken more seriously. Taking her cue from Hardy's high praise of *The Bride of Lammermoor* in 'The Profitable Reading of Fiction,' the occasion for Björk's remark, Jane Millgate has demonstrated the significant structural similarities between that novel and *Tess of the d'Urbervilles*,[24] and a similar comparison might usefully be made with *The Woodlanders*. Although he claimed on one occasion that he 'preferred Scott the poet to Scott the novelist,' and never ceased to regret that he 'should later have declined on prose fiction' (*Life*, p. 51), this can reasonably be explained in terms of the same 'anxiety of influence' that caused Hardy to play down any connections between his own work and George Eliot's (see *Life*, p. 100).

The resemblances between Scott's work and Hardy's are in fact manifold. Most obvious, perhaps, is the concern for a strong plot containing generous quantities of incident and action; then there is the shared interest in regional romance, the ballad background to their work, and especially their common emphasis on the associations of landscape. In *The Woodlanders*, for example, Fitzpiers realizes that in Little Hintock he differs from Winterbourne, Melbury, and Grace because he lacks 'old association – an almost exhaustive biographical or historical acquaintance with every object, animate and inanimate, within the observer's horizon' (ch. 17), and this is precisely what Scott emphasizes and what Hardy as narrator is able to provide. Again, Frank Chapman saw Hardy's strength in portraying the dialogue of humbler rustic characters rather than that of the educated and aristocratic as an inheritance from Scott.[25] Certainly his setting of novels in the immediate past, at a time 'within living memory' (*Under the Greenwood Tree* (bk. 1, ch. 1), recalls Scott's interest in the past that was within recall through the reminiscences of the aged. The 'external incidents' in *The Trumpet-Major*, Hardy states in his preface, 'are mostly an unexaggerated reproduction of the recollections of old persons well known to the author in childhood'; this is, of course, a historical novel directly in the Scott tradition, and it is not coincidental that Hardy bought a set of the Waverley novels just before writing it.

But there is one connection that I find particularly intriguing. Here are three extracts from the *Life:*

> I can recollect the time when the places of burial even of the poor and tombless were all remembered, and the history of the parish and squire's family for 150 years back known.   (p. 336)

> On October 9 [1925] ... he walked to Stinsford in the morning. The bright sunlight shone across the face of a worn tomb whose lettering Hardy had often endeavoured to decipher, so that he might recarve the letters with his penknife.   (p. 462)

> November 4 [1927]. We drove in the afternoon to Stinsford, to put flowers on the family graves. The tombs are very green, being covered with moss because they are under a yew-tree. T.H. scraped off most of the moss with a little wooden implement like a toy spade, six inches in length, which he made with his own hands and which he carries in his pocket when he goes to Stinsford.   (p. 476)

There is no mention of Scott in these contexts, but Hardy, as Michael Millgate has recently pointed out,[26] must have known that he was here acting out the role of 'Old Mortality.' And this gives a clue, surely, to the attitude that binds him to 'the author of *Waverley.*'

The first of the extracts from the *Life* quoted above comes from the account Hardy gave to H. Rider Haggard about the changes that had taken place during his lifetime in the condition of the Dorset agricultural labourers. One of the most significant changes for Hardy is the fact that they have become 'more and more migratory,' and this, he argues, has had a disastrous effect on a local sense of historical continuity: 'Village tradition – a vast mass of unwritten folk-lore, local chronicle, local topography, and nomenclature – is absolutely sinking, has nearly sunk, into eternal oblivion' (*Life*, p. 336). This was written in March 1902, but Hardy had long before realized the necessity of preserving such traditions and records. A similar situation to that which led Scott to assume the role of antiquary caused Hardy to see himself as performing the functions of parish historian.

In the novels the evidence of Hardy as local historian is mainly to be found in the authentic detail behind the account of the Mellstock Quire, the depiction of local folklore and superstition (he insisted in a letter to Edward Clodd that all such details in his work were accurate),[27] the integration into his plots of such local festivals as the Midsummer Eve customs in *The Woodlanders* and the 'local Cerealia' in *Tess*, and the wealth of rustic anecdotes, sayings, and proverbs that fill the conversations at the Malthouse and the Buck's Head in *Far from the Madding Crowd*. In the shorter fiction, however, these details move from background to foreground. Within the smaller compass of the short-story form Hardy can preserve fragments of local tradition – often, indeed, using the motive of preservation as an excuse for telling the tale.

Despite his statement in the preface to *Wessex Tales* that 'the stories are but dreams, and not records,' Hardy's best short stories are frequently those in which the historical or antiquarian sentiment is most strong. Often enough, this shows itself in statements insisting on the difference between the present and the past. 'Though the date was comparatively recent,' he explains in 'The Withered Arm,' 'Egdon was much less fragmentary in character than now.' 'In Nether-Moynton and its vicinity at this date,' we are told in 'The Distracted Preacher,' 'people always smiled at the sort of sin called in the outside world illicit trading.' But from time to time this story is rooted more definitely in the world of historical fact. When the 'Preventive-men' discover the cache of smuggled tubs beneath the apple-tree, they totally destroy the underground cellar, and 'the hole which had in its time held so much contraband merchandize was never completely filled up, either then or afterwards, a depression in the greensward marking the spot to this day.' The last detail adds, as it were, an apparent seal of historical authenticity. Similarly, the last sentence in 'The Three Strangers' leaves us with the impression that the story, set firmly in the past, is a traditional local tale: 'But the arrival of the three strangers at the shepherd's that night, and the details connected therewith, is a story as well known as ever in the country about Higher Crowstairs.'

Some stories, indeed, *are* local tales – or, at least, are explicitly offered as such. 'The Duke's Reappearance,' an anecdote about the Monmouth rebellion, is subtitled 'A Family Tradition.' Here Hardy employs the actual names of some of his ancestors, and although the *Life* (p. 11) casts some doubts on its authenticity, it seems at least adapted from an existing story. 'A Tradition of Eighteen Hundred and Four' purports to be similar. Hardy has a characteristically awkward comment in the 1919 preface to *Wessex Tales* in which he admits it to be 'an invention of the author's,' but claims that he was later 'told that it was a real tradition' (he never discusses the possibility that the 'real tradition' may have been born from the tale). Of many of the short stories Hardy is likely to claim, as he does in the case of 'A Committee-Man of "The Terror",' that it 'had a basis in fact.'[28]

Hardy had a seemingly inexhaustible supply of ways to provide historical underpinning to his stories. The opening of 'The Fiddler of the Reels' maintains that Wat Ollamoor, the fiddler in question, was 'known well' to the seniors in the party at which his story is told. 'Master John Horseleigh, Knight' takes its origin from an entry in a marriage-register which Hardy derived from John Hutchins's *History and Antiquities of the County of Dorset.* Some stories, like 'A Tradition of Eighteen Hundred and Four' and 'A Committee-Man of "The Terror"' already mentioned, reproduce the circumstances of oral tradition by introducing frameworks in which the narrator claims to recollect hearing the tales told by elderly people themselves recollecting events in their youth. In the latter (which appears in *A Changed Man),* 'old Mrs. H-, whose memory was as perfect at eighty as it had ever been in her life, interested us all by the obvious fidelity with which she repeated a story many times related to her by her mother when our aged friend was a girl.' By such means Hardy reproduces the sense of lived experience, of living history, which he derives from Scott.

Most impressive of all, perhaps, are stories where the narrator himself acts out the role of village historian. Here, for instance, is the opening paragraph of 'The Grave by the Handpost' (also in *A Changed Man):*

> I never pass through Chalk-Newton without turning to regard the neighbouring upland, at a point where a lane crosses the lone straight highway dividing this from the next parish; a sight which does not fail to recall the event that once happened there; and, though it may seem superfluous, at this date, to disinter more memories of village history, the whispers of that spot may claim to be preserved.

Here, surely, we find a congregation of Hardy's chief concerns: a locality to which is attached a story; a historically minded narrator, himself a solitary figure in an ancient scene; an argument for the preservation of memories. The story itself is a grimly effective 'satire of circumstance,' not the least of the ironies being the fact that the village memory dutifully preserved is 'a barbarous custom they keep up at Sidlinch, and ought to be done away wi'' – the burial of a suicide at the crossroads 'wi' a new six-foot hurdle-saul drough's body, from the sheep-pen up in North Ewelease.' Characteristically, Hardy had investigated the historical background; 'Burial of suicides at crossroads abolished c 1830' reads a note jotted down prior to the writing of the story.[29]

In 'The Melancholy Hussar' *(Wessex Tales),* a tale based on an authentic incident verified by Hardy from Batcombe parish register, the voice of the local historian is even more evident:

> Here stretch the downs, high and breezy and green, absolutely unchanged since those eventful days. A plough has never disturbed the turf, and the sod that was

uppermost then is uppermost now. Here stood the camp. ... At night, when I walk across the lonely place, it is impossible to avoid hearing, amid the scourings of the wind over the grass-bents and thistles, the old trumpets and bugle calls ...

It was nearly ninety years ago ...

Phyllis told me the story with her own lips. She was then an old lady of seventy-five, and her auditor a lad of fifteen.

This is Hardy's habitual frame to his historical stories, designed to demonstrate the line of oral tradition. But the 1896 preface to *Life's Little Ironies* (in which this story originally appeared before being transferred to *Wessex Tales*) provides an additional frame, Hardy's personal account of the circumstances under which the story was preserved:

> 'The Melancholy Hussar of the German Legion' has just such a hold upon myself for the technically inadmissible reasons that the old people who gave me their recollections of its incidents did so in circumstances that linger pathetically in the memory; that she who, at the age of ninety, pointed out the unmarked resting-place of the two soldiers of the tale, was probably the last remaining eyewitness of their death and interment; that the extract from the register of burials is literal, to be read any day in the original by the curious who recognize the village.[30]

The opening lines of the story display the distinctively regional quality that pervades Hardy's work when the local historian is to the fore; the introductory comment explains how the centre of Hardy's story is not so much the tragedy of the hussars as the way in which their story has become a part of the region to which they were strangers.

But Hardy's most substantial claims to the title 'Historian of Wessex' (the phrase is J.M. Barrie's)[31] are to be found in two collections of stories that first appeared in 1891, *A Group of Noble Dames* and 'A Few Crusted Characters.' *A Group of Noble Dames* hardly represents Hardy at his best, but the idea unifying the volume is of considerable interest. An afternoon excursion of the Wessex Field and Antiquarian Clubs is cancelled because of torrential rain, and the members, storm-bound in the Casterbridge Museum, pass the time by telling stories of the local aristocracy derived from local records. As the narrator remarks, 'many, indeed, were the legends and traditions of gentle and noble dames, renowned in times past in that part of England, whose actions and passions were now, but for men's memories, buried under the brief inscription on a tomb or an entry of dates in a dry pedigree' ('Dame the First'). Hardy doesn't exploit the artistic possibilities of his scheme; though each story is told by a different speaker, the style and approach remains for the most part monotonously the same. Rather, it is the antiquarian aspects of the idea that interest him (one wonders if John Cowper Powys took a hint from the book in portraying Squire Urquhart's obsession with a book of local Dorset scandals in *Wolf Solent*). Hardy told Edward Clodd that 'most of the tales [were] founded on fact,'[32] and half of them use information from Hutchins, but Hardy has altered, added, and superimposed. His admission, apropos of 'A Tradition of Eighteen Hundred and Four,' that 'he added a circumstantial framework describing it as an old local tradition' (*Life*, p. 424) should always be borne in mind. The stories are primarily of interest for the light they cast on Hardy's capacity to provide acceptable regional roots for his imaginative inventions.

'A Few Crusted Characters' (which originally appeared under the title 'Wessex Folk') follows a similar pattern, but achieves a far greater sense of local authenticity. The story-tellers are not middle-class antiquarians but a representative cross-section of villagers; the scene is not a museum but a carrier's cart plying between Casterbridge and Longpuddle; above all, the occasion for tale-telling is not an extraneous rainstorm but the return of a native who asks for information about the local history (and gossip) of the community which he left as a child. These stories range from farcical tall tales and amusing anecdotes, through a piece of local folklore, to a number of satires of circumstance. The whole might almost be described as an anthology of narrative kinds, offering a variety of tone and to be accepted on different levels of seriousness. Together they make up a hoard of village story and demonstrate the abundance of artistic possibility within the apparently limited context of an isolated rural community. Nothing, Hardy seems to be saying, is unworthy of attention for the committed parish historian or narrative artist.

'A Few Crusted Characters' has been described by Kristin Brady as 'a frozen image of a world actually both static and fluid, lost in the past yet constantly changing and always present to the minds of its local narrators.'[33] Hardy, I suggest, is continually exploring the coexistence of stasis and change. Even in *Tess of the d'Urbervilles*, in which the impact of change is painfully conspicuous, Hardy's role as local historian is still strong. David Lodge has observed that, 'although no dates are specified in the novel, we are often made to feel ... that it is already finished, that it took place in living memory, and is being told to us by someone who lived in the locality, who knew her, though only slightly.'[34] But in the larger compass of the novel form, the historian of Wessex, while recording and helping to preserve the continuities, has a better opportunity to record change and the effects of change, and it is to this aspect of Hardy as regionalist that we must now turn.

CHANGE IN THE REGION

When we come to examine the regional elements in Hardy's novels, we find that a development is discernible in his presentation of the increasing tensions between country and town, between local traditions and national objectives, between dialect speech and 'standard English,' between regional culture and a rootless cosmopolitanism. This is not, I suspect, a conscious policy on Hardy's part; rather, it develops naturally as he explores the rural situation in his own time. While he wished to preserve an awareness of conditions in the past, and while he was deeply disturbed by many of the trends of the period (especially the decline in community values), it is important to stress that his novels are in no way attempts to put back the clock. His Wessex is not a closed, immutable society; on the contrary, it is buffeted on all sides by the forces of change.

Although *Under the Greenwood Tree,* focused as it is upon Mellstock village, suggests the parochial rather than the regional, when examined with the advantage of hindsight as a segment of the Wessex series, it comes to be seen as curiously representative – one is tempted to say proleptic – of the whole regional pattern. The Mellstock Quire becomes a rural community in miniature: it is a historical entity of which the individual members form a part, and within which they are defined. Much of the poignancy of the novel derives from the fact that the choir sees itself as the end of a tradition – that is, within a historical context. Dick Dewy, the central figure, gains a bride but at the cost of membership in a communal, rustic activity. He is originally introduced to us as a member of the choir and it is through the traditional carolling that he first sees and falls in love with Fancy Day. That Fancy with her 'educated ideas' (bk. 2, ch. 6) is the organ-player who will ultimately replace the choir is ironic, and she is the first in a series of Hardy heroines to be educated out of the traditional communal ways. Like Mr Maybold, the young vicar, she speaks the standard English, and it is worth noting that at first Dick is struck as dumb and ineffective in her presence as the choir in its interview with Maybold (Hardy deliberately sets the scenes side by side). The novel is split, effectively, between the comic and the elegiac because our regret at the obliteration of the choir and all it stands for is mitigated, at least to some extent, by the successful union of the two lovers. Though set in a minor key, the novel presents one aspect of the basic tension that is to control and unify the whole of Hardy's fiction.

In *Far from the Madding Crowd,* as we have seen, Hardy begins consciously to develop Wessex as a regional entity. Although there is nothing uniquely local about the rural background, we gain a much greater sense of an organic rural community; Morgan describes Weatherbury as 'a perfect example of the nucleated settlement, with its farms, inn, malthouse, church, and great monastic barn.'[35] We find, moreover, a significantly greater social range here, from Boldwood the gentleman-farmer down to Fanny Robin. Above all, the regional emphasis on rural work is conspicuous, as the well-known sheep-washing and shearing scenes testify. It should be noted, however, that these scenes, excellent as they are, serve for the most part as background to the love-plot, which focuses on those characters at the upper end of the social scale – with Boldwood and Bathsheba, of course, but also with Gabriel Oak and Troy, both of whom are seen rising (by very different methods) within the village hierarchy. Such figures as Joseph Poorgrass, Cain Ball, and Liddy Smallbury, though memorable, are decidedly supernumerary. In this novel at least, to speak of the choric function of the rustic characters is *(pace* Raymond Williams) both legitimate and accurate.

I labour this point because one of Hardy' s main contributions to regionalism is a sense of the growing importance of social distinctions that inevitably weaken the cohesion of a local community. The basis of these distinctions is predominantly and increasingly presented in terms not only of financial position but also of educational attainments and social grace. This trend, implicit in the very title of *The Poor Man and the Lady,* can be seen clearly enough in *Under the Greenwood Tree,* especially in the scene where Dick Dewy asks Keeper Day for the hand of Fancy (bk. 4, ch. 2), though in this instance the obstacle can be surmounted without undue difficulty. None the less, Fancy's love of 'refinement' and her concern for 'respectability' (bk. 4, ch. 7; bk. 5, ch. 1) are traits which will become more and more conspicuous in Hardy's later heroines, and their implications for regional customs and values are considerable.

In *Far from the Madding Crowd,* social distinctions are already more prominent. Although at the time of Gabriel's first proposal Bathsheba admits, 'you are better off than I,' she adds, 'I am better educated than you' (ch. 4). Later she tells Liddy, 'he wasn't quite good enough for me'(ch. 9); but by this time, of course, Bathsheba has risen on the class-scale (through succession to her uncle's farm) while Gabriel has lost his independent status and slipped back into the role of employed worker. True, the young Bathsheba places sophisticated manners and sexual attractiveness in Troy above money and position in Boldwood and uprightness and devotion in Gabriel, but my point is that all these factors – financial position, educational standard, social refinement (and, as we shall see later, even use of language) – unite to complicate and often frustrate the traditional norms of community life. I am not denying, of course, that the seeds of many of these problems were always present in the rustic communities; it can hardly be denied, however, that they were fostered and multiplied by centralizing, unifying pressures at the time of the Industrial Revolution. They represent, then, forces in the nineteenth century that can legitimately be described as anti-regional. I believe we miss much of the significance of Hardy's work if we fail to recognize the multifaceted ironies implicit in his presentation of increasingly anti-regional elements within a developing regional series.

The Return of the Native can legitimately be described as Hardy's first full-scale regional novel, and the tension between regional and anti-regional is explicitly noticeable. Regional awareness is immediately stressed in the title. With *Under the Greenwood Tree* and *Far from the Madding Crowd*, the literary allusions in the titles implied sophisticated detachment; the rustic locale exists 'out there,' and the attitude is reflected in Hardy's surprisingly condescending presentation of his rural characters in these early novels – what Frank Chapman described (with, alas, only slight exaggeration) as 'an unpleasant effect of performing animals going through their tricks.'[36] But *The Return of the Native*, on the contrary, presupposes 'here'; the novelist, like his protagonist, has come home, and the rustic labourers are presented with amusement but also with respect. Hardy is at last speaking, we feel, from within his region.

The importance of the region is further stressed in the famous opening which, though in a sense pre-regional, at once asserts regional significance. Hardy begins with the immediate environment, which is firmly established before 'Humanity appears upon the Scene, Hand in Hand with Trouble' (bk. 1, ch. 2). Egdon Heath dictates both the form of the novel and its boundaries. 'Every scene in the book,' Joseph Warren Beach observes, 'takes place within the horizon of one standing upon Rainbarrow,' and John Paterson has shown how Hardy alters the geographical position of the tumulus, which in Dorset is located on the outskirts of the heath, so that 'it appears in the novel, for reasons that have to do with its symbolic meaning and with the focus of its action, at the heath's very center.'[37] (Later, as the regional series develops, we sense that, just as Rainbarrow forms the centre of Egdon, so the heath itself becomes a disturbingly unpredictable, untamed centre of Wessex.) Moreover, there is a deliberate emphasis on Egdon not only as a microcosmic image of an indifferent universe but as an image of life itself. So, for Clym, 'there was something in its oppressive horizontality which too much reminded him of the arena of life; it gave him a sense of bare equality with, and no superiority to, a single living thing under the sun' (bk. 3, ch. 5).

But there is a complicating irony about the regionalism of *The Return of the Native*. The same novel in which Hardy establishes the strongest feeling of a unique locality is the one in which regionalism is most surely challenged. That Egdon is the bleakest area in Wessex accounts to some extent for its memorableness, but for the first time words like 'isolation,' 'loneliness,' and 'solitude' become key concepts, and this militates against any sense of vital community. The inhabitants of Egdon are in the original sense of the word 'heathen.' The cohesive influence of the Church, prominent in *Under the Greenwood Tree*, is conspicuous by its absence, and there is no place to congregate like the Malthouse in *Far from the Madding Crowd* (the 'Quiet Woman' is significantly at the edge of the heath, and its character seems more divisive than communal). Egdon has no human centre – only the exposed

Rainbarrow. Hardy specifically refers to 'the scattered inhabitants' of the Heath (bk. 2, ch. 4) and their 'remote cottages' (bk. 6, ch. 4). Moreover, the attitudes of the rustics towards their environment are noteworthy. It is instructive, for example, to recall the scene in *Far from the Madding Crowd* in which Cain Ball reports upon the exotic sights of Bath (still, be it stressed, within the boundaries of 'Wessex'). To the inhabitants of Weatherbury, his news is strange and doubtful: '"Well, 'tis a curious place ... ," observed Moon; "and it must be curious people that live therein"' (ch. 33). By contrast, when Clym tries to explain the motives for his return to Fairway and his cronies, he finds it virtually impossible to persuade them that he prefers Egdon to Paris (bk. 3, ch. 1). It is as if the local populace has lost its regional cohesiveness and its regional morale – it sees itself as a backwater.

Against this equivocal regional background are set the two protagonists, Clym and Eustacia, one a native who returns, the other (and it needs to be stressed that Eustacia is a native of Wessex if not of Egdon) yearning to escape. Although we first see her as indistinguishable from Egdon, although her ability to follow the faint, indeterminate footpaths places her among 'the regular haunters of the heath' and shows that she is not 'a mere visitor' (bk. 1, ch. 6), she hates the place and has a passionate longing for 'all the beating and pulsing that is going on in the great arteries of the world' (bk. 4, ch. 6). She is Hardy's most uncompromising anti-regional figure. Thus Clym and Eustacia represent diametrically opposed positions in the regionalist/cosmopolitan controversy.

In his detailed textual study *The Making of 'The Return of the Native'*, John Paterson has drawn attention to some interesting changes in Hardy's conception of this novel – changes that prove highly relevant to my present concern. Originally, for instance, Clym did not go to Paris but to Budmouth (so remaining within the Wessex boundaries); the cosmopolitan theme must therefore have increased in importance as the novel developed. And at an earlier stage the characters themselves were not so carefully differentiated in social terms. Virtually all the main characters, Paterson shows, were elevated socially in the course of the writing, and part of the distinction is achieved through language. Whereas in the 'Ur-version,' as Paterson calls it, all spoke at least to some extent in dialect, in the completed text there is a clear difference between the language of such people as the Cantles, Timothy Fairway, and Olly Dowden, and that of the more central characters in the book.

This seems to me highly significant. It is true that such distinctions have occurred earlier. Fancy Day, educated outside Mellstock, speaks in 'National English' (as Barnes called it) like Mr Maybold, but Farmer Shiner and Fancy's socially conscious father both speak in dialect. A similar split occurs in *Far from the Madding Crowd*, where Gabriel is differentiated from Bathsheba's other suitors by his speech and manners.[38] In *The Return of the Native*, however, this split is decidedly more pronounced; only Diggory Venn, whose position as sometime dairy-farmer and sometime reddleman is continually equivocal, moves with any ease between dialect (in his conversation with Johnny Nunsuch, for instance) and standard English. This process is developed, almost relentlessly, in later novels.

Hardy (and this distinguishes him from 'run-of-the-mill' regional novelists) does not reproduce local dialect merely in the interests of realism or verisimilitude – still less for the introduction of local colour. In fact, he is making a serious social point. In the older communities, the use of dialect did not necessarily imply a class difference. This is particularly clear in *The Mayor of Casterbridge*. Michael Henchard, holding the highest position of secular responsibility in the Wessex hierarchy, did not feel the need – for himself, at least – to adopt a standard English. But my qualification is necessary, since in this novel (and the process is developed still further in *The Woodlanders*) Hardy catches a crucial shift in allegiances between acceptance of the old regional standards and insistence on the newer dictates of Victorian bourgeois society. The young Elizabeth-Jane has already been initiated into a sense of what is 'respectable' (she uses the word twice in chapter 3, once each in chapters 6 and 7), and Mrs Newson becomes known as the 'genteel' widow (ch. 13). Yet Henchard, though 'uncultivated' himself (ch. 20), is determined that Elizabeth-Jane shall rise in the social scale, and the tension caused by this determination comes to a head in the brilliant but painful scene in which Henchard actually uses dialect in order to rebuke her for doing the same. Settling into Henchard's ways, she follows local precedent in what Hardy calls 'her occasional pretty and picturesque use of dialect words – those terrible marks of the beast to the truly genteel.' But Hardy's sardonic irony becomes deadly earnest in Henchard: 'Good God, are you only fit to carry wash to the pig-trough, that ye use such words as those?' (ch. 20).

The Woodlanders is positively dotted with words like 'genteel,' 'respectable,' 'fashionable,' 'refined.' Melbury's obsession with his daughter's education and prospects is both pathetic and extreme. Grace's very name is eloquent in implication, and with the scene at Winterbourne's hut an alien sense of 'propriety' derived from Victorian but not rural England becomes an important feature of the plot. In this novel, despite the sequestered situation of Little Hintock, class divisions have hardened. Mrs Charmond, the anti-regional figure corresponding to Eustacia Vye and Lucetta Templeman in earlier books, is a dictatorial lady-of-the-manor, 'not sufficiently local' (ch. 8), who, though owning an estate in a woodland area, can hardly tell 'a beech from a woak' (ch. 34); Winterbourne, once of yeoman status and close to Melbury, is slipping into the condition of a migratory labourer; Fitzpiers, looking down from a window in the 'Earl of Wessex' hotel, catches the trend of the times when he tells Grace:

'I feel as if I belonged to a different species from the people [Winterbourne and his regional, dialect-speaking cider-makers] who are working in that yard' (ch. 25).

Both *The Mayor of Casterbridge* and *The Woodlanders* can be studied with profit from a regional perspective. In the former, Casterbridge is described as 'the pole, focus, or nerve-knot of the surrounding country life' (ch. 9). In the latter, High-Stoy Hill provides a focal point not unlike that of Rainbarrow, which had been 'the pole and axis of this heathery world' in *The Return of the Native* bk. 1, ch. 2); High-Stoy dominates and as it were defines the regional setting, being described as 'the well-known hill, which had been the axis of so many critical movements [in the lives of Grace and Fitzpiers] during his residence at Hintock' (ch. 45). Moreover, the setting of the novel, as the title suggests (and as Phyllis Bentley notes with some relief), is integral to the plot. Melbury's lumber business, Winterbourne's cider-making, Marty South's spar-making all depend upon the nature of the locality. The woodlands are as essential, economically, to the fortunes of the protagonists as they are, artistically, to the mood and texture of the whole novel. But the action chronicles a perilous balance. Grace falls from 'the good old Hintock ways' (ch. 6), and Winter-bourne's decline and fall are emblematic of larger patterns of change. *The Woodlanders* presents 'a modern Wessex' with a vengeance.

It is not necessary, I think, to prolong this study with any detailed consideration of Hardy's later novels. Arnold Kettle and Douglas Brown have emphasized the wandering, increasingly migratory quality of rural labour as embodied in Tess and Jude, and, while we may wish to make certain quali-fications, the basic pattern is clear enough.[39] In choosing his protagonists from the humbler 'work-folk' of Wessex, Hardy is moving closer to the regional norms, but he does so only to demonstrate that, in the later Victorian period, their regional and communal backgrounds had been eroded. Tess knows only the fag-end of a regional village community in Marlott; Blackmore Vale, which had once been for Tess 'the world, and its inhabitants the races thereof' (bk. 1, ch. 5), can no longer sustain her. Hardy, having by this time established Wessex as a coherent fictional entity, can present her wandering within it, from sub-region to subregion, her family moving on Lady Day, the age-old traditional time for rural moves and changes, but her association with her native village has now finally snapped.

And the nadir is reached in *Jude the Obscure*, which could legitimately be subtitled 'The Departure of a Native.' The preface, Gregor has recently insisted, 'announces ... a world no longer framed by a remembrance of Wessex.'[40] Dispossessed of one way of life, Jude fails to establish himself in another. His dilemma is classified by Hardy, continually emphasizing the universal pattern in the particular regional example, as 'his form of the modern vice of unrest' (bk. 2, ch. 2); and Jude himself recognizes Sue as 'a product of civilization' (bk. 3, ch. 2). The issues raised by the novel are essentially those of 'modernism.' The break-up of regional society, its deliberate destruction in the interests of an alien process, is relentlessly chronicled in the opening chapter:

> Many of the thatched and dormered dwelling-houses [at Marygreen] had been pulled down of late years, and many trees felled on the green. Above all, the original church, hump-backed, wood-turreted, and quaintly hipped, had been taken down, and either cracked up into heaps of road-metal in the lane, or utilized as pig-sty walls. ... In place of it a tall new building of modern Gothic design, unfamiliar to English eyes, had been erected on a new piece of ground by a certain obliterator of historic records who had run down from London and back in a day.

Here regionalism receives its *coup de grâce:* Jude is deprived of both his context and his roots.

The passage just quoted from *Jude the Obscure* describes the destruction of a regional locale. For an equivalent, concise account of the destruction of a regional personality we may turn to an important but rarely quoted passage from *The Well-Beloved.* It is worth noting that, although this is in most respects the least regional of his works, Hardy's preface stresses the regional uniqueness of Portland. His uncharacteristic and rather absurd plot has no necessary connection with Portland, and part of the weakness of the book derives from this lack of relation between plot and setting. Yet, as so often with Hardy, this awkward clash of elements within the novel is a significant part of the intention. Avice Caro's situation is representative, and brilliantly sums up the pattern of regional history as Hardy saw it:

> Every aim of those who had brought her up had been to get her away mentally as far as possible from her natural and individual life as an inhabitant of a peculiar island: to make her an exact copy of tens of thousands of other people, in whose circumstances there was nothing special, distinctive, or picturesque; to teach her to forget all the experiences of her ancestors; to drown the local ballads by songs purchased at the Budmouth fashionable music-seller's, and the local vocabulary by a governess-tongue of no country at all. ...
> ... By constitution she was local to the bone, but she could not escape the tendency of the age. (Pt. 1, ch. 2)

Hardy's twentieth-century readers are for the most part products of the educational process described here. The 'tendency of the age,' continued and even stepped up in our own, has been so successful that our awareness of earlier regional differences and alternative attitudes is in danger of being expunged. If we are to understand the past and our own relation to it, we must take note of what has been lost. This is a final reason why a regional approach to Hardy's fiction can emphasize an easily overlooked aspect of his work that Hardy himself considered central.

SEVEN

Regional Realism

EDEN PHILLPOTTS AND DARTMOOR

The Moor is apart; its people are apart. By reason of their geographical situation, and the distinctiveness of their industries, the character of the people has a quite special savour and quality. What a district for a novelist – compact, complete, withdrawn, exceptional, traditional, impressive, and racy! Eden Phillpotts found it and annexed it.[1]

Arnold Bennett's account presents what would seem to be an ideal recipe for the regional novel. Though born in India, Phillpotts had been brought to England and Devon as a child and grew up within reach of Dartmoor. After a brief period as an insurance clerk and journalist in London, he settled once again in Devon and spent the rest of an unusually long life (he lived from 1862 until 1959) in social seclusion there as an extraordinarily prolific writer. He produced approximately two hundred and fifty books (many of them under pseudonyms), embracing poetry, plays, school stories, and detective novels. But he is best known for the stories of Dartmoor, twenty of which (including two volumes of short stories) form a coherent series of regional fictions.[2]

Phillpotts appeared to possess all the qualities and advantages requisite for an important regional novelist. Dartmoor itself was a well-defined area with distinctive physical features and a unique atmosphere that had not been extensively portrayed in fiction. Blackmore, whom Phillpotts admired greatly and to whom he dedicated his first Dartmoor novel, *Children of the Mist* (1898), had already popularized Exmoor, and Hardy had alerted the novel-reading public and the literary tourist to the attractions of the west country. Superficially, the geography of Dartmoor, with its separate communities of human beings in the villages and combes surrounded by the spectacular and lonely scenery of the moorland, was admirably fitted for regional treatment. Phillpotts himself was a conscientious and dedicated writer with a fine ear for dialect speech, stylistic variety, an ability to develop both comic and tragic themes, and the main technical resources of a skilled story-teller. His knowledge of the area was encyclopaedic, and he had a particular interest in the archaeological remains for which Dartmoor is famous and in all aspects of natural history, especially botany. As early as 1899 no less a critic than Bennett hailed him as 'the greatest of our younger writers, yet very imperfectly recognized at present.'[3] Only seven years later, he had progressed sufficiently for F.J. Snell, in his preface to *The Blackmore Country*, to remark that 'one instinctively associates [Dartmoor] with the names of Baring-Gould and Eden Phillpotts.'[4] The mantle of Hardy seemed destined to fall upon him.

Yet although Phillpotts's name will be familiar to most students of popular fiction in the first half of the present century, and although he was in fact an accomplished and respected writer (as the collected edition of the Dartmoor novels testifies), he has failed to create a lasting reputation. Two reasons are generally brought forward to explain this: first, he produced far too much and so dissipated his talents; second, he was unfortunate in writing under the shadow of Hardy. Both reasons are cogent but neither, I think, quite fits the case. A better explanation is to be found in his position within the whole context of English regionalism.

Phyllis Bentley maintained, as we have seen, that the golden age of regional fiction lasted from 1840 until 1940. It began with the discovery of regional variety as an indirect result of improved communications following the macadamization of roads and the development of the railway system. Hardy, born in 1840 itself, grew up not merely to present his native region in all its historical, geographical, and above all human richness, but to reflect the changes it was undergoing and the serious dangers that threatened it. Phillpotts, though only twenty years younger than Hardy, did not begin his regional series until after Hardy's fiction-writing career was over. *Jude the Obscure* had appeared in 1895; *Children of the Mist* followed in 1898. But although the latter is set in the period from the middle 1870s to Queen Victoria's Golden Jubilee in 1887, it seems to belong to an earlier world than the former. On Phillpotts's Dartmoor 'The citizen's *Then*' is 'the rustic's *Now*' with a vengeance. The almost contemporary reference is of little significance; it exists merely so that the Queen's pardon for deserters can conveniently resolve the plot. We get no clear impression of a region developing and changing through time.

Phillpotts's problem, I suggest, was not so much that he wrote under the shadow of Hardy as that he began where Hardy began and chronicled a world that by his time belonged to the past. Dartmoor was indeed 'apart,' to use

Bennett's term. Compared with Dorset, it was far more removed from the central concerns of Victorian England than the few extra miles from London would suggest. Phillpotts's own retirement to Devon (he is said never to have visited London afterwards, not even to attend a performance of his triumphantly successful play, *The Farmer's Wife*) was a retreat from the world very different from Hardy's life at Max Gate with its regular visits to London and excursions elsewhere. It seems as if Phillpotts wanted to avoid most of the complex issues that dominated the world of his day. His final novel in the Dartmoor series, *Children of Men*, appeared in 1923. A foreword to the book suggests that it renders the design of the cycle 'orbicular and complete,' and this is borne out by the chiming titles of the first and last novels. But the Dartmoor world presented is hardly different. A passing reference to trouble in Ireland in *Children of Men* suggests that the setting is roughly contemporary with the date of publication, but it must have seemed extraordinarily (to some, no doubt, attractively) remote from the years of *l'entre deux guerres*. Hardy's world was indeed 'a Wessex under Queen Victoria'; that of *Children of Men* gave little indication of a Dartmoor living under King George V. Phillpotts was undoubtedly inspired by Hardy but he failed to comprehend Hardy's essential message.

The influence of Hardy upon Phillpotts has been challenged on account of various claims, lacking authority, that Phillpotts had established himself as a regional writer before reading the Wessex novels. The circumstance seems on the face of it unlikely, and it is effectively refuted by Arnold Bennett, who records in his *Journals* details of a visit paid to Phillpotts as early as 1899, just after the publication of the first Dartmoor novel, *Children of the Mist:* 'He said he had been influenced by Hardy ("Talking about your god, are you?" said his wife, coming in).'[5] Certainly, it is difficult to read far in Phillpotts without being reminded of Hardy, though this may be explained in part by the latter's comprehensive treatment of rural themes, which makes it difficult for a successor to sound original. Perhaps the most obvious examples are the record of a woman 'burn[ing] the chap in a wax image stuffed with pins' in *Sons of the Morning*,[6] a drowning scene at the climax of *The River* that inevitably recalls *The Return of the Native*, the mock-burial in *The Whirlwind*, which is close to the skimmity-ride in *The Mayor of Casterbridge*, and the account of the Mummers' Play referred to frequently in *The Three Brothers*. Besides, *Children of the Mist* is especially full of what seem to be Hardyesque echoes. Thus the following remark seems calculated to remind the reader of Egdon Heath: 'Modern man has also fretted the wide expanse, has scratched its surface and dropped a little sweat and blood; but his mansion and his cot and his grave are no more; plutonic rock is the only tablet on which any human story has been scribbled to endure.' And when we are told of Damaris Blanchard that 'the Moor possessed no terrors for her' the image of Thomasin Yeobright inevitably springs to mind.[7]

The Hardy novel which appears to have made the greatest impression upon Phillpotts was *The Return of the Native*, and there is an obvious reason why this should be so. The desolate, untamed stretches of Dartmoor bear a close resemblance to Egdon Heath. But whereas Egdon, though a haunting presence in the Wessex series as a whole, is the centre of only one novel, Phillpotts's Dartmoor is the centre of the whole novel-cycle. It is true that Phillpotts, like Hardy and far more obviously, sets his individual novels in different parts of the moor,[8] but the local differences are minimal. Dartmoor as a whole remains Dartmoor; the human beings inhabit the outskirts of the moor, their habitations penetrating into the combes, with occasional farming, mining, and quarrying activity on the uplands. But the area provides none of the agricultural variety that we find in Hardy's Wessex, and Phillpotts persuades us of the unity of Dartmoor as a regional entity but not as a viable economic unity. There is no 'unity in *diversity*' here. In consequence, there is a tendency towards monotony in Phillpotts's series; his Dartmoor becomes a formula setting as Hardy's never does.

It would be reasonable to suppose, indeed, that Phillpotts derived a formula for writing regional fiction from his study of Hardy. Once again *The Return of the Native* was probably his immediate model. It is the only Hardy novel in which the first chapter is devoted entirely to landscape description, but this becomes a common feature of Phillpotts's work; examples include *The Thief of Virtue, The Beacon*, and *The Forest on the Hill*. Even more common is a detailed initial description of scenery (as in, among others, *Sons of the Morning, The River, The Secret Woman*, and *Miser's Money*) before – in Hardy's hallowed phrase from the second chapter-title of *The Return of the Native* – 'Humanity appears upon the Scene, Hand in Hand with Trouble.' In Hardy, the one opening that verges on formula is the introduction of a solitary figure or group of figures moving across an otherwise empty landscape, and this is conspicuously echoed – almost parodied – in *The Virgin in Judgment:* 'It was at this stage in the unfolding phenomenon of night that life moved upon the void: a black amorphous smudge crawled out of the gloom and crept tardily along. At length its form ... divided and revealed a brace of animals, one of which staggered slowly on four legs, while the other went on two.'[9] More often in Phillpotts we find a single figure on the top of a hill ('The Man on the Cairn,' to quote the opening chapter-title from *The Whirlwind*) who looks down upon the particular section of the moor in which the novel is set. Used once, this is an effective device; used too often – and Phillpotts employs it quite frequently – it becomes a mere trick of the fiction-writing trade.

Phillpotts's regional preoccupations manifest themselves clearly in these scenes, and often, like Hardy, he uses them to present a detached narrative perspective. To cite one brief example, in *The Portreeve* we are told that from the summit of Yes Tor, 'the spectator of imagination thus surveying a whole centre of human activity, as he might view a nest of ants, or the commonwealth of a hive, ascends from merely manlike perception to the comprehensive discrimination of a god.'[10] Moreover, a related formula involves the use of the moor as a place where characters may find solitude in order to think things out in times of crisis. In regional terms, this looking down on the area from above leads to the employment of theatrical imagery, the landscape being regarded as scenery against which human comedies and tragedies are played out. In *The Secret Woman*, 'Dartmoor is an embodiment of reality and a theatre of elemental force'; in *The Whirlwind* it is 'chosen by nature for a theatre of worship and work'; and in *The Beacon* the slopes of Cosdon are 'a playground for light and shadows and a theatre for storms.'[11] The image is especially recurrent in this last novel, and recalls Hardy's famous remark in *The Woodlanders* about Sophoclean dramas taking place in a circumscribed, regional locale.

The sense of formula writing in Phillpotts increases as the Dartmoor series proceeds, and it is his chief artistic limitation that his basic effects become too visible and forecastable. All novelists, of course, must face the challenge of smoothly combining the four main ingredients of fiction: plot, character, theme, and setting. In general, the integration of character and setting presents no difficulties for Phillpotts. The vast majority of his characters are presented as natives of the moor whose ancestors have lived there for centuries, and we never feel (as we do sometimes even in Hardy – in the case of Eustacia Vye, for example) that their personalities are unlikely to have developed within the environment in which we find them. They are also refreshingly free from the myth of rustic innocence. Phillpotts claimed to be in active revolt against what he considered the falseness of romantic rural conventions, even in Scott, and he habitually presents 'the petty bickerings, jealousies, and strifes of ordinary country existence.'[12] His human beings are as accurately and realistically presented as the setting they inhabit.

The relation of setting and plot, however, proves a little more questionable. Phillpotts's tendency to describe the scene first and then to set the narrative moving in front of it can accentuate the sense of setting as *mere* background, and this is encouraged by the theatrical imagery just mentioned. Phillpotts claimed that he 'never took a plot to Dartmoor for its background but approached every new scene with empty mind, confident that a story awaited [him] there,'[13] yet we often feel that his plots, in Ernest A. Baker's words about *Wuthering Heights* already quoted, 'might have been played out on any stage.' There is nothing local, for example, about the plot of *The Secret Woman*, where a wife murders her husband when she discovers his infidelity, but is observed by her two sons, who disagree about whether she should confess her crime. The characters are credible, the plot believable, and the setting vivid, but the three are certainly not inseparable.

I suspect, however, that Phillpotts's greatest difficulty was to reconcile his thematic concerns with the other elements of the novelist's art. Certainly the relation of theme and plot can be awkward. Especially in the later novels, readers become increasingly aware of how one character visits another to talk over a matter of mutual interest (the theme in question) and then the second character goes on to a discussion with a third. As soon as we notice the formulaic structure, it becomes conspicuous as an intrusive mannerism. It is as if Phillpotts's honest and preponderant realism cannot disguise – is even, perhaps, duty-bound to reveal – the relentless sameness of so many rural lives.

But Phillpotts's themes are most often associated with his own ethical rationalism, and the connection between this and the Dartmoor locale is tenuous at best. Whereas Hardy had been able to relate his own experience of 'the ache of modernism' to a deeply entrenched Wessex fatalism, Phillpotts has no such recourse and can only assert his views from the narrator's stance. Hardy, while no longer a believer, could present rustic pieties with a sympathy that often seems to verge on the envious, but Phillpotts has the assurance of an advocate, and his evolutionary humanism is always apparent even when it seems remote from the cultural attitudes of his characters. In consequence, his educated narrator is always somewhat detached from – even superior to – the people about whom he writes. In the terms that J. Hillis Miller uses in reference to Hardy, we find the aesthetic distance but not the balancing desire. Although there is usually at least one character in each novel who breaks away from 'superstition,' the authorial attitude gets in the way of a general sympathy. This suggest an anti-regional centralism curiously at odds with Phillpotts's local loyalties. It causes him not to transcend regionalism but to supersede it.

With Phillpotts, then, whatever is 'universal' in his work is imposed upon the regional rather than drawn out of it. Dartmoor is always a backwater, never a microcosm. No alternative to village ways is offered within the fiction itself. The human communities may vary from novel to novel in order to encompass all parts of the moor, but they are all much the same – societies of working farmers with occasional presentations of local gentry (the Squire of Godleigh in *Sons of the Morning*, for instance) or the local labourers who resemble Hardy's garrulous countrymen but are generally commonplace (more realistically portrayed but less forceful artistically). Phillpotts's main characters, however credible and moving, inevitably lack the representative significance of, say, Grace Melbury or Tess or Jude. They are seen against a background of history – or, more generally, prehistory – but the image implied is one of a human continuity that varies little through the millennia. In *The Three Brothers*, for example, Humphrey Baskerville insists to his nephew that the builders of 'the roundy-poundies – the circles of stones cast about on the hillsides and by the streams' were 'men like ourselves.'[14] Socially (as distinct from philosophically), there is little emphasis on change and development. Life on Dartmoor, we gather, is only superficially altered by the technological discoveries and historical events of the last hundred years or so.

In his heyday Phillpotts was, one suspects, read primarily for the image of Dartmoor that he communicated so well. He prided himself on his fidelity to the Dartmoor of actuality. Hardly any of his place-names are invented, and an appropriate Ordnance Survey map lays his countryside before readers as if, like so many of his protagonists, they were looking down from one of the tors. But this very accuracy (itself verging on a formula to convey authenticity) can be limiting. The more Phillpotts equates his fictional world with the existing area in Devon, the less room he leaves for the workings of the creative imagination. By never completely identifying Casterbridge with Dorchester or Weatherbury with Puddletown, Hardy retained control of an imaginative possibility that Phillpotts relinquished.

The Dartmoor series will always retain a sociological value, but its repute as literature is never likely to return to the peak that it attained briefly in the 1920s. Individual novels are often impressive, but the whole cycle fails to sustain a consistent level of interest. So far as a regional perspective is concerned, Phillpotts's most satisfying book may well be *Widecombe Fair*, a novel content to present not so much a vision of life as, simply, life itself. It centres upon the best known of the moorland villages, and is unusual in the Dartmoor series for being a comedy. Framed by the arrival and departure of Tryphena Harvey, an orphan child from Exeter, it presents Widecombe first through the eyes of a patronizing outsider, Blatchford the lawyer, who brings her to the village (one is reminded of Lockwood in *Wuthering Heights*); we are then introduced to the inhabitants and their ways through the experience and increasing devotion of Tryphena herself. The novel contains a wide range of characters, all with their different quirks and problems; instead of a continuing plot, we are offered a series of interlinked short stories with the leading characters in one playing supernumerary roles in the others. The emphasis falls on the village rather than the encompassing moor, and as a result we gain a strong impression of the local community as a social organism. But the success of *Widecombe Fair* is bought at a price. A pleasant, gentle, leisurely narrative, it lacks a sense of any larger significance. Although we are supposed to reject Blatchford's cosmopolitan myopia, it is difficult not to regard the book, even while enjoying it, as a kind of 'escape.' Phillpotts's most satisfying example of regionalism, then, presents a severely limited regionalism. While his aims were ambitious, his achievement resembles what Hardy's would be if *Under the Greenwood Tree* were judged to be, artistically, the best of the Wessex series.[15]

SHEILA KAYE-SMITH AND THE WEALD

According to her own testimony, Sheila Kaye-Smith's first story, written at the age of fifteen and entitled 'Northward of Brede,' began: 'The river Tillingham floweth out of the west and loses its waters in the silent Rother. On its way it passes many a gaunt farm-house with neglected pastures sloping down to the streamlet's bank, but never one more gaunt or neglected than Ellenwhorne.'[16] Shades of *Cold Comfort Farm*, but the most remarkable thing about this beginning is the way in which, from her first fumbling attempts at fiction, she zeroes in on the region that was to preoccupy her through a long writing life. Brede is some seven miles or so above Hastings, and the country to the north of it is the stretch of agricultural land on the borders of Sussex and Kent known as the Weald. It is a beautiful, gentle region with a rather surprising history, since it was the centre of the English iron industry from Tudor times until the greater convenience of coal as fuel for the furnaces led to the transfer of the industry from the south to the north of England in the late eighteenth century. The novelist herself was born in Hastings in 1887, the daughter of a doctor, and eventually made her home at Doucegrove, a community that appears in many of her novels and is itself 'northward of Brede.'

Her first two published novels, *The Tramping Methodist* (1908) and *Starbrace* (1909), are both set in the eighteenth century and take the form of picaresque stories full of violent action and swashbuckling adventures that seem to derive from Defoe and the early Smollett. They are essentially immature work, the details and characters far removed from her own experience. In later life she readily admitted, when reminiscing about the former novel, 'that my protagonist was really the country of the Rother Valley and my plot a map of the Kent and Sussex borders.'[17] She also admitted that she knew nothing of Methodism at that time; none the less, region and religion are the two most conspicuous ingredients in all her work, and it is interesting to see them interwoven from the start of her writing career.

The Tramping Methodist opens at Brede Parsonage, and in the first few chapters we find Starvecrow, Spell Land Woods, Udimore, the Rother marshes, Doucegrove Farm, and Beckley Furnace, all of which are to reappear in later work. The background is sometimes expressed in excessively 'fine' writing ('The sun was setting fast, and hung low in the sky above Witherenden – a scarlet wafer on the brink of a cloudy chalice into which it was rapidly sinking' [ch. 2]) but it is none the less effective in establishing a specific countryside. In chapter 10, for instance, John Palehouse and the narrator, Humphrey Lyte, climb the tower of Tenterden Church and look down at the view:

All round us lay the wonderfully contrasted yet wonderfully blended colours of the weald – red and yellow farm-houses, with their white-capped oasts and black barns, emerald pastures, olive-green hop-fields, green-bice woods, brown and purple commons where the gorse-fires flared, and above all the blue sky across which the clouds were scudding. Due south stretched a strip of apple-green, with a blue ribbon winding along the centre. It was the Rother Marsh with the Rother. And on the further side huddled the fields and woods of Sussex.

It is easy to criticize such a passage, with its hint of painting by numbers, and the scene draws only too obviously on the standard regional formulae that became so conspicuous in Phillpotts, but it conveys none the less a distinct if heightened sense of the kind of countryside that she made her own.

Indeed, the heightening may itself be significant, a desperate attempt to inject into a delightful but unostentatious countryside a more vivid and dramatic quality than the locality in fact contains. There is a curious combination in these early stories of a rather cruel realism with a romantic vigour and bravado, and the setting is not in itself adequate for the effects she needs. In the later fiction, when she writes of a period close to if not contemporaneous with her own time, and offers what one commentator has called 'an entirely naturalistic picture of the rural community,'[18] her work recalls Phillpotts without Dartmoor. Her setting is just not noteworthy enough to sustain interest, to be more than background. As I noted in discussing Phillpotts, his stories are often only minimally related to his region, but the overriding presence of Dartmoor helps to give them a certain magnitude; in Kaye-Smith's Weald, however, this magnitude is lacking and the relation between plot and setting becomes noticeably slack.

It is not coincidental, I believe, that *Sussex Gorse* (1916), a book generally accepted as one of her more successful novels, if not her best, is most prominently concerned with the theme of man and the land. Reuben Backfield is consumed with an obsessive passion to make the wilderness blossom as the rose. The Boarzell, the gorse-crowned hill-waste above the Backfields' farm property, is as dominating a physical presence as Egdon or Dartmoor. It is the continual focus of the story. From the outset, man is pitted against the land:

> He, Reuben, would never be happy till he had torn up that gorse and lopped those firs from the top of Boarzell. ... That sinister waste, profitless now to every man, should be a source of wonder, wealth and fame. ... He could fight this cruel, tough thing only by being cruel and tough himself. He must be ruthless as the wind that blustered over it, wiry as the grass-roots that twisted in its marl. (Bk. 1, ch. 1)

We are immediately made aware (in ways that anticipate the character of Gideon Sarn in Mary Webb's *Precious Bane)* of a far subtler integration of plot and setting. This is a story of conflict that, in a curious way, leads to an identification. A little later, Naomi, Reuben's first wife, 'noticed a kind of likeness between him and Boarzell – swart, strong, cruel, full of an irrepressible life' (bk. 2, ch. 5). In another scene where, after watching Naomi and Harry together, Reuben literally embraces the earth, his sexual association with the landscape is emphasized (bk. 1, ch. 5). And the narrator subsequently observes: 'In challenging Boarzell he had challenged the secret forces of his own body, all the riot of hope and weakness and desire that go to make up a man' (bk. 5, ch. 7).

When she came to discuss the novel in her autobiography, Kaye-Smith went so far as to find a weakness in *Sussex Gorse* because 'it is too big to be true.'[19] Certainly there are times when Boarzell as symbol and unifying image becomes oppressive and the constant reference to it almost mechanical. But it remains a centre of power. Backfield is both horrifying and impressive in his single-minded determination to conquer Boarzell and make it fruitful, and at the close we cannot avoid being split between grudging admiration and stern disapproval. The novel represents the closest that Kaye-Smith ever gets to the rich possibilities of imaginative regional fiction.

As if to compensate for her presentation of Reuben Backfield as a giant in the land, she turns in her next rural novels to the portrayal of ordinary men and women, often inarticulate, often failures, but all in their own ways bound to the soil. *Little England* (or, in its American form, *The Four Roads*) was published in 1918 and its muted and touching patriotism represents the novelist's response to the First World War. It deals with a small area of unremarkable Sussex farming country just north of the Pevensey marshes. The focus is mainly on Tom Beatup, a young farmer who goes reluctantly to war and dies in battle, and Jerry Sumption, scapegrace son of a local preacher, who volunteers but, after absenting himself from his regiment on a love-escapade, is court-martialled and shot for desertion. The fate of Thyrza, Ivy, and Nell Sumption and the perils of marriage are well-presented (Nell's fear – not that her husband will be killed but that he will return – has great power), and Mr Sumption, blacksmith turned unsuccessful preacher, is a complex and moving character. The novel depends on its form for its local cohesiveness, the contrasted, juxtaposed, and interrelated fortunes of members of a single community. The title is indicative not only of a patriotic stance but of a rural microcosm.

Little England, then, is both poignant and impressive, but its larger theme detracts from the more exclusively regional interest that it attempts to foster. The countryside is special only in so far as it is one of the parts of southern England where the guns in France could be clearly heard. Kaye-Smith reports, indeed, that hearing the guns in this area gave her the first germ for the book.[20] One gets the impression that the novel is included in the regional series merely because the series already exists and provides a convenient framework; there seems to be no pressing artistic reason. As usual, Kaye-Smith floods her novel with place-names verifiable on local maps – but the area possesses no unique qualities. 'When later in France [Tom Beatup] thought of England,' we are told, 'he thought of it only as that willow-pond at the opening of Sunday Street, and Thyrza Honey lying heavy and warm and sweet against his breast' (pt. 2, ch. 15). The sentiment rings true, but Sunday Street remains no more than a name. Its associations become meaningful only for Tom; it is not transformed, as places in Scott and Hardy are transformed, for the reader.

The same reservations have to be made about *Green Apple Harvest* (1920). The central figure here is Robert Fuller, a young farmer with a 'wild' reputation who is suddenly converted and tramps the countryside with an idiosyncratic gospel. Torn between love and religion, between the seemingly conflicting demands of flesh and spirit, he fails pathetically and embarrassingly in both areas of human experience. Once again the novel is accomplished in construction, characterization, and dialogue (especially dialect). Its weakness lies first in the difficulty of evoking tragic sympathy or empathy with a character who is basically a failure, both weak and confused, and second (more to the point here) in its lack of the imaginative conception and dimension that one finds not only in such writers as Scott, Emily Brontë, and Hardy, but in Kaye-Smith's contemporaries such as Mary Webb and Constance Holme. Once again Kaye-Smith resembles Phillpotts in being somewhat monotonously competent.

Joanna Godden (1921), set in the Romney Marsh area, was one of her most popular novels, partly because of the originality of the leading character who gives her name to the story. A vigorous, unconventional woman who flouts tradition by running her own farm, Joanna Godden dominates the book. But it is essentially an episodic novel. Divided into four parts it deals with her early attraction to the 'looker' (= shepherd), Socknersh; her 'first love' with Martin Trevor, son of the local squire, who dies just before the wedding; her younger sister Ellen's marriage with Joanna's farmer suitor, Arthur Alse, and Ellen's running away (temporarily) with Sir Henry Trevor, Martin's father; and finally Joanna's affair with a suburban clerk, Albert Hill, her leaving him before the wedding and then realizing that she is to have a child. As this synopsis suggests, there is nothing particularly regional about the book; although a case might be made for interpreting it as a study of the clash between Joanna's human instincts and her inherited regional mores, this is not sufficient to hold the novel together.

The book contains, moreover, a number of puzzling and rather disturbing resemblances to *Far from the Madding Crowd*. After taking over the farm, Joanna acts as her own bailiff (pt. 1, ch. 2), dismisses her shepherd (pt. 1, ch. 7), is seen with the new shepherd in his hut at lambing-time (pt. 1, ch. 14), and rebukes him at a sheep-shearing (pt. 1, ch. 15). In addition, the relation between Joanna and Martha Tilden recalls that between Bathsheba and Liddy, the conversation in the Woolpack Inn suggests a Hardyesque chorus, and such dialect comment as 'everyone staring and fidgeting so as pore mus' Pratt lost his place in the Progress and jumped all the way from the Belief to the Royal Family' (pt. 1, ch. 3) has a familiar Wessex ring. The echoes are doubtless unconscious on Kaye-Smith's part; the difficulty is that her approach to her characters does not create a sufficiently new interest and concern to make them seem more than a pale imitation. Again, I know of no evidence to prove that Kaye-Smith read Phillpotts (though it seems highly probable), but Thyrza Honey in *Little England* has a Phillpottsian name – Thyrza Tapper appears in both *Widecome Fair* and the play *The Farmer's Wife* – and her position as general store-keeper and her relation to Tom Beatup is close to Barbara Hext's situation in *The Thief of Virtue*. Like Phillpotts's own apparent echoes of Hardy, these resemblances suggest that, so far as a basically realistic presentation of rustic locales is concerned, the regional vein was showing signs of running thin.

The novels I have already mentioned constitute Kaye-Smith's best known work. Her fiction continues with remarkable regularity and consistency (her last novel appeared in 1954, two years before her death), but she never developed beyond the level of the good popular novelist achieved in the years beginning with *Sussex Gorse* (although her Catholic conversion and religious writings earned her further attention in extra-literary circles). But mention needs to be made of the fragments of an ambitious novel-series which she projected in the 1920s and early 1930s.

It began with *The End of the House of Alard* (1923), the ruthless chronicle of the decline of a great estate in the years immediately following the First World War. As always, it is set solidly in the Weald, though it is perhaps too representative to be tied to a specific region. A powerful novel grappling boldly with an important issue of the time, it paints a convincing and by no means sentimental picture of the rural aristocracy, and provides in some ways a stimulating comparison with Constance Holme's treatment of the estate question a decade earlier. Once again, religion rivals the land as the main theme (one of the sons goes into a monastery and, succeeding at the end of the novel, causes a sensation by selling the crippled estate), but the two themes are united in a concern for the continuity – in historical, economic, and personal terms – of a tightly knit community.

The opening chapter traces the history of the Alards from the Crusades to the First World War in what appears to be history, the effect being not dissimilar to parts of D.H. Lawrence's opening to *The Rainbow*, though without his imaginative scope. The Alards, in fact, are larger than the novel, and it is clear that, once the book was finished, they refused to leave the novelist alone. Her most pressing interest lay in the events following the sale of the estate, and this led to the writing of *The Ploughman's Progress* (1933, published in the United States as *Gipsy Waggon*). This is a chronicle-story, organized by years, and often reads more like social history than fiction (' ... the first months of 1928 saw the beginnings of a regional slide into bankruptcy' ['1928']). It is not strictly a sequel to *The End of the House of Alard*, since there is a narrative shift from the gentry to the labourer. We see most of the action from the viewpoint of Fred Sinden, the ploughman of the title, and some from that of Jim Parish, a small independent yeoman. Sinden, losing his job as a ploughman, is forced by circumstances to take to a caravan and the life of migratory labour. He and his wife adapt to this regular job (as a *mechanized* ploughman) when the latter comes into a legacy. Since we see the action from two different viewpoints, it remains uncertain whether this is indeed a progress (i.e., a finding of freedom) or – as Parish sees it – the breaking of a good countryman. Since it covers ten crucial years of British agricultural history with a documentary concern, the book has distinct sociological value. But as a novel it hardly rises above the level of average competence. Kaye-Smith herself was later to confess that it was 'a patchwork of local events and observations, held together by my indignation that England should in such a manner throw the best of herself away.'[21] It is, however, more genuinely regional than most of her books – mainly because, although the governmental attitudes to agriculture are national in scale, the plot derives from regional elements that reflect a local situation.

But Kaye-Smith was not yet finished with the Alards. Two subsequent novels, *Superstition Corner* and *Gallybird* (both published in 1934), turn back to the Alard past. The first is set at the time of the defeat of the Spanish Armada, and the tension between Catholic and Protestant is conspicuous. The emphasis, which makes the novel truly regional, is on the Sussex iron industry, and Kaye-Smith makes clear that she is portraying the area at yet another period of crisis: 'The country was being destroyed – eaten up by the love of money expressed in fire and waste. Near the furnaces woodmen were at work cutting down the forests to feed them' (ch. 7). Unfortunately, the plot belongs to Hollywood historical romance (it contains religious betrayal, a fatal duel, a public execution, and sudden death from the plague), but the attempt to fill in the history of the district is of some interest. Similarly, *Gallybird* is set just after the accession of William of Orange (at another period of Catholic/Protestant crisis), and concerns a priest who gives up his church because of the split in allegiances. The iron industry is once more prominent, and a concern for magic adds some rather fantastic spice to the plot. Here Kaye-Smith could be described as inventing regional history (the story of Kate in the previous novel has now become a local legend within the text); at the same time there is a hint of *Rogue Herries* romanticism about the whole book. Though an odd story, requiring a generous amount of willing suspension of disbelief, it is strangely powerful.

In *Three Ways Home*, published three years later, she writes that

Superstition Corner was originally intended to be 'the title of an immense book which should give the story of the neighbourhood from the banishment of the Mass in 1559 down to the return of the Mass [at Little Doucegrove, where she and her husband – a sometime Anglican clergyman turned Catholic – then lived] in 1930. The story should not be only religious, but historical and social as well.'[22] At the same time she records a doubt 'that I shall ever finish the history of the Alards,'[23] and she did not, in fact, return to them. The four books remain as oddly disparate fragments of what might have been an impressive regional series.

Sheila Kaye-Smith enjoyed an inflated reputation in her lifetime and, perhaps as an inevitable reaction, has been neglected ever since. She is generally classified as a realist, and is one of the few regional writers unresponsive to Scott.[24] Yet her early work set in the eighteenth century contains many of the ingredients of historical romance, and in the 1926 foreword to a reprint of *Starbrace* she acknowledges Harrison Ainsworth as part of what she calls 'her wide reading of the romances of the period.' Subsequently realism (sometimes, however, with a distinct touch of romanticism) came to dominate her writing, but as a result her fiction loses some of its imaginative power while sloughing the exaggerated absurdity of the early plots. It may be significant that in 1937, while discussing *Green Apple Harvest*, she wrote of 'the middle light between realism and romance which is the best to read human nature by.'[25]

Despite the romantic ingredients, however, she seems to me closer to Phillpotts than most other regional writers. Her Catholicism, like Phillpotts's humanistic rationalism, tended to get in the way of her regional concerns. Though she insists that she found it 'impossible to visualize human beings apart from their surroundings,'[26] her plots are not always fully integrated with her settings. Both writers are skilled in presenting rural characters at work, yet both find difficulty in raising their characters above the level of the commonplace. Kaye-Smith's topography is almost as accurate as Phillpotts's; most of her names are authentic, though she is capable of altering distances and architectural details in the manner of Hardy. Thurston Hopkins, who wrote an early topographical book about her work, observed that, despite seeming 'very punctilious in her description,' she 'set many traps for the would-be discoverer.'[27] Above all, she resembles Phillpotts in lacking the urgency that gives rise to major fiction. Her books are convincing as we read but rarely haunt the memory. The countryside of the Weald remains (with the exception of the Boarzell in *Sussex Gorse)* a geographical area faithfully presented but not imaginatively transformed. The limitations of verisimilitude as a criterion for regional literature are nowhere more evident than here.[28]

EIGHT

Regional Romance

THE 'ENCHANTED LAND' OF CONSTANCE HOLME

Constance Holme's region is the area of Westmorland (or what used to be Westmorland) bordering on Morecombe Bay just south of Wordsworth's Lake District. Its geographical boundaries are conveniently identified in *The Things Which Belong*— as 'the hills, – the mountain-land and moorland which ring in all this part of the country, except where, on the one side, it runs rolling to the sea' (pt. 1, ch. 7). It is an agricultural area of manor-houses, farms, and estates, dominated by hills serving as sheep-fells and the all-powerful sea, which is alternately loved and feared. In her first novel, *Crump Folk Going Home*, these regional determinants are caught in a single sentence where Deb Lyndesay 'could hear the big tide filling the river, and wondered if the sheep were safe on the mosses, and whether the low-lying farms were trembling for the sea-wall' (ch. 20). Phyllis Bentley rightly emphasizes how Holme concerns herself with 'the peculiar geographical conditions of life in the district,' especially 'the Kent tidal wave, which daily runs its swift and irresistible course and may in time flood the marsh farms and bring ruin and death to their inhabitants.'[1] Like Blackmore, Holme is particularly sensitive to atmospheric conditions and skilled at portraying the effects of storms. Like Hardy, her region is both a social and an economic unit; Witham (= Kendal?), the market-town, appears in virtually all her books, and a number of houses and physical features recur and so help to suggest a local cohesiveness.

Little is yet available about Constance Holme's life (she lived from 1880 until 1955), but her origins are more important than her biography. As she notes in her introduction to the World's Classics edition of *The Old Road from Spain*, her ancestors had lived from time immemorial in the region about which she wrote: 'There was little that I could look at that those forebears had not looked at first; no place where I could walk where they had not walked long before. Their homes were still to be seen in village, on marsh or on fell; their dust was in the churchyards.' Moreover, she both married a land-agent and was descended from three generations of land-agents. Her own position is reflected in Deb Lyndesay's situation in *Crump Folk:* 'Kilne Lyndesays had been Crump stewards for centuries, serving the fine estate from father to son with inherited and increasing devotion' (ch. 1). Holme is concerned, then, not merely with the region itself but with regional attachment on the part of the characters, whatever the station in life to which they belong. For Christian Lyndesay, one of the gentry in *Crump Folk,* the local form of wrestling is cherished, over and above its qualities as a sport, for its regional distinctiveness ('It's a fine thing for a county to have its own game' [ch. 9]); for Lanty Lancaster, the land-agent in *The Lonely Plough,* 'no other place called him. The whole of his heart was here' (ch. 2); for Wolf Whinnerah, tenant in the same novel, life is indistinguishable from 'the view of a summer evening, and the sea washing at the wall, an' – an' all the other things meaning Ninekyrkes and no other spot whatever!' (ch. 1). Throughout her work stress is laid upon what she calls, in a fine phrase from *Crump Folk,* 'the fierce passion of heritage' (ch. 9). Such heritage, it is insisted in *The Old Road from Spain,* is 'not merely a matter of houses and lands' (ch. 15); rather, these become its potent representatives, even its symbols.

This tradition of loyalty and connection gives her not only a major theme but a structural principle for her fiction. Love of land, duty towards the land, a rootedness in the land: these are her main subjects and in turn they help to generate her plots. 'There was a centralising power about the mansion of a big estate of which those who had never been connected with one could have no knowledge,' she writes in *The Things Which Belong*—; it was 'a background against which you could see yourself' (pt. 1, ch. 7). And this centralizing power gives form to her novels. *Crump Folk Going Home,* as its title implies, is centred upon Crump and the family that controls the estate; *The Lonely Plough* is similarly focussed on the Bluecaster estate and *The Old Road from Spain* on Thorns. In *The Lonely Plough* the land-agent is the main figure, while the landowners, the Lyndesays of Crump and the Huddlestons of Thorns, dominate the other novels. But in each case the responsibilities of the estate inevitably bring the main characters in contact with those who live and work on the land, and in this way each novel encompasses and presents a rich and varied human society.

Perhaps Holme's most original contribution to the regional novel in her early fiction was the sense of a bustling, crowded, active rural society. She is fond of scenes where characters meet and mingle – sheep-dog trials, horse-shows, market-day, a local concert, rent-audit, workhouse treat, charity bazaar. There are, of course, scenes of traditional rural labour, where the sense of interconnection is also prominent: 'Folk were making hay in half a dozen fields stretching out to the faint earth-line on either hand. When they could not be seen, or only vaguely, like figures moving in some rite, the whir of the cutter linked them all across the land' (Old Road from Spain, ch. 16). But Holme is especially fond of emphasizing the organizational aspects of country life – the world of public meetings and committees. Often these are parodied, as in the whirl of social engagements that engulfs Helwise Lancaster in *The Lonely Plough* or the passion for arranging functions that become an obsession with Mrs Garnett in *The Old Road from Spain*. Their genuine importance, however, is seen in the efforts of landowner and agent alike to maintain the traditions and responsibilities that they have inherited.

Holme writes, then, of 'old-fashioned' attitudes and assumptions; her rural world is one that has passed into history. But she was writing of it at the very moment that it was passing into history, and she is acutely aware of the radical changes that are transforming, even destroying, the society that she portrays. *Crump Folk Going Home* was published in 1913 and documents a rural world that seems confident, entrenched, and for the most part unchallenged. While there are within it elements of doom and threat (which I shall be discussing later), these come from the past rather than the future. To a reader encountering the novel in the year of its publication, it would doubtless have seemed an engaging and relatively carefree presentation of 'things as they are' in a rural backwater which, if a little behind the times in many respects (the word 'provincial' might well spring to mind), gave no signs of being overwhelmed by a flood. But when the novel was reprinted in the World's Classics edition in 1934, Holme wrote in an introduction:

The authors of 1913 have more reason than most to believe they were different creatures in a different universe. The world *was* different, then. ... Only another year, and the great slide was to begin which was to alter, not only the whole face of the countryside, but the outlook of its inhabitants. Country life was at that stage which, it is said, may be seen in the sinking of a vessel, when the water seems to pause for a moment before it swamps the boat.

The Lonely Plough, which first appeared in May 1914, superficially presents the same kind of world, but there is a significant – and troubling – difference in tone. The novel opens with a one-sentence paragraph: 'He felt very old.' The reference is to Lanty Lancaster, the land-agent, who is only thirty-seven, and across the table from him sits a tenant, Wolf Whinnerah, who 'was over seventy, but until recently he had carried his years with an almost miraculous lightness. Now, at last, however, the rigorous hand of Time had touched him suddenly, breaking him in a few weeks' (ch. 1). We encounter in later chapters the energetic activity of a thriving rural society, but the opening scene, which involves the refusal of Wolf's son to succeed to the tenancy and the subsequent breaking of a traditional arrangement, is proleptic of disaster to follow. It fosters 'a sense of tragedy lying in wait' (ch. 4). This time the threat *is* from the future, and the main action concerns a prophecy that the Lugg, a large sea-bank built by Lancaster's father as part of a land-reclamation project, is unreliable and a threat to the safety of the area. An oppressive feeling of foreboding hangs over the whole book, as chapter-titles like 'The Trouble Shaping,' 'The Beginning of the End,' 'The Trouble Coming' sufficiently indicate. In the event, the prophecy is fulfilled: a freak storm breaches the Lugg, and Wolf Whinnerah, who has moved into a house on the reclaimed land as a gesture of confidence in Lancaster and the traditional ways of the estate, is drowned along with his wife.

The novel ends conventionally (and not very convincingly) on an optimistic note; moreover, the original contained a cover-summary stressing 'the loyalty of the north-country character' and 'the value of the three-cornered relationship between landlord, agent, and tenant.' But *The Lonely Plough* is ultimately memorable for its intimations of decline and collapse. It is difficult not to read the novel in the allegorical terms suggested by my necessarily foreshortened account just given – and it is similarly difficult after the event not to equate the flood and the breaching of the sea-bank with the outbreak of war and the collapse of the traditional rural civilization. When Holme came to write an introduction for the reprinting of the novel in 1931, she made specific reference to the cover-summary: 'This was written at almost the last moment of the old order of things. ... Many estates have been broken up either wholly or in part; electricity and the motor-bus have changed the conditions of the countryside; ... the land itself seems to be disappearing under the wave of building sweeping across it.' True, the next paragraph begins, 'Yet much remains ...' but the sense of a changed world is obvious. Moreover, the imagery employed – 'a wave of building sweeping across [the land]' – indirectly supports a symbolic reading of the Lugg and the flood.

The third novel, *The Old Road from Spain*, was published in the middle of the war, in 1916, and although it deals with the old society, and although there is no direct mention of current affairs, the impress of war can be seen upon its pages. One of the legends upon which the book is based, derived by Holme from a story connected with her mother's family, involves the casting up of a waif from a shipwrecked vessel of the Spanish Armada in Morecombe Bay. It is not illegitimate, I think, to translate the sense of national danger form 1588 to 1916. The mood and tone of the book seems far away from the contemporary world of the trenches, but its nightmare suggestion of doom is anything but escapist.

Significantly, this is the first of her novels not to end within the sanctioned traditions of comedy. *The Old Road from Spain* concludes with the death by drowning of the last of the Huddlestons. History repeats itself with a difference: the modern shipwreck is fatal.

All this might suggest that Holme belongs to the 'realist' camp of regional fiction. Certainly, there is a strong sense of authenticity and verisimilitude in her work. We 'believe' in her characters, and the majority of their actions seem both credible and representative. But there is, at the same time, a very different dimension to her fiction, one that distinguishes her radically from her contemporary, Sheila Kaye-Smith. Hers is an imaginative as well as a realistically accurate world. In *He-Who-Came?* (1930) she remarks that 'people in lonely country districts live so close to the psychic border that to slip over it every now and again seems nothing out of the common' (ch. 5). Holme's border-country, then, is not so much between one geographical region and another as between the everyday world and a strange, visionary dimension. Sometimes this involves literary ingredients that traditionally accompany tales of mystery and horror. Thus the one-sentence opening paragraph of her first novel – 'The curse of the old place was upon it – sudden death' – offers intimations of Gothic melodrama that are discernible through much of her work. 'Curse' and 'doom' are recurrent words, but they are localized through their connection with regional superstition. In *Crump Folk Going Home*, for example, one of the Lyndesay ancestors is said to have hanged himself on a yew tree in the grounds and tradition maintains that no Lyndesay of Crump will die a natural death while the tree stands (ch. 7). In *The Old Road from Spain* the Herdwick sheep only leave their 'heaf' on the fells and descend to the lowland to announce the approaching death of the master of Thorns. The heafed sheep may be seen as emblems of rootedness in human beings. Moreover, the superstitions themselves are as deeply rooted as the families about which they tell. We accept them as convincing examples of local legend, but Holme goes further and, as it were, vindicates them through her plots. The Lyndesay curse, the Lugg prophecy, the sheep that anticipate death are all sustained within the narratives. Many of her books contain this brooding sense of mystery, which is chilling in parts of *Crump Folk*, merely whimsical in *He-Who-Came?*, while *The Old Road from Spain* comes as close to the supernatural as any novel outside the realm of the ghost- or horror-story. This is a world in which legend and superstition evoke a new imaginative dimension as in the best work of Mary Webb.

But Holme's novels contain another, less controversial, but still problematic imaginative world. Her characters frequently inhabit (to quote Hardy's phrase once again) 'a partly real, partly-dream country.' In her most widely known but by no means her best book, *The Lonely Plough*, Lanty Lancaster feels the need to escape from time to time from the oppressive problems of the Bluecaster estate to 'a capricious lane' that offers him glimpses over gates and stiles of another kind of reality. 'Lancaster called the peeps his Green Gates of Vision' (ch. 2), and the capitalized phrase recurs in chapter-titles. In *Crump Folk*, an equivalent emblem of otherness is the wishing-well in the Pixies' Wood (ch. 11) alluded to on a number of occasions, but green lanes make their appearance in other novels as indications of the visionary life. Luis Huddleston in *The Old Road from Spain* has a similar experience in a rural lane while two other characters are able to walk in what they call 'our country of the mind' (ch. 7). Kirkby, the head gardener in *The Things Which Belong*—, has a more 'realistic' version of the same experience:

> Hurrying in the same almost slinking fashion along the central walk, he came to the cliff-side, and stood looking across the beautiful, dangerous stream to the mountain-wall beyond. ... The wide view, passing over the wooded cliff across, and rising by green and russet slopes to that last long line of loveliness above, sometimes many-coloured and strong, and sometimes faint and phantasmal as a cloud, had been all that he had ever wanted by way of 'escape.' (Pt. 1, ch. 7)

The sense of 'vision-country' *(Old Road from Spain*, ch. 10) is strong in all her work, and although it sometimes declines into a sentimental whimsicality, it also enables her, in a way that Phillpotts and Kaye-Smith never managed to find, to create an original imaginative world independent of the geographical locality on which it is based.

The 'race-feeling' out of which she writes had, in her own words, 'sanctified a certain countryside with the light that never was on sea or land' (*Old Road from Spain*, Preface). The Wordsworthian quotation seems to have been a favourite – it appears again in *Beautiful End* (ch. 1.) – and it emphasizes the essentially creative element in Holme's work. No complete identification is possible between the historical Westmorland and the 'enchanted land' *(Old Road from Spain*, ch. 18) that we encounter in her books. Whereas the stories in Phillpotts and Kaye-Smith are successful or otherwise for their intrinsic qualities as narratives, Holme's (and Mary's Webb's) depend to a great extent upon the way they are told. A sense of artistry and artifice is always present. In her later books this is achieved in part through a dramatic simplification of story. Characters are reduced to a minimum, and the time-scheme is often limited to a single day.[2] These books are less obviously regional than their predecessors, if only because the emphasis on a small number of characters precludes the broader sense of social panorama in the earlier work. But *The Splendid Fairing* (1919) is almost ballad-like in its weirdness and rough justice, and the plot is regional to the extent that it depends for its climax upon a peculiarity of a treacherous local tide. And *He-Who-Came?* contains a tale-telling within the tale – one of the characters, Tim Walker, recounts part of the story to the narrator, and the occasion of the telling is a sharply etched regional event. The emphasis is consistently upon 'making' and one of the things made is a recreated world of the past that perhaps never was on sea or land and is certainly extinct. For this reason, Holme's work partakes of 'romance.' Her general attitude could be described as backward-looking, but she writes with intelligence and, although on occasion she may brood nostalgically on a lost world, at no time does she wallow in sentiment. While never more than a minor writer, she is both original and accomplished; as a skilled practitioner within regional fiction she deserves to be better known.[3]

MARY WEBB'S ALLEGORICAL TOPOGRAPHY

Mary Webb is one of the most original, possibly idiosyncratic, of regional writers, and for this reason literary critics have been ill at ease with her fiction. It cannot readily be fitted into an existing narrative tradition; it eludes categories. Thus Glen Cavaliero, in a generally appreciative study, finds himself bound to point out that 'there is no social awareness in Mary Webb's novels, no knowledge shown of agricultural problems, no attempts at social criticism.'[4] Nowhere, perhaps, is the habitual realistic emphasis in the approach to regional fiction so clearly manifest. The observation is true yet, given her interest and the kind of novels that she writes, irrelevant. It belongs, one feels, with the complaint that Jane Austen ignored the Napoleonic Wars. Webb's preoccupations do not lie in the direction of social criticism, and there is no *a priori* reason why they should. She is concerned instead with personal values, with man's inhumanity to man – and to woman – and above all with the intimate relation between human beings and their natural environment. Hers, like T.F. Powys's, is essentially an imaginative world; moreover, she portrays men and women (generally women) who inhabit their own imaginative worlds.

More substantial is Cavaliero's claim that 'there is no real sense of an England existing outside her fictional Shropshire, no sense of that Shropshire being a part of something greater than itself.'[5] Certainly, the microcosm/macrocosm argument that Hardy insisted on in defence of his circumscribed Wessex hardly applies here. The problems of her protagonists are universal problems – faith and doubt, love and lust, selfishness and selflessness – but their wider implications do not manifest themselves in either social or national terms. It is probably significant that, when her novels were issued in an illustrated edition in the late 1920s, they contained not local photographs, like the almost contemporaneous Widecombe edition of Phillpotts's Dartmoor novels or the much earlier 'Wessex Novels' edition of Hardy (1895-6), but curiously effective, half-caricature drawings and paintings that catch the sense of an eccentric but decidedly individual way of looking. Once again, a comparison with T.F. Powys seems in order. Both writers proceed by means of a radical simplification of character and action that does not ultimately distort but instead throws certain human traits into excessively high relief. Similarly, both writers owe a considerable debt to Bunyan (a point to which I shall return); an 'Englishness' pervades their work as it does his, but it is a psychological rather than a geographical Englishness.

Webb's novels, none the less, belong indisputably to the Shropshire landscape even if they depart dramatically from that landscape in certain respects. T.F. Powys's backgrounds are quintessentially rural rather than regional (which explains why he is not considered in detail in this book); although his Dodders and Madders bear a definite resemblance to the Dorset villages of Chaldon Herring and Mappowder where he lived for many years, they do not depend on that resemblance. But Webb's work is steeped in the physical features of south Shropshire. Her novels share a common topography even when the central area, the ridges of the Long Mynd and the Stiperstones with the vale in between, is transformed almost out of recognition. *The Golden Arrow* is dominated by the Devil's Chair, a gaunt outcrop of rock about which D.H. Lawrence was to write a few years later in *St. Mawr*.[6] For Lawrence, 'It was one of those places where the spirit of aboriginal England still lingers, the old savage England, whose last blood flows still in a few Englishmen, Welshmen, Cornishmen,' and this same timeless, primeval quality in the native inhabitants is what preoccupies Webb. Throughout her books, place is more important than time. With the exception of *Precious Bane*, the plot of which takes its origin in the agricultural activity following the instituting of the Corn Laws, her fiction exists in a timeless realm, pre–First World War and pre-motorcar, but otherwise unspecified. This is not escapism, however. Webb focuses her attention on eternal realities rather than the superficial details that change from decade to decade. As she remarks, controversially, in her preface to *Precious Bane*, 'there is a permanence, a continuity in country life which makes the lapse of centuries of little moment.'

There is a final reason why Webb's novels are difficult to assess, and this is best seen in contrast to those of Phillpotts. Whereas his novels are all part of a unifying series, and so, although varied in tone, resemble each other in certain basic respects, Webb's, while sharing a family resemblence through the force of their creator's personality, are always different. Webb never repeats herself; certain recurring traits are readily discernible, but she eschews any formula. The atmosphere of one novel is never identical with what has gone before or what will come after. *Gone to Earth* implies a related but decidedly different world from *The Golden Arrow*, and *The House in Dormer Forest* is distinct from both. Indeed, one of the artistically admirable qualities of her work is the progression and change that can be traced from one novel to another. My subsequent discussion will therefore proceed from book to book, concentrating of course on the regional aspects that are involved.

Though a story of regional 'hill-folk,' the plot of *The Golden Arrow* (1916) has in itself no intrinsic regional quality. Read with an eye to the English fictional tradition, the novel seems compounded of many simples drawn from earlier writers. In presenting the story of Deborah Arden and Stephen Southernwood in counterpoint, as it were, with that of Joe and Lily, Webb appears, like the young Lawrence, to have followed George Eliot's plan 'to take two couples and develop their relationships.'[7] Mrs Arden has a tinge of Mrs Poyser in her makeup, and an important phrase, 'the other side o' silence' (ch. 46) reads as a direct borrowing from *Middlemarch* (bk. 2, ch. 20). The descriptions of the Devil's Chair ('Nothing ever altered its look. ... It remained inviolable, taciturn, evil' [ch. 4]) recalls Hardy's Egdon, while Stephen Southernwood, an outsider who brings challenge and discontent into a closed community, represents a type with whom we are familiar from the Wessex novels. Again, Eli Huntbatch is in many respects the Joseph of *Wuthering Heights* writ large, and 'the age-long feud between storm-tossed greatness and sheltered littleness' (ch. 51), symbolized by the contrast between the wild hills and the protected valley, suggests an atmospheric connection with Emily Brontë's novel. In addition, the use of seasonal festivals – Lammas, All Hallows Eve, Martinmas, Thomastide, Christmas – to indicate the passing of time is, of course, a device frequent in regional fiction.

In listing the traditional origins of effects in Webb's first novel, I am in no way implying that her work is derivative or in any way stale. On the contrary, I want to demonstrate how her unique contribution transforms conventional material into strikingly new forms. She achieves this in large measure through the rooting of her characters within a particular environment so that her universally applicable story of love and faith and doubt and despair becomes quintessentially regional. We are confronted here with 'a race that had come of the soil' (ch. 30), perfectly integrated with its locality, and Webb insists continually on the interconnections between man and nature. In the opening paragraph, the Ardens' weather-boarded shippen (which has an important function within the plot) is described as 'lichen-grey, like the house, stone and wood having become worn as the hill-folk themselves, browbeaten and mellowed by the tempestuous years, yet tenacious, defying the storm.' It is impossible to separate the inhabitants from the local features that surround them, and characters are constantly being linked to natural objects through simile. John Arden's 'brown, thin face ran into kindly smiles as easily as a brook runs in its accustomed bed,' and Deborah's hair is 'brown as a bark-stack, and had the soft sheen of a wood-lark's wing or a hill-foal's shank' (ch. 1). Deb's full realization of her love for Stephen is 'like coming to a sudden splendid valley, full of deep colours, after walking a bare hillside' (ch. 20). Stephen, the outsider, effectively sums up this interconnection of local man and local environment when he remarks of Deb: 'She seemed to belong to this country of mountains; he could not imagine her anywhere else' (ch. 39).

We soon learn to interpret the implications of language in this book, and these extend far beyond the dialect distinction through which Stephen is differentiated from the rest. It is not so much the dialect words as the local richness of association that is involved. Often enough, this is achieved through the rural application of biblical speech by means of which natural references apply to human situations. '"There's a sheep gone astray over yonder," Deborah said absently; "hark at her crying"' (ch. 23). The sheep serves, in T.S. Eliot's sophisticated phrase which is not as out of place in reference to this novel as we might expect, as an objective correlative of Deb's own state. And when her father says, '"God help all poor folk benighted"' (ch. 42) we recognize it in a spiritual as well as a physical sense. Nor is Stephen exempt from this effect: his urban rationalism is deliberately satirized by being presented in rustic terms when he is seen as 'hag-ridden by thoughts, longings, despairs' (ch. 42).

Above all, her characters are constantly seen against the transformed Shropshire countryside – 'huge, primeval' (ch. 12) – which, as I have said, is to become the setting for all her work. It is always conspicuous, ever-present in the imaginative lives of her protagonists, frequently dwarfing the characters who live within it and infusing them with both its wonder and its menace. In a typical effect, Eli is made at the end of a chapter to depart into the shadows, 'a hunched and grudging little figure in the frank and splendid hills' (ch. 14). Although based accurately enough upon the area of the central Shropshire hills, the landscape is presented without any undue deference to the canons of realism. The place-names intimately associated with individual characters – Lostwithin, where Stephen lives and works; Bitterley, home of Eli Huntbatch – alert us (though Bitterley is an authentic name from another part of Shropshire) to Webb's essentially moral geography. At the opening of the novel John Arden is described as 'lifted by his simple love of all creatures as far above right and wrong as his cottage was above the plain' (ch. 1), and the chapel is deliberately 'poised between the lowland and the heights' (ch. 3).

Local topography and tradition present Webb with an appropriate place-name in the Devil's Chair, a name at once symbolic and authentic, but she improves upon actuality by renaming the range of the Stiperstones of which it forms a part 'the gaunt Diafol ridge' (ch. 1), thus investing it with an inescapable sense of the diabolical. The Long Mynd, on the other hand, becomes Wilderhope (another local name transferred from elsewhere) and here she places the Flockmaster's signpost 'that makes the shadow of a cross in the light of the moon' (ch. 41). That the two extremes, Devil's Chair and Flockmaster's signpost, are consciously intended as fixed points in Webb's Manichean imaginative universe is evident from the following crucial passage:

> Day by day the Devil's Chair shook in the heat haze as though it would fall. Opposite, by the Little Wood on the Wilderhope range, the shepherd's signpost, blistered in the sun, confronted it whitely. Between the ranges lay the valley, shadowed alternatively by each. (Ch. 19)

We soon realize, indeed, that the movements of the characters within this symbolic landscape are arranged according to a moral graph. Local topographers may insist that John Arden's cottage is based on Nill's Cottage, near Pontesbury, in which Webb had not set foot when she wrote the novel but which was destined a year or so later to become her home. In the text, however, 'Upper Leasurs' is clearly placed on the Wilderhope range – i.e., on the 'right' side of the landscape – not far from the Flockmaster's signpost (and close to the Little Wood, which is a garden of sensual delight potentially good but – like Eden – a place of danger for the weak or easily subverted). When Stephen and Deborah set up house together before marriage, Deb moves across the valley to a partially ruined cottage between the Devil's Chair and Lostwithin. Lily and Joe are not made for either the heights or the depths and appropriately take a cottage at Slepe on the neutral plain. That the places can be charted on a local map helps to give them a local habitation and a name but their position on a moral map, stressing the verticals rather than the horizontals, is ultimately more significant.

The folklore which Webb draws upon and adapts to fit her own purpose also supports this moral dichotomy: on the one hand, the story of Christ the shepherd localized into the Welsh legend of the Flockmaster, 'him as lights shepherds whome and carries the dropped foals' (ch. 14); on the other, the throne of the Devil who is never seen but always felt as an oppressive presence. A related contrast is well represented by the Arden parents, John preoccupied with a mystical Christianity, Patty (the local midwife, and so committed to the physical) harking back to 'them wold, unrighteous tales' of the Dark Riders (ch. 6). It is a countryside of intense superstition, ranging from the charming to the chilling. And the legend of the golden arrow itself, expanded and transmuted from an authentic Shropshire folk-tale (Webb separates it from its traditional locality on Pontesford Hill), becomes an allegory of love that encompasses both sorrow and 'a vast of joy' (ch. 14).

The Golden Arrow is a strange mixture (though a typical Mary Webb blend) of the simple and the sophisticated, the tough-minded and the mildly sentimental. Her fictional technique is formidable, and her ability to catch the amusing and painful nuances of dialogue, to control tone and balance scene with scene, makes Phillpotts seem flatfooted and even Hardy appear somewhat gauche. There is a Forsterian detachment about her authorial voice, though it must be admitted that the polish of her artistry sometimes seems at odds with the primitive rusticity of her material. But she is too often criticized for not providing what she had no intention of providing, and frequently appears more incisive (and often more radical) than her critics. There is a Lawrentian intensity about her attitude to sex and love which prevents her mysticism from ever descending into the vague and abstract. Her simplifications, like Bunyan's and T.F. Powys's, are never simplicities. Deb Arden, like Prue Sarn after her, is a 'good' heroine who is always credible and never over-sweet. Her story is genuinely moving, and her spiritual growth is indicated in a culminating passage that illustrates once again how inextricably character and environment are fused.

> She looked across at the Devil's Chair. ... It seemed to her that there was no hostility now between the two ranges, between the towering throne and the small white cross. Always before, she had superstitiously regarded the Chair as wholly evil, the Flockmaster's signpost as wholly good. Now she saw good and evil mingled, and felt a slumbering terror in the protecting cross, a hidden beneficence in the inimical stronghold across the valley. ... She was naturally religious, and she felt an almost mystical comfort and rapture in the peace of the Flockmaster's green pastures. ... But away in the black night, among the tomb-like rocks, ... she had heard devils laugh, had felt a dark power brood on the crag. Instinct told her that the two visions were one. She was content with the balance of life as she found it, being dimly aware that the terror and the beauty intermingled in something that was more wonderful than beauty.   (Ch. 51)

This is her penultimate position, immediately prior to the return of Stephen, who 'had found the golden arrow, to his own agony and ennobling' (ch. 52). If this is 'romance,' it is a romance that can encompass subtle psychological states. It argues eloquently that regional romance deserves to be treated with respect.

   With *Gone to Earth* (1917) Webb's art had moved closer to fable, and her landscape has in consequence become increasingly allegorical. The heroine, Hazel Woodus, is pulled to and fro between Reddin, the lusty squire of Undern Hall, and Edward Marston, minister of the chapel at the top of God's Little Mountain. Although both locales are based on actual places in the countryside south of Shrewsbury, Wilderhope Manor and Lordshill respectively, the associations of underworld and a Christian hill of truth are clearly primary.

And Webb emphasizes this moral topography in her accounts of Hazel's dilemma:

She looked up at the round wooded hill that hid God's Little Mountain – so high, so cold for a poor child to climb. She felt that the life there would be too righteous, too well-mannered. The thought of it suddenly made her homesick for dirt and the Callow.

She thought of Undern crouched under its hill like a toad. She remembered its echoing rooms and the sound as of dresses rustling that came along the passages while she put on the green gown. Undern made her more homesick than the parsonage. (Ch. 14)

All the references here suggest allegory: the Bunyanesque mountain that is hard to climb; the toad reference that suggests one of Satan's disguises in Eden; the traditional meaning, so common in Elizabethan literature, of the green gown. At the same time, the Callow is a genuine place-name, and God's Little Mountain itself is only a fictional heightening of the actual Lordshill. Webb's allegory may universalize her theme, but it develops from a regional matrix.

Hazel herself, with her appropriate name in a novel whose pages are studded with references to wild flowers, is a creature of the earth. Her association with Foxy links her with all wild things; 'all animals,' she tells Mrs Marston, 'be my brothers and sisters' (ch. 9). She was 'enchained by earth, prisoner to it only a little less than the beech and the hyacinth – bond-serf of the sod' (ch. 9). And later we are told: 'She had so deep a kinship with the trees, so intuitive a sympathy with leaf and flower, that it seemed as if the blood in her veins was not slow-moving human blood, but volatile sap' (ch. 21). Her natural innocence is central to the meaning of the book, though it creates difficulties when the detail within the narrative suggests conventional novel rather than stylized allegory. She is closer to W.H. Hudson's Rima than to Hardy's Tess, and belongs more comfortably in a world of folklore and myth. Indeed, the book operates on a number of symbolic levels, with Hazel as a natural creature caught between extremes, victim in 'the deathless quarrel of the world and the monastery' (ch. 4), 'the world-old conflict between sex and altruism' (ch. 9). The Bunyanesque moral dichotomy of heaven versus hell, good versus evil (though Webb's terms are never quite as simple as these divisions would suggest) is continually being overlaid with mythic structures, and Hazel the flower-spirit may reasonably be seen as a Persephone figure carried off by Reddin-Pluto. Moreover, her story blends into the specifically local legend of the Black Huntsman and 'the tale of the death-pack' (ch. 36).

Once again, therefore, Gone to Earth returns to its regional origins. Local history and folklore combine to root the book in the Shropshire countryside.

Webb's best biographer, Gladys Mary Coles, sees the ending as based on the story of the Major's Leap on Wenlock Edge, where Major Smallman escaped from his Roundhead pursuers by leaping with his horse over a precipice, and she even records an Actaeon-like story in which a local keeper of hounds near Stanton had been torn to pieces by his own pack.[8] Doubtless such stories provided the seed out of which the plot grew. Similarly, Webb bases the folk-charms employed in the narrative, though as always adapted and transformed in the interests of her story, on the traditional lore of her native countryside. Even a detail like the surname of Reddin's servant Vessons is borrowed from a local place-name. Webb was careful to set her novel in recognizably the same landscape that she had used in *The Golden Arrow* (the two books share the names of Silverton and Bitterley), and although on its own *Gone to Earth* might not qualify as a regional story, it is, I believe, intended to be read as a tale of the countryside whose features had been firmly and fully established in the first book.

Initially, *The House in Dormer Forest* (1920) suggests a traditional regionalist formula. As Thomas Moult, himself a regionalist, commented in his study of Webb, she 'adopted the method of Hardy and Eden Phillpotts in opening the story of her house at the edge of the forest of Dormer, for no human character appears upon the scene until the second chapter.'[9] We are offered instead a detailed atmospheric description of the house and its immediate environs. It 'lay low' (ch. 1), unlike the Arden cottage in *The Golden Arrow*, and the dichotomies in this novel – Man and Nature; Law and Impulse, individual and herd, etc. – are all subsumed into that of House (book 1) and Forest (book 2), which represent respectively the depths and the heights, both geographical and moral. Whereas *Gone to Earth* was dominated by images of flowers and birds, this novel is full of spiders, funguses, death's-heads, etc. The scheme fits well enough into the physical features of Webb's Shropshire, but is hardly intrinsic to it. Dormer itself is said to be based on the house of her parents at Meole Brace, the grotto adapted from one at Hawkstone, and the church modelled on Hope Church,[10] while Cantlop and Velindre are both borrowed from local place-names. But the parody Gothic of much of this novel is general rather than particular in application, and, although a unique imaginative world is created, its regional qualities are muted.

Although we are told that Webb's father loved the Waverley novels and that her mother 'claimed kinship with Sir Walter Scott,'[11] there is little evidence of Scott's influence on her own work. But *Seven for a Secret* (1922), though in no way resembling Scott's fiction, depends for its unusual effect on the idea of 'border country' (ch. 1). The scene is set, as the opening sentence insists, 'in the country that lies between the dimpled lands of England and the gaunt purple steeps of Wales – half in Faery and half out of it.' Something of this quality pervades *The Golden Arrow*, but it only becomes explicit in this fourth novel. The phrase 'over the border' reverberates throughout the book, and in characteristic Mary Webb fashion the regional border blends into a psychic one. Regionally, the distinctions are summed up in the description of Trewern Coed, 'a typical border village, not quite sure of its nationality, mingled in speech, divided between the white, blue-roofed cottages of Wales and the red thatched ones of Shropshire' (ch. 10). The Welsh element comprises the world of dream and poetry – in a word, perhaps, 'romance' – while the Englishness comprises a spectrum ranging from practicality and organization to selfishness, class-consciousness, and insensitivity.

The allegorical side of Webb's nature is less prominent here, but its place is taken by a corresponding emphasis on romance fantasy. The supernatural (or at least semi-supernatural) element in the novel is unusually strong: a gipsy prophecy, Gillian's half-physical, half-mental scar that eventually disappears; the mysterious 'unket' place called the Gyland 'where summat'll come to pass' (ch. 6). And the last example shows that, here as always, Webb is eager to root her fantasy in a specific place, albeit an imaginary one. Although the emphasis in this novel is on remoteness – 'At Dysgwlfas people were often snowed-up for a week at a time' (ch. 4), even the pigeons recognize in slight changes of routine on the farm 'some intrusion of the outer world' (ch. 1), and we are told that Aunt Fanteague, the intruder in question, 'lived in the great world, at Silverton itself' (ch. 3) – there is a strong sense of local history. This is centred upon Jonathan Makepeace, who with his continual tale-telling represents, as it were, the folk-history of the region, which has an earthiness and a concreteness that distinguishes it from Gillian's music and Robert Rideout's poetry. His local stories continually punctuate the text, and in the final chapter, which ties up the strands in a way that deliberately draws attention to the artifice of the whole, we are informed that 'the story' – that of *Seven for a Secret* itself – 'has made for itself a place in the annals of the country, and has become one of Jonathan's tales, which the other Jonathans will tell' (ch. 32). The novel is dedicated to Hardy, and, although the tone is anything but Hardyesque, this idea of the narrative becoming part of the local history out of which the author gets material for fiction is close to an aspect of Hardy that I have emphasized as part of his regionalist concern (see pp. 97–100 above). It is in this sense that *Seven for a Secret* legitimately qualifies as a regional work, and this may explain why Martin Armstrong, one of its original reviewers, remarked: 'On laying down *Seven for a Secret* our first impression is that we have penetrated deeply into the country.'[12]

But it is *Precious Bane* (1924), Webb's last completed novel, that assures her an honourable place in the history of both fiction and regionalism, and the advance is achieved by the seemingly simple and obvious means of making the regional heroine the narrator of her own story. Prue Sarn is the voice of the region out of which she speaks; her dialect, her superstitions, her local stories are the speech, the folklore, the history of her community, and these elements are no longer 'background' but essential strands in the texture of the fiction. In responding to the book we are required, as in *Lorna Doone*, not merely to appreciate regional attitudes but to look at the world through regional eyes.

The Sarns take their name from the land 'where Sarns had been time out of mind' (bk. 4, ch. 6). Curiously, since this is the most vividly realized of Webb's books, the topography is in dispute. The map that appears in the larger editions of this frequently reprinted book place Sarn, Plash, and Lullingford in the northern extremities of 'Shropshire. But, as Stanley Baldwin noted in his introduction to the first collected edition, 'the scene of *Precious Bane* is the country of north Shropshire meres – the Ellesmere district, but the dialect is that of south Shropshire.' Not only dialect, we may add. The reference to Diafol Mountain (bk. 2, ch. 2) and Mallard's Keep (bk. ch. 2) link the novel with the locales of *The Golden Arrow*, *The House in Dormer Forest*, and *Seven for a Secret*, and it may be worth mentioning that a passing reference to Lady Camperdine in *The House in Dormer Forest* (ch. 7) associates the locality of that novel with the local gentry here. Sarn Mere seems to be a composite of Ellesmere and Bomere Pool, a favourite haunt of Mary Webb just south of Shrewsbury, while Lullingford, sometimes identified by topographers as Ellesmere and sometimes as Ludlow, is in the text described with what seems to be deliberate ambiguity as 'by the mountains' (bk. 1, ch. 3). It seems impossible to unravel the various accounts of the topographical relationships between Sarn Mere, Lullingford, and Silverton. Had she lived, Webb might perhaps have regularized her topographical references like Hardy; on the other hand, the strong romance elements here may have dictated a less exactly topographical approach. The important point is that she here creates her most convincing imaginative region, which, while dependent upon an intimate knowledge of Shropshire history and tradition (she acknowledges her debt to Charlotte Burne's *Shropshire Folk Lore* in her foreword), is decidedly her own creation.

The superficial regional qualities are abundant in *Precious Bane*: the impressionistic but convincing description of a rural market-town (bk. 2, ch. 2), the accounts of hiring-fair (bk. 3, ch. 1) and Harvest Home (bk. 4, ch. 1). Prominent, too, are the references to folk-custom, whether sin-eating, the 'game of costly colours' (a local version of cribbage virtually confined to Shropshire), songs like 'Green Gravel' and 'Barley Bridge,' or the ducking-stool for witches. But Webb goes much further. In having the accounts of these regional features communicated by Prue Sarn, she reveals the folk-mind in process. A sense of extraordinary immediacy is achieved by means of casual references to local tales and beliefs that Prue takes for granted. The story of the wizard Beguildy who keeps the soul of a dead squire in a bottle will strike us as bizarre, but Prue's acceptance of the story (at least on the level of story) gives it a local authority, and we are not surprised to find similar accounts preserved in *Shropshire Folk Lore*. Again, reference is made at one point to 'the roaring bull of Bagbury' (bk. 3, ch. 4). The story is never explained in the text, but Charlotte Burne gives a detailed account of it, writing that it 'is still talked of about Bishops's Castle and all along the Shropshire side of the border.'[13] Such casual allusions give us far more insight into the folk-mind than any anthropologically systematic version of the legend.

As in *Seven for a Secret*, the concept of 'story' remains highly important. In her foreword Webb describes her good fortune 'in having many friends in farm and cottage who, by pleasant talk and reminiscence have fired the imagination, but also in having the companionship of such a mind as was my father's – a mind stored with old tales and legends that did not come from books.' The novel is steeped in such stories, and when Gideon starts seeing ghosts just before his death, the event is seen as 'not so very different, after all, from many a tale of frittening we'd heard' (bk. 4, ch. 5). Once again the narrative blends into the fabric of the tales out of which it is made: 'the coming of Jancis, and the child, and the drowning, made such a tale as hadna been in our part of the country' (bk. 4, ch. 4).

I emphasize this because an understanding of the kind of story Webb is writing can profoundly affect both our reading of the novel and our appreciation of her art. She has been underestimated in the past because critics have judged her work according to the norms of the intellectually fashionable fiction of her day, fiction that she had no desire to emulate. She shows no interest in psychological realism and makes no attempt to avoid the traditional artifice of story-telling. Of all her work, *Precious Bane* proclaims itself unabashedly as romance, and the romance structure is evident throughout. Even as sympathetic a critic as Gladys Mary Coles complains that 'ultimately it fails to convince and satisfy because of the weak, almost fairy-tale "happy ending".'[14] 'Fairy-tale' weighs down the balance in the direction of juvenile wish-fulfillment; if we substitute the more accurate 'folk-tale,' we see that the observation in no way implies weakness. The whole narrative has been based on the spirit of folk-tale, and it is told by a story-teller who measures experience according to folk-tale conventions. In its own terms, the ending is decidedly satisfying in that it conforms to the narrative logic of the whole. This is not, admittedly, the logic upon which the 'great tradition' of modern fiction is based, but to criticize *Precious Bane* because it does not conform to a model like *Nostromo* or *To the Lighthouse* is as foolish as to dismiss these two modernist masterpieces because they do not follow the pattern of *Precious Bane*.

Webb's novels have also been criticized for escapism, as if they were somehow evading the issues of modern man. In my introductory chapter, I quoted Raymond Williams on 'flight to the edges of the Island'; certainly, the idea that novels about a sheltered rural life (itself a curious urban myth) are somehow escapist and second-rate is widespread. There are many possible answers to this objection. First, until recently a significant percentage of the population of England indeed lived in isolation, and some still do; the assumption that their way of life and particular problems somehow do not matter seems curiously arrogant. Why, one might ask, are sociological studies of isolated communities legitimate but not literary ones? The modernist theory that all subjects are available to the serious artist seems not to be accepted in practice. But in the case of Webb there is, I think, a more telling argument. Just as *The Golden Arrow* is a book about awakening, *Precious Bane* is a study of isolation both personal and communal. Not only is Sarn Mere isolated but Prue, because she is 'hare-shotten' and because of all the superstition that accompanies this condition, is herself isolated within this circumscribed community. While on one hand Prue is a figure of ballad and traditional story, moving in a world remote from most educated modern experience, on the other hand she is a resonant and representative figure, the type of all our lonelinesses.

In *Gone to Earth* Webb offers a description of a book that Mrs Marston was reading:

> It had no relation whatever to life. Its ideals, characters, ethics and crises made up an unearthly whole, which, being entirely useless as a tonic or a balm, was so much poison. It was impossible to imagine its heroine facing any of the facts of life, or engaging in any of those physical acts to which all humanity is bound. ... It was impossible to imagine also how the child, which appeared discreetly and punctually on the last page, could have come by its existence, since it certainly, with such unexceptional parents, could not have been begotten.   (Ch. 19)

If Webb's own work qualifies as 'romance,' it does not avoid the facts of life. She did not, of course, go to the lengths of D. H. Lawrence, but her own heroines are women of flesh and blood, and it is not as surprising as it might at first seem that her writings have enjoyed some attention recently in the wake of feminist criticism. Lacking Constance Holme's sense of the claims of community, she was on Lawrence's side in championing the individual against the drab conventions of society, and the thinness of social texture that has been discerned in her work can be explained in these terms. She was, moreover, so steeped in the regionalist tradition that, however individualistic her characters may be, they never burst out of their environment. They realize their selfhood ('coming into being' in Lawrence's term) *within* their landscape, not outside it. The journey outside one's own region is never initiated, and as a result Mary Webb remains within – some might claim, imprisoned within – the regional consciousness. It was Lawrence who ventured outside, not only beyond his native countryside but beyond regionalism itself.[15]

PART THREE: BEYOND REGIONALISM

D.H. Lawrence

'THE COUNTRY OF MY HEART'

The first visual image to arise in our minds when Lawrence's name is mentioned is, I suspect, one of a pit-head, and the first sound that clink of the colliery locomotive engine which so impressed Ford Madox Ford when he read the opening paragraph of 'Odour of Chrysanthemums.' D.H. Lawrence, the miner's son: that is the favoured designation – and it is, of course, a true one, though it is only part of the truth. Arthur Lawrence was certainly a miner, but he was also, at heart, a countryman. Lawrence himself describes how his father, getting up at five o'clock to work in Brinsley pit, 'would set off in the dawn across the fields at Coney Grey, and hunt for mushrooms in the long grass, or perhaps pick up a skulking rabbit, which he would bring home at evening inside the lining of his pit-coat.'[1] And Lawrence's sister Emily recalled, 'Father was very good on wild life. ... He knew the names of the birds and animals and that.'[2]

Lawrence inherited his father's knowledge of the countryside and the natural objects within it. What in Arthur Lawrence had been a peasant's practical know-how – mushrooms as free vegetables, the rabbit as a welcome addition to the family's larder – became in his son an enthusiasm that combined the passionate and the intellectual. Emily is one of many to note how her brother's interests became infectious on rural walks: 'he was so quick, he could notice things that you would just walk past and never see.'[3] Ada, the younger sister, describes other excursions taken with Lawrence in their youth: 'Those walks were full of interest. Not a flower, tree or bird escaped Bert's notice, and he found wonderful adventure in seeing the first celandine or early violet.'[4] She remarks later that he was always the first to see rabbit, pheasant, or primrose, 'or the fascinating male and female flowers of the larch.'[5] The last remark, of course, recalls the botany lesson in *Women in Love*. Virtually all the memoir-writers who have recorded their impressions of Lawrence make similar observations.

His knowledge of places and their associations was equally strong. As a youth, when he went with his family and friends on holidays and excursions, he had clearly read up in guide-books and local histories so that no site of importance was missed. Jessie Chambers's account of a day's outing by train from Eastwood to Skegness must stand as one instance among many. She records how he seemed to know all the landmarks on the way, how he would make his companions rush from one side of the compartment to the other to get glimpses of Gedling Church or Belvoir Castle or the famous Boston Stump: 'But it was not merely *seeing* these landmarks; it was kind of immediate possession, as though to have missed seeing them would have been to lose an essential moment of life.'[6]

In these accounts we see the beginnings of Lawrence's preoccupation with the 'spirit of place' which forms so important a foundation for his later fiction. The phrase occurs most prominently in the opening chapter of *Studies in Classic American Literature*, and in such novels as *Kangaroo* and *The Plumed Serpent* we can see Lawrence's efforts to communicate the sense of local place in Australia and Mexico. But it is in the fiction set in his own countryside that this spirit of place is most conspicuous. In a well-known letter to Rolf Gardiner the ruralist, written from Italy in 1926, Lawrence describes the view from the home in Eastwood, the mining village just north of Nottingham in which he was brought up. He remembers the view over Crich (which shares its name with several local families and with a main character in *Women in Love*), the High Park Woods and Annesley (transformed into the gamewoods of *Lady Chatterley's Lover*), Engine Lane and its level crossing (suggestive of though not identifiable with the setting of 'Odour of Chrysanthemums'), and the Haggs Farm (see *Sons and Lovers*). He remarks poignantly, 'That's the country of my heart,' adding of a somewhat broader area of the same country: 'It's real England – the hard pith of England.'[7]

As my parentheses indicate, it is not merely the country of his heart but the setting for most of his English fiction. Indeed, this part of the midlands has become known as 'the Lawrence country' in much the same way – and for much the same reason – that the area around Dorchester has been christened 'the Hardy country.' There are some notable similarities, as we shall see later, yet it is the contrasts that are most immediately obvious, and these are determined, as usual, by geographical and geological factors. When Elizabeth Gaskell called one of her novels *North and South* she drew attention to the fact that, in the mid-nineteenth century, the north of England contained the centres of industry while the south remained predominantly agricultural. The Lawrence country, it is fair to say, exists on the borderland between the two. It is midland in two senses of the word: almost exactly in the middle of the country (one thinks also of George Eliot's Middlemarch), it represents simultaneously an uneasy blend of the rural and the industrial. Lawrence catches the essence of this region in the title of a late essay, 'Nottingham and the Mining Countryside.'

The blend is a complex one, most easily seen in historical terms. Although mining had been carried on in the area for centuries, the Industrial Revolution brought radical and sweeping economic changes. These are reflected in population growth, economic patterns, technological development, and education opportunities, all of which transformed the way of life of the inhabitants.[8] Lawrence was born into the middle of this remarkable transitional period. Much of the traditional rural culture remained with its special local customs and associations. As a boy Lawrence used to bathe 'in the dipping-hole, where the sheep were dipped,' and he could recall a time when the nearby mill still ground the local corn.[9] In the highly autobiographical and realistic *Sons and Lovers*, we remember, Paul Morel could cycle out from the mining environment of Bestwood (Eastwood) to Willey Farm and a virtually unspoilt countryside. Life, Lawrence insists, 'was a curious cross between industrialism and the old agricultural England of Shakespeare and Milton and Fielding and George Eliot.'[10]

The mention of Eliot provides an important link with the particular literary tradition I am tracing in this book. Their respective midland regions lie almost side by side (a convenient link is established, albeit accidentally, by the reference to Cromford in the first chapter of *Adam Bede* and the eighth chapter of *Women in Love*), yet they are treated very differently. The view provided is on the one side that of an estate-manager's daughter, on the other that of a miner's son. Inevitably, perhaps, Lawrence offers us far greater concrete detail. Eliot's Loamshire and Stonyshire make a literary point but we do not believe in them as regions in the same way that we believe in Lawrence's more specific countryside. The difference is best established, perhaps, by means of a diagrammatic model. For Eliot Loamshire is juxtaposed spatially with Stonyshire, each representing a different regional landscape; for Lawrence the two coexist as in a cross-section. In Lawrence's world the miners labour underground at the coalseams, while on the surface crops are grown and cattle raised. This bordercountry is on a vertical rather than a horizontal axis.

I emphasize the point since it is crucial to any understanding of Lawrence's achievement as an artist. Here we can see the regional inheritance transforming itself into a larger myth. The model corresponds remarkably closely to the revolutionary pattern of the Romantic world-picture most conspicuous in

Blake, where energy comes from below rather than from above, where the standard heaven-earth-hell pattern of medieval Christianity (and Milton) is replaced by one in which vital energies within the earth attempt to overthrow the oppressive abstractions of the sky god. Related to this pattern, of course, are the well-known Romantic image-concepts of tree versus machine, organism versus mechanism, life versus death, that are present in so much of Lawrence's writings and particularly conspicuous in *Lady Chatterley's Lover*.

An illustration especially convenient for my purpose is to be found in the fourth chapter of *The Lost Girl*. Alvina Houghton, the central figure, is described as 'hidden like a mole in the dark chambers of Manchester House,' her appropriately named home in Woodhouse (another slight disguise for Lawrence's native Eastwood). One day she goes down the pit-shaft in her father's mine – 'it was as if she were in her tomb forever' – and when she returns to the surface, in a form of psychic rebirth, what had first seemed, and in fact still is, ugly appears transformed: 'What a strange and lovely place, bubbling iridescent-golden on the surface of the underworld.' She gains insight into 'the force of darkness' and comes to believe that, whereas the world was seeking 'a new Jesus, another Saviour from the sky, ... what was wanted was a Dark Master from the underworld.' The passage needs to be read in full, but I have quoted enough, perhaps, to suggest how it begins in an accurately presented regional world (one is frequently reminded of Arnold Bennett's Potteries in *The Old Wives' Tale*) but breaks the bonds of its regional beginnings to take on mythic resonance. Eventually, Alvina is 'lost' to the solid, traditional, but ultimately narrow and oppressive world into which she had been born.

Like Alvina, Lawrence was torn – between regional and anti-regional forces, between his father's working-class poverty (both material and intellectual) and his mother's bourgeois ambitions, between the demands of community and the urgings of individuality (a theme he sees as the central preoccupation of Hardy's novels),[11] between a nostalgic yearning for the older world he had half known and an awareness that it could never satisfy him, between a middle class that he found 'charming and educated' but 'shallow and passionless' and a working class 'deep and passionate' but 'narrow in outlook, in prejudice, and ... in intelligence.'[12] This is one reason why Lawrence was drawn towards Hardy; as Raymond Williams has observed, both came from 'a working community,' and shared 'connected desires and the frustration of desires.'[13] Lawrence loved the old regional world, the country of his heart, but came to realize that it could not sustain him. Like many other writers of his time, Lawrence found that he had to leave his native area, yet he was continually returning to it for his literary inspiration. And he found a major theme in the painful process of separation. Not only does he transcend his regional boundaries by his remarkable capacity to transmute local detail into the universal patterns of myth, but he chronicles the process of moving out into the wider physical and intellectual environments. He begins in fact where Hardy, in *Jude the Obscure*, ended. There are, of course, many ways of responding to Lawrence's artistic challenge, and I shall be considering only a small part of his literary significance in this context. I believe, however, that there are many less promising ways of approaching his work than studying him, in the way attempted here, as a displaced regionalist.

REGIONAL BEGINNINGS

Thanks to Jessie Chambers's memoir, *D.H. Lawrence: A Personal Record*, we have a clear picture of Lawrence's literary awareness when he began to write his first novel, *The White Peacock*. Her account of his 'Literary Formation' lists a large number of the writers and texts that I have discussed in earlier chapters. Both Jessie and Mrs Lawrence were fond of Scott, and Jessie records that she discussed with Lawrence in some detail the characters and scenes in the Waverley novels,[14] though a reference in *Sons and Lovers* (ch. 7) suggests that the non-Scottish romances, like *Ivanhoe* and *The Talisman*, were just as popular with them as *Guy Mannering*, *Rob Roy*, and *The Bride of Lammermoor*. But Scott does not, in fact, seem an immediate presence behind Lawrence's work. Far more important are the Brontës, George Eliot, and of course Hardy. It is interesting to note, however, that *Cranford* and *Lorna Doone* were also early favourites, and that in addition Lawrence showed an interest in a local regional novelist James Prior (who wrote about Sherwood Forest), and seems to have been aware of the work of Eden Phillpotts.[15] Not too much, perhaps, should be made of this evidence; at the same time, Lawrence's response to the spirit of place would be likely to lead him towards an interest in regionalism, and it is worth noting that the prestige of regional writing was at its peak when he was embarking on his career as a novelist.

Lawrence's debts to Eliot and Hardy are well known and need be reviewed only briefly here. Most significant is Lawrence's remark just as he was beginning to think about novel writing: 'The usual plan is to take two couples and develop their relationships. ... Most of George Eliot's are on that plan. Anyhow, I don't want a plot, I should be bored with it. I shall try two couples for a start.'[16] Moreover, Lawrence's reaction to the love (Jessie erroneously writes 'marriage') of 'the vital Maggie Tulliver' and 'the cripple Philip'[17] is profoundly relevant to Lawrence's preoccupations from the early 'Daughters of the Vicar' to the late *Lady Chatterley's Lover*. Similarly, his interest in Hardy at the time he was concerning himself with the material that eventually became *The Rainbow* and *Women in Love* is often discussed, but Lawrence had been familiar with Hardy's work much earlier (Jessie makes this clear, and Lawrence specifically recommends *Jude the Obscure* to Louie Burrows in 1910).[18] Despite the autobiographical foundation of *Sons and Lovers*, the resemblance of the basic triangle to *Jude* and (with the sexes reversed) to *Tess* is doubtless a factor in the structure and does much to explain the composite and balancing figure of Clara Dawes. But both Eliot and Hardy impressed upon Lawrence the importance of a well-established background in any fiction. The 'circumambient universe' (to use Lawrence's favoured phrase) is prominent in Eliot and central in Hardy. When Lawrence set to work on his first novel, compromising between a presentation of situations that he knew and the production of what he believed to be expected in fiction, it is not surprising that he should begin from a strong regional base.

The alternative titles for the first novel – 'Laetitia,' emphasizing a leading character; 'Nethermere,' focusing upon the local setting; and finally *The White Peacock*, employing a teasingly enigmatic image – are indicative of Lawrence's uncertainty concerning the central interest of the book. But the opening chapter, 'The People of Nethermere,' appropriately sets the characters against an encompassing background, and to read the novel with the conventions of regional fiction in mind is to see it, perhaps freshly, as at the end of a generic tradition just as it marks the beginning of a personal creative career. We can readily imagine a version of the book in which the life of the valley itself would be the central concern. But Lawrence, like Hardy but a generation or so down the line, knew that regional awareness, regional cohesiveness, was declining, even doomed. 'The whole place,' we learn in the third sentence, 'was gathered in the musing of old age.' And we soon realize that the community described is in decay. The Squire is specifically presented as head of 'a now decayed house' (pt. 1, ch. 6), fertile agricultural land is being turned into more profitable rabbit-warrens, and there is a memorable description of a derelict farm (also pt. 1, ch. 6); the church, too, as in *Wuthering Heights*, is deserted and overgrown.

Furthermore, the society Lawrence portrays is an uneasy, somewhat disturbing blend of the 'cultivated' and the earthy. All commentators remark on the way Lawrence uses incidents from autobiographical experience but raises the families which he treats to a higher class-level, but there are other reasons for the change besides snobbery and social ambition. The working-class novel – or, at least, the working-class industrial novel – was barely known in Lawrence's day. With an eye to the literary market, and to the practice of recognized novelists of his time, Lawrence was merely providing what was customary (this is the age, for example, when Meredith, Maurice Hewlett, and the early Galsworthy were popular). But Lawrence had, I believe, a more pressing reason. As the painful but decidedly effective chapter entitled 'Pastorals and Peonies' shows, Lawrence's very subject is the odd mixture of natural and artificial, rural and would-be sophisticated, in the society of

Edwardian England. He can be seen as making a deliberate social – and regional – point when he has Cyril Beardsell, the narrator, take over Lawrence's own detailed knowledge of natural objects – of birds, beasts, and flowers – but with none of his passionate response. To Cyril they are subjects for sensibility, essentially external and extrinsic. They are converted into art, not accepted as co-ordinates of the earth. The regional setting still remains, but the old regional culture, the accustomed regional ethos, is conspicuous by its absence.

We are introduced to a motley group of young people who have been born and have grown up in the valley. These include the fickle Letty, Emily (with whom Cyril has a love affair that fades out), and George Saxton, the farmer who is given a vision of a larger life he can never attain. But no cohesive society is to be found. Inevitably, they disperse; to use the imagery of *The Rainbow*, which is less emphatic but just as appropriate here, the circle widens. The centre of interest seems to lie less in the fortunes of the individual characters – the 'plot' with which Lawrence claimed at the outset that he would soon get bored – than in the pathos of this particular diaspora. After some months of acute homesickness but increasingly sophisticated intellectual growth in London, Cyril looks at the regional from a new, non-regional perspective:

> Nethermere was no longer a complete, wonderful little world that held us charmed inhabitants. It was a small, insignificant valley lost in the spaces of the earth. The tree that had drooped over the brook with such delightful romantic grace was a ridiculous thing when I came home after a year of absence in the south. (Pt. 3. ch. 3)

On visiting Strelley Mill, he finds it occupied by a family of labourers, 'strangers from the north.' As the native inhabitants move away in one direction, strangers appear from another. The once crowded and warm farm kitchen now had 'the barren air of a cell,' and is presided over by a woman speaking 'Glasgow-Scotch' who keeps five cages of canaries. 'I could not believe the brooding Mill was in her charge.'

But a surviving example of a traditional regional community is introduced right at the end of the novel. This is Swineshed Farm, the home of Tom Renshaw whom Emily eventually marries, and it is significantly set apart from Nethermere, some miles deeper into the country. Emily has earned her retreat, which is also presented as a fulfillment, but even this idyllic setting is shadowed by the presence of the dying George and his pathetic failure. To readers of the later Lawrence, indeed, Swineshed Farm is one of the 'chinks' left by the sprawling, urbanized 'children of men' that Birkin speaks of in *Women in Love* (ch. 26). It is interesting to note, however, that both Strelley Mill and Swineshed Farm are based, in detail if not in geographical location, on the Haggs Farm, home of the Chambers family and the 'Miriam' of *Sons and Lovers*.

Indeed, the topography of *The White Peacock* and most of Lawrence's English fiction exists firmly within the regional tradition. As in Hardy (and Webb who began to write a few years later), the setting is precise enough to be mapped – maps are now being provided in the Collected Edition in progress from Cambridge University Press – but fictitious names are substituted for the real names within the immediate vicinity. So Moorgreen becomes the 'Cossethay' that is going to become so prominent in *The Rainbow*. On the other hand, the names of places further afield (Matlock, Nottingham, Sherwood Forest, etc.) are retained, and these recur in later novels and so constitute the beginnings of a continuing topography. This is a small, perhaps obvious point, but it is important in demonstrating Lawrence's seemingly automatic adherence to the established tradition of literary regionalism.

The same regional concern, far more accurately reproduced, characterizes *Sons and Lovers*, and here the overlap of rural and industrial-urban is given special emphasis. Although everyone remembers the dour-sounding opening of the novel – ' "The Bottoms" succeeded to "Hell Row" ' – the initial paragraph as a whole lays stress on the still rural aspect of the area: 'There lived the colliers who worked in the gin-pits two fields away. The brook ran under the alder-trees, scarcely soiled by these same mines. ... And all over the countryside were these same pits, ... little black places among the cornfields and the meadows.' Here, far more faithfully than in *The White Peacock*, Lawrence presents his own experience of the transition. Many of the reminiscences about rural excursions described by the memoir-writers find an appropriate place within the fictional structure of the novel. But this society, too, is doomed to dispersal. As soon as Paul Morel enters the Co-op reading room to 'look for advertisements for a job,' he finds himself 'a prisoner of industrialism' (ch. 5). And the death of the mother leads directly to the absorption of Paul into the town. At the beginning of the final ('Derelict') chapter, he 'took lodgings in Nottingham' and 'was always in the town at one place or another, drinking.' And later, even the appreciation of flowers, so important throughout the book and derived in both fact and fiction from the mother, lapses after her death: 'Things had lost their reality. The first snowdrops came. He saw the tiny drop-pearls among the grey. They would have given him the liveliest emotion at one time. Now they were there, but they did not seem to mean anything.' Paul is divorced, by the demands of life and by social pressures, from the earth that nourishes him. And however we interpret the significance of the famous last sentence of the novel, in which he 'walked towards the faintly humming, glowing town, quickly,' what is indisputable is that his future, for good or ill, lies in the urban world.

I have no wish to play down the father-mother-son relationship – the Freudian pattern, if you will – that has attracted so much attention in critical studies of the novel. Rather, the two readings should complement one another. The father's tragedy is that his rural instincts are inexorably destroyed by the industrial system as it develops in the mines – the system to be analysed and condemned in a well-known chapter of *Women in Love;* the mother's tragedy is that of a drive towards betterment and respectability, the vision of a beyond (the process is examined further in the opening chapter of *The Rainbow)* that is destined to blight her relations with her husband and spiritually cripple her son. Similarly, the Paul-Miriam-Clara triangle has implications which have little in common with regional concerns, although one element in the split is that Clara belongs to the town and an intellectually sophisticated culture that attracts Paul while it erases the traditional values centred on Miriam. The familial situation – that of parents, sons, and lovers – is in many ways a microcosmic reflection of an 'inevitable' historical as well as psychological pattern. The juxtaposition of the modern, urban-generated Freudian pattern on to the local, regional context embodies the very process that Lawrence is chronicling.

Sons and Lovers, as Graham Holderness has argued in *D.H. Lawrence: History, Ideology and Fiction,* is supreme in the warmth, complexity, and cogency of its 'realism.' It represents that position in Lawrence's development where the regional matrix has yielded all that it can provide. Its popularity derives in part from its traditional qualities. While Lawrence displayed a section of working-class life that had never been presented with such immediacy – or, perhaps, such authority – it did not depart drastically from the forms of established fiction. But Lawrence was too original an artist to remain satisfied with this achievement. He knew that he had to explore further, and as a result he had to break out of the regional assumptions that hitherto had served him so well.

WIDENING CIRCLES: 'THE RAINBOW' AND AFTER

When, just before the beginning of the First World War, Lawrence decided to write a short book on Thomas Hardy, he probably saw the enterprise as a deflection from his main path as a novelist. In fact, it helped him to clarify both the debt he owed to Hardy as a forerunner in fiction and the extent to which his own views differed. The 'Study of Thomas Hardy' (not published till after the deaths of both author and subject) is well known as a Lawrentian reading of Hardy's novels in which the emphasis falls not so much on what they say as on what Lawrence considers that they ought to say. Both *The Rainbow* and *Women in Love* were gradually evolving at the time, and Lawrence's comments on Hardy throw revealing light upon the new directions that his own fiction was taking.

Lawrence's main points about Hardy are threefold: first, his heroes and heroines are all 'struggling hard to come into being'; second, their tragedy lies in the fact that they so often die 'in the wilderness' after having left the 'imprisonment' of 'established convention'; third (which he sees as particularly conspicuous in *The Return of the Native*), 'there exists a great background, vital and vivid, which matters more than the people who move upon it.'[19] He goes on to explain the rich but disturbing tension present in Hardy's work by arguing that, while Hardy's sympathy always lay with the individual against the community, he is forced to 'represent the interests of humanity' by taking his stand with the average and the conventional against the exceptional and the rebel.[20] *The Rainbow* and *Women in Love* can legitimately and profitably be read as Lawrence's own commentary on these positions. Ursula Brangwen is the representative of the Brangwen family who is determined to 'come into being'; her mother is one of those who remains 'in the wilderness' without climbing down Pisgah (though Lawrence does not treat this as a tragic theme); most important is the fact that for Lawrence, essential as a vital background may be, it can never take precedence over its human denizens. In this last instance lie the limits of Lawrence's regionalism. His characters are never overwhelmed by their environment; moreover, whether Ursula and Rupert Birkin or Connie Chatterley and Mellors are in question, the individual is invariably supported against the 'community,' whether that community is regional or cosmopolitan.

As we have seen, from the beginning of his fictional career Lawrence followed the regional Hardy in so far as he chronicled aspects of the decline of the regional consciousness. But in *The Rainbow* this process is explored more deliberately, more ambitiously, and more comprehensively. In this novel Lawrence takes the transition from the rural/regional to the urban/industrial, with all its attendant complications for human relationships, as his dominant theme. Its particularly urgent quality stems from the fact that this was the main pressure that Lawrence recognized as the pattern within his own life. The dilemma which *The Rainbow* explores has been isolated most skilfully, I believe, by F.R. Leavis in his last book, *Thought, Words and Creativity*: 'In the old rural civilization the lively intellectual milieu in which Lawrence found and nourished his genius wouldn't have been possible. Yet Eastwood was a characteristic product of the developing civilization regarding which he was sure that, of its very nature, it was heading to the most final of disasters.'[21] Though it may be expressed too negatively, this seems to me profoundly true. Despite the haunting lyricism of many of its scenes, the novel *is*, as Leavis had argued earlier in *D.H. Lawrence: Novelist*, about a historical process; this process may be imaginatively foreshortened, adapted in the interests of fictional rather than sociological 'truth,' but it provides a cogent analysis and embodiment of a tradition. But whereas Leavis, who seriously underestimated Hardy's significance as a central figure in English fiction, roots Lawrence firmly in his own 'great tradition' as a successor to George Eliot, I would insist that *The Rainbow* belongs more closely to the documentation of regional decline offered in Hardy's Wessex series. We have here Lawrence's – of course, highly individual – version of a 'movement' in English provincial history from, say, the Weatherbury of *Far from the Madding Crowd* to the Christminister of *Jude the Obscure*.

The opening chapter of *The Rainbow* is justly famous, but it can easily be misread. The tendency to allegorize or intellectualize needs to be resisted: its essential ruralness must be acknowledged. I would suggest, however, that it is decidedly more rural than regional. Lawrence is concerned with the ultimate emergence of the individual out of the impersonal 'blood-intimacy' of the folk. A remark by George Sturt ('George Bourne'), the contemporary writer on English folk-culture, is relevant here: 'the true antithesis to *Folk* is *Individual*.'[22] The Brangwens in the opening chapter are deliberately undifferentiated. Lawrence presents, first in the form of lyrical myth, then in this own brand of somewhat impressionistic history, the gradual development of personal individuation. 'How Tom Brangwen Married a Polish Lady' chronicles the first step towards a larger world, the foreign, the 'other,' to what makes Ursula's adventure possible. And it leads to Tom's turning away from communal, regional values to private, domestic ones. Several commentators have noted the lack of any real sense of regional context in the book; the Marsh Farm seems, though in a different way, as isolated (or as a-social) as Wuthering Heights. Lawrence may be concerned with what he calls 'the reality of Cossethay and Ilkeston,' but it is certainly not presented through detailed regional verisimilitude. Only briefly, in the 'Wedding at the Marsh' chapter, do we get a sense of English regionalism – a fine example of a regional culture, though even this scene is predominantly familial rather than local or (in Sturt's sense) tribal.

The 'Wedding at the Marsh' chapter may be seen, in some respects, as a watershed in Lawrence's art. It reminds us strongly of his traditional allegiances to Eliot and Hardy. In *The Mill on the Floss* too, we remember, the emphasis is on family rather than community, and the last remains of the old order so dear to Hardy (the sharpness of dialect, the proverbs, the folk-customs) are close to the surface in references to 'the old mystery-play of St. George' – shades of *The Return of the Native*! – and the carolling of the newlyweds at the close of the chapter. But Lawrence is driven, while still following his mentors, well beyond them. If the rest of the book occasionally recalls Hardy, it does so because the seeds of rural/regional decline are already evident. The wedding is a conjoining but also a separation. Anna Brangwen enters 'a new world' (ch. 6), and the order of the Marsh Farm is thereby diminished. In her life with Will the bonds are loosed still further: 'They would leave this cottage at Cossethay ... they would leave Cossethay, where the children had all been born, and where they always kept to the same measure' (ch. 14). The parallel to the movement in *The White Peacock* is painfully evident throughout. But henceforward Lawrence is more interested in 'the widening circle,' a pattern that recalls Maggie Tulliver's story, though Ursula leaves her far behind. The two themes are linked, however, since the decay of the old order is the price paid for the widening circle. *The Rainbow* is, in a sense, an elegy for the regional.

Of course it is many other things as well. Lawrence's well-known 'systole-diastole' principle is in operation here, and the decline in the regional is offset by the adventure into the unknown – an adventure that requires a looser and more exploratory literary form to contain the new attitudes transcending Eliot's and Hardy's rural/regional mode. As early as the first chapter, the men of Cossethay seem 'dull and local' to the women. Ursula later feels the pull of the larger world, as her mother did before her. In the sixth chapter we are shown Anna 'on the Pisgah mountain' attracted to the land stretched out before her but also reluctant to advance towards it. According to the chapter-title she is 'Anna Victrix' but her victory is simultaneously a defeat. And so, to a considerable extent, is Ursula's. Both in the closing section of *The Rainbow* and at occasional but crucial moments in *Women in Love*, Ursula feels painfully, excruciatingly, the pull of the Marsh Farm and all it stood for. She feels it in the brief, curious scene where Anthony Schofield, market-gardener brother of her friend Maggie, proposes to her; and she feels it again when, believing herself pregnant, she thinks back to the life-pattern of her mother.

Critics have generally interpreted these scenes as temptations to be over-come, and there is much truth in this. Schofield represents the past, and Ursula knows that you can't go home again. Anna 'relinquished the adventure to the unknown' – the adventure Ursula must follow. But we must not underestimate either the force of the temptation or the pain involved in resisting it. It is worthwhile to quote from both passages. Here is Ursula on Schofield after she has rejected him: 'Her soul was an infant crying in the night. He had no soul. Oh, and why had she? He was the cleaner' (ch. 14). And here is a passage from the final chapter:

> Suddenly she saw her mother in a just and true light. Her mother was simple and radically true. She had taken the life that was given. She had not, in her arrogant conceit, insisted on creating life to fit herself. Her mother was right, profoundly right, and she herself had been false, trashy, conceited.

Stephen Miko argues that here 'Ursula shows a further confusion which Lawrence clearly does not share.'[23] Other critics agree, but the matter is not as simple as that. Both Ursula and Lawrence are, I am convinced, profoundly torn in their loyalties and preferences. This self-division is not a matter that can be dismissed in terms of romantic nostalgia or sentimental reaction. Whether communicated in imagery of uprooting and transplanting or of death and birth, the process is traumatic and complex. Characteristically, Lawrence portrays it in all its human discomfort and suffering. Moreover, he is never closer to Hardy, I suggest, than on this subject. Both novelists knew that they had benefited from their own widening circles; both were conscious that their own lives would have been stifled by the narrowness of the 'provincial,' regional life they both escaped and nostalgically missed. They also knew that their literary success depended upon the patronage of an urban middle class that they found uncongenial. Both were deracinated; Hardy found fellow-feeling with Jude, while Lawrence recognized Ursula's story as, in a sense, his own.

In *Women in Love*, it might be said that the break has been made but that the wounds are still sore. The novel shows us, indisputably, a modern, urbanized world. The setting described in the opening chapter (so different from that of *The Rainbow*) is 'this defaced countryside.' In *Sons and Lovers* the original coal pits punctuated, even blended into, the rural scene; now it is a matter of 'ugliness' only occasionally 'overlaid with beauty' (ch. 9). 'Coal-Dust' (the title of chapter 9) is over all. In her search for being, for something beyond, Ursula goes with Birkin, Gudrun, and Gerald beyond England and any English tradition to the continent, to Switzerland, and on two occasions the sight of a man going to feed cattle in a barn reminds her of the limited but rooted world she has left behind. In the second of the two incidents she watches a man with a lantern move across a farmyard and enter the dark cattle-stalls:

It had reminded Ursula again of home, of the Marsh, of her childhood. ...
Oh, God, could one bear it, this past which was gone down the abyss? Could she bear, that it had ever been! ... She wished it could be gone for ever. ... She wanted to have no past. (Ch. 29)

But it is Gerald Crich, losing 'all his sense of place,' as Lawrence says of him just before his death (ch. 30), who ultimately denies his past. Ursula pulls back from the abyss she contemplates. We must not forget that, at the end of *Women in Love*, she and Birkin return – whether temporarily or finally is not made clear – to England and the Mill. Perhaps it is not too much to suggest that they return where they start from and know the place for the first time. At any rate, the pull between past and future, origin and goal, remains.

Henceforward, of course, Lawrence's circles widened to such an extent that any regional origin is abandoned. In *The Lost Girl*, which recent scholarship has demonstrated was all written in its present form after *Women in Love*,[24] Alvina breaks from Woodhouse/Eastwood and ends in a rural Italy that bears no resemblance to her own origins. She is 'lost' to Woodhouse; whether she has found an alternative 'being' is left uncertain. Aaron, too, makes a similar break in *Aaron's Rod*, Lou escapes to South America in *St. Mawr*, and a similar pattern is found in *Kangaroo* and *The Plumed Serpent*. The emphasis in these books is on response to foreign 'spirits of place.'

These novels need not concern us, but in *Lady Chatterley's Lover* Lawrence returns to his native countryside. By this time, however, mythic qualities clearly take precedence over regional ones. The novel may be discussed as a version of pastoral, with the gamewoods as a haven into which Connie and Mellors may retreat and play out a relationship unthinkable in the 'real' world,[25] but its regional associations are minimal. Significantly, Lawrence made no serious attempt to locate his novel in a consistent area within the country of his heart. Tevershall, Stacks Gate, and Wragby Hall itself seem to correspond to certain places in the area of Derbyshire just south-east of Chesterfield, but other details are incorporated from Eastwood and Annesley. But Lawrence's attitude to the whole area has darkened. It is now 'the hopeless countryside' (ch. 11), not only because of the oppressive ugliness but because of the total collapse of regional awareness: 'the younger generation were utterly unconscious of the Old England. There was a gap in the continuity of consciousness' (ch. 11). The only connection discoverable between environment and human society is bleakly negative: 'The people were as haggard, shapeless, and dreary as the countryside, and as unfriendly' (ch. 2).

All the regional characteristics are negated. Dialect indicates not regional specificity but class-distinction. Mellors is as isolated in the working-class society of the area as Connie is among the gentry. As individuals they have nowhere to turn except to each other. Society, for them, is reduced to the gamekeeper's hut in the woods. Above all, of course, they play out their parts in moral fable that has developed far beyond either regional or social realism. Sir Clifford is not representative in any human sense; as cripple, he is an emblem of modern man, and as landowner and mine owner he is a kind of parody of industrial capitalism. Connie embodies certain feminine instincts and attitudes but is certainly not offered as a social model. Mellors is constructed out of a variety of Lawrentian impulses that make him a spokesman for certain social, political, and sexual attitudes, but he hardly exists, in any traditional sense, as a character. All this suggests that Lawrence, by the end of his life, had ventured far beyond the possibilities of regionalism – even, perhaps, beyond the boundaries of fiction itself.

TEN

John Cowper Powys

REGIONAL ANCESTORS AND REGIONAL DISTINCTIONS

John Cowper Powys had many literary heroes – Homer, Rabelais, Balzac, Dostoievsky, etc. – but Scott and Hardy were his chief mentors in the British fictional tradition. The Powyses' most recent biographer records that their mother read them Scott's romances while they were children.[1] In the *Autobiography*, Powys describes Scott's works as 'by far the most powerful literary influence of my life' (ch. 2), though it seems that he had not read them since boyhood.[2] While the books he most often mentions are the later romances like *Ivanhoe* and *The Talisman* rather than the Scottish historical novels, casual references to *The Bride of Lammermoor* in *Rodmoor* (ch. 15) and *Ducdame* (ch. 16) may well be significant. At all events, he loved the long and leisurely pace of Scott's narratives – 'that massive solidity, that slow-moving convincingness' (*Autobiography*, ch. 2). But it was Scott's blurring of the divisions between 'novel' and 'romance' that most obviously intrigued Powys. 'Romance,' he wrote in the section on Emily Brontë in *Suspended Judgments*, 'implies, above everything else, a long association with the human feelings of many generations,' and this quality, together with a skill for mixing modes and conventions, invariably delighted him. Norna of the Fitful Head (from *The Pirate*) is mentioned on several occasions in his *Autobiography*, and the scenes which juxtapose her performing spells for Minna Troil (whose very name is Powysian) with a conversation between Triptolemus Yellowly, whose 'ruling passion' is agricultural improvement, and Claud Halcro (a local poet who can never forget that he once met Dryden) suggests a temperamental closeness between Scott and Powys. It also suggests, however, that Powys knew better than Scott how to extract an effect of amused grotesqueness out of his odd and oddly mixed characters.

But it is, of course, in Powys's later historical novels, in *Owen Glendower* and *Porius*, that Scott's influence is most clearly evident. G. Wilson Knight records that, when he asked Powys how he had succeeded in incorporating so much historical detail into *Owen Glendower*, 'he said that Scott's narratives helped him, which was scarcely an answer.'[3] To my mind, however, this *was* an adequate answer. The border setting, the scenes set 'on the verge of great events' (ch. 11), the relation of the mainly fictional Rhisiart to the romantically conceived but historical Glendower, all are part of Powys's debt to *Waverley*, and these novels could hardly have been written without Scott's example. Angus Wilson has recently compared the effect in *Porius* to equivalents in *Rob Roy* and *Ivanhoe*, 'yet,' he goes on to admit, 'how different it is.'[4] In the final analysis, Powys's romances are indeed different from Scott's. Powys was a great innovator, despite his profound connections to the numerous cultural traditions from which he sprang. Among these he inherited a taste for regional romance that was beginning to seem stale and outmoded. His importance stems from the way he transformed this tradition to make it a vehicle for his backward-looking but essentially original artistic vision. Powys, it might be said, illustrates his blend of traditionalism and originality by introducing his own inimitable form of romance into Hardy's Wessex.

His devotion to Hardy is even more evident than his admiration of Scott, though there is uncertainty concerning the age at which he became familiar with Hardy's work. Since the Powyses lived in Dorchester in the early 1880s, one would expect him to have encountered the writer and his work at that time, and in a letter he wrote as an old man to Glen Cavaliero he refers to 'my passionate devotion to Hardy who taught me *everything* as a boy.'[5] In the *Autobiography*, however, he asserts that he had not even heard of Hardy until he left Cambridge (ch. 5). The discrepancy may not be as puzzling as it first appears, since Powys apparently saw his 'boyhood' as unusually prolonged. What seems certain is that a serious acquaintance with Hardy himself and with his novels coincided with Powys's first awareness of the significant differences between English regions. Because this realization has a crucial effect upon his subsequent work, it will be necessary to trace the connection in some detail.

While he was still at school in Sherborne, Powys records, he 'began to grow conscious of a more definite response to different kinds of natural scenery'; this was encouraged by his father, who urged his sons 'to note every undulation, every upland, every spinney, every ridge, every fen and the effect produced upon all these by every variety of season or weather' (*Autobiography*, ch. 4). We can recognize here the origins of the atmospheric particularity that is so important an ingredient of the early landscape descriptions in his novels, but it was not until he left Cambridge in 1894 that a full sense of regional differences was dramatically brought home to him. At that time he applied to a teaching agency and was assigned a position in a girls' school in West Brighton. Powys caught the next train and, as he looked out of the carriage window, was amazed at the subtle contrasts between the Sussex countryside and that of the Dorset-Somerset border that he knew so well:

> Sussex scenery ... was certainly different from any scenery I had ever seen. Those huge Sussex barns whose vast sloping roofs were encrusted with orange-coloured lichen that was as strange to me as were the 'orange-tipped' butterflies I saw on the railroad banks, in place of our Dorset 'marble-whites,' those mellow Sussex cottages where old dark woodwork was so cunningly mixed in with brickwork and flintwork, those Sussex bricks themselves that ... gave a look to the whole scene so much warmer and sunnier than the Dorset thatch or the Somerset stone, those enormous Sussex wagons, painted blue and scarlet, and of a size so large that they would have astonished a Somerset farmer, the trim, neat, picturesque Sussex villages themselves, where it seemed as though everyone was so much more well-to-do than in the West Country, all these things struck me, sank into me, and abode with me. (*Autobiography*, ch. 6)

This is, I suggest a central text for an understanding of literary regionalism. Not only does it isolate the details of architecture, building materials, the colour and design of farm wagons – details themselves dependent on the more fundamental differences of geology and climate whose impact upon regional culture was about to be studied and discussed by such writers as George Sturt and H.J. Massingham – but it conveniently demonstrates the extent to which generalized rural backgrounds (the kind of descriptions we find in George Eliot, for example) differ from the minute particularities noticed and lovingly reproduced by the committed regionalist. Powys, who lived in the county for a time after his marriage, used this Sussex landscape as background for his recently discovered novel *After My Fashion*, just as he used the Norfolk background with which he was familiar for *Rodmoor* and the opening chapter of *A Glastonbury Romance*, but the importance of this period of Powys's life for his later work derives from the fact that it impressed upon him the unique qualities of his own landscape, of Montacute and its environs.

Powys goes on to liken the impact that this Sussex landscape had upon him to the experience of reading Sir Thomas Browne or Hardy and then suddenly being confronted with the work of Walter Pater. The reference to Hardy at this time can scarcely be fortuitous. As I have already noted, he claimed earlier that he had not heard of Hardy until he left Cambridge – that is, at about the time of his move to Sussex. And a little later in the *Autobiography* (still ch. 6) he recounts how he bought his first Hardy book, *Far from the Madding Crowd*, at Hove. This discovery led to a (bad) poem in praise of Hardy included in his first published volume, *Odes and Other Poems* (1896), which in turn led to his sending a copy to Hardy and receiving an invitation to Max Gate.

Years later Powys acknowledged himself as 'a hero-worshipper of old Hardy,'⁶ a statement borne out by his account of how, on the day Hardy was reciprocating his visit to Max Gate, he announced to his family 'that the greatest writer *then living on this earth* was coming to visit [them]' (*Autobiography*, ch. 6). And it is further borne out, of course, by the way in which Hardy is continually being recalled, either through indirect similarities or specific allusion, in Powys's fiction. Above all else, Hardy gave him a landscape. The west country is always 'Wessex' to Powys because he sees it through Hardy's eyes. Yet when, in his essay on Hardy in *Visions and Revisions* (1915), he writes that Hardy is identified 'with that portion of England where the various race-deposits in our national "strata" are most clear and defined,' we can see that he is also capable of seeing Hardy's Wessex through his own eyes. *Wood and Stone*, his first novel, is fulsomely dedicated 'to the greatest poet and novelist of our age THOMAS HARDY,' and the close of the preface to that book is a careful statement of his debt to Hardy but at the same time a denial of direct imitation. 'Mr. Hardy cannot be imitated,' he insists, but he also admits that one could 'hardly have the audacity to plant one's poor standard in the heart of Wessex without obeisance being paid to the literary over-lord of that suggestive region.' Montacute is in fact only on the shadowy edge of Hardy's Wessex (it is the 'Montislope' of the short story, 'Master John Horseleigh, Knight'), but, though he skirts Hardy's main Wessex locales, Powys was to move much closer to the heart of the older novelist's 'suggestive region' in *Wolf Solent, Weymouth Sands*, and particularly *Maiden Castle*, which is not only set in the original of Hardy's Casterbridge but opens with an affectionate parody of the main incidents in *The Mayor of Casterbridge*. Yet Powys is correct in denying that he imitates Hardy. By the time he came to write his 'Wessex romances," Powys had come to recognize not only the objective differences between regions but the subjective ways of differentiating *between* landscapes. Powys's Wessex is ultimately no one's but his own.

AN ALTERNATIVE WESSEX

Powys's first novel, *Wood and Stone* (1915), is clearly conceived within the established conventions of regional fiction. It begins with an introductory chapter concentrating on the locality in which the action is to take place; this is identified geographically as the borderland of Somerset and Dorset, and its most significant features, the natural landmark of Leo's Hill and the human community of Nevilton, are singled out for detailed attention. Particular stress is laid on geographical and historical determinants. Leo's Hill (in reality, Ham Hill) is the source of local and more than local building-stone, while Nevilton (Powys's own Montacute) has important antiquarian links with the past of religion and legend. Bernard Jones has compared this chapter with the prose of Hardy and Phillpotts;[7] I am convinced, however, that the similarities derive more from a regional perspective than from the stylistic cadences of the writing. Like Egdon Heath and Dartmoor, Leo's Hill is the dominant natural feature that ultimately controls the destinies of those who live in its vicinity; Nevilton, like Casterbridge and, to a lesser extent, Phillpotts's Okehampton, is the country town that serves as a human centre. But Powys differs from Hardy and especially from Phillpotts in emphasizing what he calls the 'spiritual influence' of place. For the purpose of the novel Leo's Hill is 'the impious heathen fortress' while Nevilton, where a fragment of the Holy Rood is said to have been discovered, is 'the consecrated repository of Christian tradition,' and Powys recognizes 'a strange supernatural conflict' between them. The basic polarities are those intimated in the title, the qualities of stone and wood, and these are soon developed into representative symbols of a vast occult struggle between materialism and mystery or, in the terminology he favours, between the impulse to Power and the impulse to Sacrifice.

But the main difference between Powys and his immediate predecessor in regional fiction is to be found in the extraordinary characters that he introduces against this background. Here his predilection for 'romance' and imaginative fantasy holds full sway. Hardy's major work was at one and the same time concerned with universal problems and local, rural trends; Tess, for example, contributes to debates on 'the woman question' and 'the ache of modernism' but is also a Wessex dairymaid affected by the moral, economic, and historical movements of the west country. Phillpotts's characters are humble, often inarticulate people encountering the standard human temptations and dilemmas in their own way, playing out their lives within the context of isolated traditional communities. But Powys's characters are fantastics – obsessed materialists, hermit philosophers, eccentric poets – presented as chess-board figures in a cosmic, binary game. The background is often vividly evoked, but the connection between the human beings and their environment exists for the most part on the plane of intellect and emblem. An orchard based on rock, one of the philosophers muses, 'is an admirable symbol of what this place represents. Clay at the top and sandstone at the bottom! I wonder whether it is better, in this world, to be clay or stone?' (ch. 10). Wood and Stone is full of subjects and effects that will be developed and refined in later novels, and it is valuable in illustrating, albeit in extreme form, Powys's characteristic quiddities, but he has not yet solved the problem (which he clearly recognizes as crucial) of how to present the all-important relation between human individuals and their local world.

Towards the end of his literary life, Powys described himself as 'a romantic-minded and yet realistic-minded novelist.'[8] The dichotomy is at the root of his art, and the achievement of his own balance between the two modes exercised him from *Wood and Stone* onwards. For his next novel, *Rodmoor* (1916), he transferred his attentions to a very different kind of landscape, the East Anglian coast presented in terms of 'the monotonous stretch of grey sky, grey dunes and grey sea' (ch. 3). Powys's concern to connect his characters with their background (which should function as more than background) is reflected in the following statement about Brand Renshaw: 'His ancestors had lived so long in this place that there had come to exist between the man's inmost being and the voracious tides which year by year devoured the land he owned, an obstinate reciprocity of mood and feeling' (ch. 6). But for the most part, the characters are as fantastic and grotesque as those in *Wood and Stone*, and despite the continued reference to tides, erosion, and monotony the relation between plot and setting is tenuous.

In *After My Fashion* (written around 1918 but not published until 1980), Powys moved to Sussex, and we are closer here to his mature manner. The leading character, Richard Storm, has just returned from France after twenty years, craves for 'some foothold in his native land,' and on arriving at the village in which his grandparents are buried expresses 'a deep thrill of pure delight to be once more in the land of his own people' (ch. 1). Here the physical relation – Powys's novels are full of scenes in which characters commune with their dead relatives in graveyards – becomes far more integral, though the love affair between Storm and Nellie Moreton and the sequence of events that leads all the main characters to transfer themselves to New York ultimately has few connections with regionalism. But we can detect in this book an advance in Powys's quest for his own landscape. The following passage describes Robert Canyot's vision behind the picture that he is painting:

> He had concentrated all his powers upon the reflection in the water of that rank herbage and those mossy walls, indicating as well as he could the shadowed presence there of a spirit of the spot, carrying the mind down a long dim vista of obscure memories, gathering itself, out of the colours and shapes of the moment, into a kind of eternal vision – a platonic archetype, that was more than a crumbling wall and a bank of hemlocks.   (Ch. 9)

Three central Powysian concerns have been brought together: the idea of 'a spirit of the spot'; the voyage of the mind in its association with a memoried, atavistic past, and, above all, an emphasis on 'rank herbage' and 'mossy walls' rather than the more conventionally beautiful elements in a local landscape. Here, I suggest, we can see Powys learning from Hardy while at the same time establishing his own independent regional landscape. The passage just quoted may not immediately suggest Hardy, but intimations of such a landscape may be found in the older novelist's work. Consider, for example, this well-known description of Tess moving through the uncultivated garden 'damp and rank with juicy grass' past 'tall blooming weeds emitting offensive smells' to get nearer to Angel Clare as he plays his harp on a summer evening:

> She went stealthily as a cat through this profusion of growth, gathering cuckoo-spittle on her skirt, cracking snails that were underfoot, staining her hands with thistle-milk and slugslime, and rubbing off upon her naked arms sticky blights which, though snow-white on the apple-tree trunks, made madder stains on her skin. (Tess of the d'Urbervilles, ch. 19)[9]

This is a comparatively uncommon effect in Hardy, but entirely characteristic of Powys, and it is doubtless significant that he lists it among his favourite passages in Hardy's prose.[10] Scenes of vegetable profusion and decay, with emphasis on smells and such details as lichen and fungi and the lesser-known flowers and butterflies rather than the traditionally sanctioned beauties of nature, are habitual in his work.

With Ducdame (1925) Powys's mature style is more distinctly and consistently adumbrated. First, he returns to a Wessex landscape (it is unambiguously offered as a Dorset story, though the descriptions of water-meadows and marshland suggest Somerset); second, the plot with its emphasis on the need of a male heir for the ancient and indigenous Ashover family integrates setting and theme; third, the grotesque characters are more deeply explored and more closely identified with an acceptable if idiosyncratic 'romance' landscape that can be associated with an authentic west country (though he evokes a pre-1914 rural ethos that had virtually disappeared by the time the novel was written); ultimately, however, it exists as a separate imaginative realm which can encompass figures as diverse as the witchlike Betsy Cooper and the idiot Binnory Drool, the eccentric clergyman William Hastings (who seems to have wandered out of T.F. Powys's related but distinct fictional world), and the Ashover Brothers, who, like so many fraternal pairs in Powys from the Andersen brothers in Wood and Stone onwards, reflect the complementary but differing personalities of Llewelyn Powys and John Cowper himself. There is a curious Gothic quality about Ducdame – it is close in places to the mood of Constance Holme's Crump Folk Going Home and the opening of Webb's The House in Dormer Forest, and became a source and target for Cold Comfort Farm – but in tone and assurance it approaches close to the level of the great Wessex romances. And it is worth stressing here that the advance is most clearly explained by the creation of a distinct and inimitable regional atmosphere.

Wolf Solent (1929) is generally regarded as Powys's first fully achieved fiction. It is in many respect his most conventional novel and therefore has found readers who cannot stomach the full feast of his rich idiosyncrasy. Though it encompasses many of Powys's recurrent concerns, it is in many respects within the tradition of regional fiction, and the landscape (if not the characters who inhabit it) is close to Hardy's in terms of both geography and mood. I have already quoted in my introductory chapter Powys's statement concerning 'that tendency to "describe scenery," which is so tedious an aspect of most modern work' ('Dostoievsky,' *Visions and Revisions*); his own practice generally stressed 'aura' and 'atmosphere' rather than description, but there are a remarkable number of conventional regional descriptions in *Wolf Solent*, especially in the early pages. This is because he records Wolf's impressions as he returns to Dorsetshire for the first time as an adult. We are shown what Wolf sees, and some of these descriptions are remarkably close to Hardy. Here, for instance, is Wolf's and the reader's introduction to Blacksod, based on Yeovil:

> The town of Blacksod stands in the midst of a richly-green valley, at the point where the Dorsetshire Blacksod Vale, following the loamy banks of the River Lunt, carries its umbrageous fertility into the great Somersetshire plain. Blacksod is not only the centre of a large agricultural district, it is the energetic and bustling emporium of many small but enterprising factories. Cheeses are made and also shoes. Sausages are made here and also leather gloves. Ironmongers, saddlers, shops dealing in every sort of farm-implement and farm-produce, abound in the streets of Blacksod side by side with haberdashers, grocers, fishmongers; and up and down its narrow pavements farmers and labourers jostle with factory-hands and burgesses.   (Ch. 4)

This reads more like Hardy or Phillpotts than Powys; it would be at home, indeed, in virtually any realistically oriented regional novel. The passage has all the raw, informative detail of a guidebook, and evinces an economic awareness that Powys rarely supplies. If it sounds somewhat familiar, the reason may be that it closely resembles a passage at an equivalent point in *The Mayor of Casterbridge* (also ch. 4) where Hardy indicates the character of the town by listing 'the class of objects displayed in the shop windows.'[11]

But these represent Wolf's initial, superficial impressions. Before long he has established a rapport with this new landscape, has isolated what he calls its 'autochthonous essence' (ch. 9), and has imposed his own (Powysian) vision upon it. On a later visit to Blacksod, we find him skirting the centre of town, finding an environment 'more congruous with his mood' as he walks 'past muddy ditches and wooden dams, past deserted cow-sheds and old decrepit barges half-drowned in water' (ch. 7). Eventually Wolf, we are told, can recognize 'the actual smell of Somersetshire, as distinct from the smell of Dorsetshire' (ch. 13), and at the close of the novel Powys's alternative Wessex, an olfactory region composed of Proust-like memories and essentially Powysian juxtapositions, creates a suitable atmosphere for the denouement. 'That smell of pigs' urine, mingled, just as it was a year ago, with the smell of the flowering hedge, gave him a thrill of delicious sadness, and all Dorset seemed gathered up into it!' (ch. 25).

Although, as I have said, *Wolf Solent* is Powys's most conventional novel, in the sense that it strays closer to the norms of traditional fiction, it contains numerous romance elements. Gerda Toop and her capacity to imitate a blackbird's song belong no more to realism than Wolf's incredible marriage to her. There are the usual Powysian grotesques – Urquhart, Tilly-Valley, Mr Malakite, Selena Gault – and the wide-ranging, multi-layered looseness of romance structure (held in check, however, by the controlled limited narration from Wolf's presence and consciousness). But here, more obviously than hitherto, Powys achieves his own version of the ideal he articulates in the 'Balzac' essay in *Suspended Judgments:* 'We need an imaginative realism. We need a romanticism which has its roots in the solid earth.' He had now created an intensely real – almost, we might say, a surreal – landscape that provided not merely a background but a physical and spiritual home for his romance creations. Unequivocally regional, it was a landscape based on a particular locality replete with architectural, topographical, and botanical details of an almost Pre-Raphaelite exactitude. His next major work was to link his special form of romance with the existing Somerset town of Glastonbury. Here, we might assume, is regionalism at its most extreme. Yet, as we shall see in the next section, *A Glastonbury Romance* is the fiction in which Powys penetrates with full confidence beyond the traditional regional boundaries. This region of the imagination extends to encompass the whole cosmos.

TRANSCENDING REGIONALISM

As the elements of 'romance' – loosely structured interweaving narratives, hints of the supernatural, defiance of the standard conventions of realism – become more conspicuous in Powys's plots, his settings become increasingly accurate and topographical. It would be both difficult and unnecessary to make confident identifications of the settings in *Rodmoor* and *Ducdame*, and those in *After My Fashion*, while identifiable, are comparatively superficial. None the less, Powys often follows Hardy in giving fictional names to places that can be readily identified on the map; so the Nevilton of *Wood and Stone* is clearly Montacute, while the Ramsgard and Blacksod of *Wolf Solent* are Sherborne and Yeovil respectively. In both these novels, however, as in Hardy's and Lawrence's, places outside the immediate vicinity of the action (Glastonbury,

Weymouth, Salisbury, etc.) are given their proper names, and from *A Glastonbury Romance* onwards his eccentric characters play out their unlikely lives against meticulously authentic backgrounds. It is not only possible but even desirable, if the full effect of Powys's obsession with topography is to be fully appreciated, to follow the movement of the characters in *A Glastonbury Romance*, *Weymouth Sands*, and *Maiden Castle* on street maps of Glastonbury, Weymouth, and Dorchester.[12] Powys again seems to have been influenced in this regard by his reading of Balzac, since he refers in the essay in *Suspended Judgments* to 'the admirable Balzacian tradition of mentioning the Paris streets and localities by their historic names, and of giving circumstantial colour and body to his inventions by thus placing them in a milieu which one can traverse any hour of the day, recalling the imaginary scenes as if they were not imaginary.'

At the same time, his settings have increasingly preternatural associations. This is less true of Weymouth than the rest, though even here the Wishing Well at Upwey and the primitive customs and beliefs of the Isle of Slingers are prominent. But three west-country locales become for Powys powerful centres for what H. P. Collins calls his 'earthy occultism.'[13] These are Glastonbury with its Arthurian legends, Maiden Castle with its pervasive suggestion of long-past actions and rituals, and Cerne Abbas with its great hill-figure representing fertility and natural magic. The first two are familiar to readers of the romances that contain their names. The Cerne Giant is continually referred to in his fiction and non-fiction writings; an important scene in *The Brazen Head* takes place on the figure, and the Giant himself appears as a character in the late fantasy *All or Nothing*.

The mature Powys is preoccupied with psychic atmosphere. I have already quoted a reference to 'a spirit of the spot' (very different from Lawrence's 'spirit of place'!) in *After My Fashion*, and such references proliferate, generally placing an increased emphasis upon mysterious emanations and extraterrestrial influence. A casual allusion to 'the old heathen aura of the Isle of Slingers' in *Weymouth Sands* (ch. 8) is typical. A passage from *A Glastonbury Romance* develops the idea to a greater pitch of subtlety: 'Everyone who came to this spot seemed to draw something from it, attracted by a magnetism too powerful for anyone to resist, but as different people approached it they changed its chemistry, though not its essence, by their own identity, so that upon none of them it had the same psychic effect' (ch. 4).

Powys's transcending of the normal boundaries of literary regionalism will now be clear. In one sense there can be nothing more intensely regional than *A Glastonbury Romance*, since the book recounts a sequence of events that, by definition, could only occur in that unique spot on the earth's surface. And we can see, too, how he needs the obsessive sense of topographical detail that is a feature of these writings: Powys's vision was breaking the forms in which he was working. As he remarked in discussing Dostoievsky as early as *Visions and Revisions*, 'there are certain human experiences which the conventional machinery of ordinary novel-writing lacks all language to express.' Similarly, he must transcend all regional limitations, extending his vision in both space and time. Spatially, this occurs in the famous (or notorious) opening to *A Glastonbury Romance*, where we are poised between, on the one hand, Brandon railway station and on the other 'the deepest pools of emptiness between the uttermost stellar systems.' Powys believes, and exploits the idea in his fiction, that a powerful human emotion or gesture can create, in the words of *The Brazen Head*, 'a psychic stir in the whole surrounding atmosphere of any particular spot' (ch. 2). This opens up Powys's subject-matter to encompass the whole of the apprehensible universe, but the 'particular spot' none the less retains an unassailable importance.

Temporally, in the novels succeeding *Maiden Castle*, where Uryen displays a mystic connection with the earthwork that associates him with a past occult tradition, Powys harks back to earlier periods in English and Welsh history, to the times of Owen Glendower and Roger Bacon and the Arthurian age of the fifth century AD, thus going back further and further towards man's prehistoric beginnings. As he remarks in *A Glastonbury Romance*, 'the submerged Cro-Magnon in [most men], or at least the submerged Neolithic man, swims up in them like a rising diver from the bottom of the atavistic sea' (ch. 16). The final short works of his old age are best described as philosophic fables set in the never-never-lands of outer space, and, whatever reservations we may have about their ultimate importance, bear witness to the almost boundless extent of his final viewpoint.

This process can be traced most clearly in *Maiden Castle* itself. Recently, it has become standard in Powys criticism to claim that Powys is less topographically concerned in this novel than in his earlier work. 'We are little aware of Dorchester as a town,' G. Wilson Knight wrote in *Saturnian Quest*, and C.A. Coates has called it 'a vague unspecified locality,'describing its background as 'thin' and 'undetailed.'[14] This seems to me a misreading. Dorchester is as accurately reproduced as Glastonbury or Weymouth. High East Street, the Hangman's Cottage, the area of the railway station and Maumbury Rings, the Hardy statue at Top o' Town, and the road to Maiden Castle are all described memorably and forcibly. It is true, however, that Powys is more imaginatively engaged in the complexity of Dorchester's past than in its present. His protagonist, Dud Noman, is a historical novelist whose fascination for the past interferes with his ability to live adequately in the here and now; other important characters include Teucer Wye, who reads nothing but Plato, Roger Cask, who is obsessed as much with the Romans as with communism, and especially Enoch (Uryen) Quirm, who is preoccupied with the Celtic past. However, we should not forget that the novel's title focuses our attention not so much on Dorchester as on Maiden Castle and its connections with a mystical prehistoric world. Powys's regional particularity, while still present, is qualified by his increasing interest in the capacity of certain places to contain and preserve emanations that transcend space and time. The two elements are perhaps most clearly balanced in *A Glastonbury Romance*; in later novels the second gains the ascendancy.

The area around Dorchester, then, fascinates both Powys and his protagonist because it is 'a region charged with so many layers of suggestive antiquity' (ch. 1). And Maiden Castle itself exists here as an enchanted realm. Ghost winds blow from its ramparts down to the contemporary market town. It is a place, in Uryen's words, of 'mists and mirages and vapours' (ch. 6), all contributing to an atmosphere Powys will exploit further in his Welsh novels. He has moved a long way from Hardy – at least, from the major Hardy. It is interesting to note, however, that Powys may well have been influenced by Hardy's short story 'A Tryst at an Ancient Earthwork,' which is set at Maiden Castle or 'Mai Dun.' Not only does Hardy offer a story of excavation and discovery (the contemporary excavations at Maiden Castle are a focal point in Powys's novel), but he presents the earthwork as a scene of storms and winds. 'Strange articulations seem to float on the air from that point,' we are told, and these are identified (albeit tentatively) as 'air-borne vibrations of conversations uttered at least fifteen hundred years ago.' We cannot be absolutely sure that Powys read this story, which was first collected in *A Changed Man* in 1913, but if not the coincidence is remarkable. Here is an uncharacteristic Hardy at his closest to Powys. It is a strain, however, that leads the latter away from mainstream Hardy towards the enchantments of his Welsh heritage.

While the writing of *Maiden Castle* was still in progress, Powys moved to Corwen in North Wales, which he describes as 'the very heart of the Owen Glendower country.'[15] It was therefore natural that at this time his thoughts should turn to his Welsh origins and the Scott-like possibilities for romance inherent in the story of the Welsh revolt against Henry IV. This is the first of his books to be set in a distant past, and it is filled with places that he knew to be instinct with the spirit of Welsh history – Glyndyfrdwy, Dinas Brân, Valle Crucis, Mathrafal. But topographical accuracy is now less important than a kind of atmospheric mysticism. The locales tend to exist on two levels – Hardy's phrase 'part real, part dream-country' is especially applicable to Powys's practice here. Thus for Rhisiart ab Owen in the opening chapter of *Owen Glendower* there is a 'real' and an 'ideal' Dinas Brân, the latter described as 'that mystic terminus of every vista of his imagination.' The point is made even more forcibly a little later. 'Its foundations were sunk in the earth, but they were sunk in more than the earth, they were sunk in that mysterious under-world of beyond-reality whence rise the eternal archetypes of all the refuges and all the sanctuaries of the spirit, untouched by time, inviolable ramparts, not built by hands!'

The character of Owen Glendower fascinates Powys for several reasons: because of his loyalty to the 'ideal' rather than to the 'real' Wales; because he is – or, at least, can be convincingly portrayed by Powys as – especially conscious of 'the spirit of the place' (ch. 12); because, after his mystic 'seizures,' Powys can make him feel 'like someone who has been dragged back from levels of life far more satisfying than any outward events' (ch. 12); but most of all, one suspects, because of the romantic possibilities that his story provides. Romance has now taken precedence over realism, and this is best indicated by the opening words of the novel, which are 'Don Quixote.' The accompanying list of characters is divided into those 'mentioned in history' and those 'un-mentioned in history,' and these last give Powys all sorts of excuses for his inventive capacities. One of these fictional creations, Tegolin the maid of Edeyrnion, is a Welsh Joan of Arc figure who belongs to one type of romance. Others, like Broch o' Meifod with his death philosophy and the vivisecting Gilles de Pirogue, allow Powys to people his narrative with characters representing a rich variety of attitudes and beliefs. Two minor figures, Tom Hardy and Jimmy Trenchard (Powys's habitual mistake for Henchard), show him in whimsical mood, indicating perhaps that the Powysian Wales is not wholly separated from Hardy's Wessex. But for the most part all is 'enchantment,' a key word in this narrative. The landscapes are often vividly recreated (especially the mist and winds that cast a magic spell over the autumnal greenery of the primeval Forests of Tywyn), but, whereas the names for the most part exist on modern maps, the structures and atmospheres that Powys evokes belong wholly to his own characteristic region of the imagination.

This process is carried even further in *Porius* (1951), a vast novel whose printed edition of 682 pages is, we are told, somewhat less than two-thirds of the original manuscript. The setting (like the unparalleled final chapter of *Owen Glendower)* is Corwen, and the action extends over only seven days, the days in question being in the last year of the fifth century AD. Powys delights in recreating, in immense fictional detail, a period of the 'dark ages' about which little is known, since it allows him a free hand for his 'romantic' propensities. But it is not wholly escapist. As he commented, 'my story combines the tricks of story-telling and the old romantic melodramatists with the modern form of psychology.'[16] The period fascinates Powys because of the combination of races that coexisted (though by no means peacefully) in North Wales at that period. In a review George Eliot once mentioned 'that *conflict of races* which Augustin Thierry has pointed out as the great source of romantic interest – witness

"Ivanhoe",'[17] evidence perhaps that Powys's scheme here is closer to Scott and the conventional romance tradition than appears at first sight. At all events, Powys emphasizes the relation of each of these races (aboriginal giants, Celts, Picts, the Welsh 'forest-people,' Romans, Saxons) with the land they inhabit.

Only the main physical features of this land are recognizable today – Mynydd-y-Gaer (the hill-fort of Caer Drwyn, which had already been used in *Owen Glendower* and which, interestingly enough, Powys describes in a letter to his brother Llewelyn as 'Corwen's "Mai-Dun" or Maiden Castle'),[18] the river Dee, the Fountain of St Julian, the Beryn range. The action is rooted in the vale of Edeyrnion, but it is permeated throughout by the Powysian equivalent of Wordsworth's 'light that never was on sea or land, / The consecration and the poet's dream.' The key images used to evoke the landscape are those of 'this mother of rivers, Dyfrdwy, Divine Water' (ch. 1) and the Welsh mists which are sometimes physical, sometimes supernatural in a way that recalls the ghost-winds in *Maiden Castle*. But the most memorable scenes, the underworld refuge of the last of the Druids, the mountain fastnesses from which the Giants descend, belong firmly to 'imagination' rather than to 'reality.'

With *Porius* Powys exploited the sense of a region only to overwhelm it. The novel can be read on two levels – as an almost shameless retreat into a world of 'what might have been' or a sophisticated allegory of the modern pluralistic universe. This romantic, enchanted realm is peopled with characters as obsessed, as 'modern,' as any in Dostoievsky. The circumscribed region that acts as microcosm appears yet again, albeit in an unusual form. But if these books shatter the more traditional form of regionalism, they also depend upon it. It can hardly be a coincidence that Powys's later writings, which abandon any regional specificity that readers can identify with, lose the immediacy that is so important an ingredient in his best work. *Atlantis* (1954) goes back to Homer's Ithaca, but it is a land to which neither Powys nor his readers can respond save through the literary imagination. More significantly, *The Brazen Head* (1956) returns to thirteenth-century Britain, but its failure to emulate its predecessor is explained in large measure, I believe, by its lack of regional connection. While it opens at an 'ancient circle of Druidic stones,' the setting is never rooted within a recognizable topography. It remains a created stage-set against which events take place; it cannot be identified, discovered on a map, visited. The result is a detachment very different from the imaginative remoteness that is so invigorating in *Owen Glendower* and *Porius*. Perhaps unconsciously, Powys demonstrates the extraordinary importance of a 'spirit of place' even when the fiction in question ventures far beyond any regional limits.

Powys is a figure of giant literary proportions who, like Lawrence, could never be confined within the boundaries, either literal or metaphorical, implied by the phrase 'regional fiction.' But, also like Lawrence, he needed a specific countryside to stimulate his best work. Moreover, it was necessary that this countryside or region reflected either his own early memories or those of the childhood of the race. Late in life, he looked back with loving nostalgia to 'the particular lanes, ponds, orchards, water-mills, gates, ditches, rivers, hills, woods round about the villages of Montacute, Tintinhull, Stoke, Norton, Martock, Ilchester, Thorn, Brympton, Odcombe, Coker, Batemoor, and Ham Hill.'[19] This is the area that might be termed 'the Powys countryside.' But he wrote these words in Corwen, and found there his second countryside, with its deeply embedded sense of his (possibly adopted) country's history. 'Not a field,' he wrote, 'not a river-bank, but there emanate from it, wavering, fluctuating, ebbing and flowing like mountain-rain, legends and rumours of an unbelievably remote Past.'[20] In one or other of these two realms of both reality and romance he produced an idiosyncratic but brilliant body of literature that is, in his own words, 'deeply local, and yet as wide as the world.'[21]

ELEVEN

Conclusion

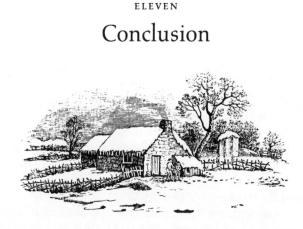

THE PASSING OF REGIONALISM

'If anything has died in the last 30 years, it is regionalism. Our society – why pretend – has made war on regionalism and has destroyed it. We may question whether, under any disguise, it can be reborn in the modern world.'[1] It is difficult to argue with V.S. Pritchett's conclusion, written over forty years ago. In earlier books on non-fiction rural writing and on 'the poetry of nature,' I have been able to conclude with an emphasis on at least probable continuity into the future, but in the case of English regional fiction the outlook is bleak indeed. Of course, novels will continue to employ rural settings so long as countryside exists, but *regional* novels – in anything like the forms discussed in this book – can hardly be written any more, since distinctive regions have now been penetrated by cosmopolitan (or, perhaps more fatally, metropolitan) technologies and communications systems, and have thus lost any sharp sense of differentiation. What were once the constituents of genuinely regional cultures now seem no more than quaint survivals within a more centralized, standardized, relatively homogeneous society that takes its values from the industrial centres. Response to individual place obviously remains important – indeed, essential – and both non-fiction and poetry are well equipped to embody a sense of unique local life.[2] But rural regional fiction has become an anachronism since it can no longer claim to be representative; the local cannot be transformed into the universal because so much of it is universal already.

Yet any adequate exploration of the decline – or collapse – of the regional novel cannot be limited to purely historical factors. In many respects, the seam had already been worked out. When the last great practitioners – Hardy and Lawrence – took regional decline rather than regional life as their main theme, the writing was already on the wall. As a result of this decline, the romance element in regional fiction necessarily increased, since regional communities were no longer to be found anywhere but in the past. Unfortunately, romance itself had by this time degenerated from an alternative literary mode – Northrop Frye has called it 'the structural core of all fiction'³ – to a calculated evasion of 'reality.' The fag-end of the form can be seen most conveniently in Hugh Walpole's Herries Chronicles, comprising Rogue Herries (1930), Judith Paris (1931), The Fortress (1932), and Vanessa (1933). The four volumes offer a saga of one family's life in the Lake District from the eighteenth century to the time of writing. The whole project may be seen as an attempt at regional fiction catering to the age of film, although it anticipates by some years the development of the technicolour spectacular.

Walpole was a lifelong admirer of Scott, and assembled an impressive collection of his works, but his own novels represent little more than a vulgarization of the genre that his mentor created. The links are obvious. The very name Herries is borrowed from Redgauntlet, and Rogue Herries (which also contains, like Rob Roy, a character called Osbaldistone) includes a section on 'Forty-Five' in which the protagonist has a predictable interview with Bonnie Prince Charlie. But most of the book is devoted to a swashbuckling romanticism for which the Lake District provides an appropriate but by no means necessary setting. All the main characters dutifully record their love of the countryside in which they live but of which they never become a part. It remains a suitably picturesque background for duels and love rivalries. Walpole's own love of the area is clearly genuine, but setting and plot are never integrated.

Above all, Scott's central concern, the exploration of a profoundly significant historical process, is wholly lacking. The personal history of the Herries clan is continued in the later volumes through the French Revolution, the Chartist demonstrations, the Great Exhibition of 1851, the Boer War, the First World War, and the General Strike of 1926, but the family loves and feuds make no necessary connection with these indicators of historical change. It is not surprising, then, that interest in the saga falters as we get closer to the contemporary period, since the romantic distortions inevitably become more and more conspicuous. John Cowper Powys possessed the imaginative sophistication that enabled him to create an idiosyncratic but original world out of the chasm that opened up between the romantic and the realistic; he was able to turn a general liability into a particular adventure. Walpole had no such gift, and could offer only the lowest common multiple of (albeit popular) romance.

'COLD COMFORT FARM' AND ALL THAT

But it was not merely regional romance that was revealing itself as vulnerable in the early 1930s. Stella Gibbons's Cold Comfort Farm appeared in 1932, while the *Herries Chronicles* were still in progress, and it parodied the whole genre of rural/regional fiction. The inspiration for the book appears to have arisen out of reaction to the cult of Mary Webb that developed immediately after Stanley Baldwin's preface that introduced a reprint of *Precious Bane* in 1928. But Gibbons's satirical aims went much further. When approached by Gladys Mary Coles, Webb's biographer, she confirmed that, in addition, she had in mind the work of Sheila Kaye-Smith, John Cowper Powys, and T.F. Powys.[4]

This is confirmed by internal evidence from *Cold Comfort Farm* itself. The concentration on a decaying farm in Sussex certainly suggests Kaye-Smith, and the reference to 'Reuben' as a typical name (ch. 2) may well allude to the protagonist of *Sussex Gorse*. The parody dialect ('Curses, like rookses, flies home to rest in bosomses and barnses' [ch. 7]) clearly hints at John Cowper Powys, while Amos's preaching, perhaps beginning in response to Kaye-Smith's books in general and *Green Apple Harvest* in particular, develops when he purchases a Ford van into a sly dig at T.F. Powys's *Mr Weston's Good Wine*. But the main target, of course, is the excesses of Gothicism and the emphasis on doom and dark secrets. In itself, this is a tradition going back, as both Tom Winnifrith and Glen Cavaliero have noted, to *Wuthering Heights*,[5] and writers as established as Emily Brontë are by no means immune to Gibbons's no-nonsense criticisms. But the obvious subjects in more recent fiction would seem to be *Crump Folk Going Home* (a title that would have delighted Gibbons), *The House in Dormer Forest*, and *Ducdame*. Nor is Phillpotts exempt. He, if anyone, is most given to Baedeker three-star landscape descriptions, and can it be a coincidence that Gibbons's family are the Starkadders while there is a character named Blackadder in his Dartmoor romance, *The Lovers?*

Cold Comfort Farm was an immense success in its time, and must have been considerably influential in exposing the weaknesses of run-of-the-mill regional novels and romances. Inevitably, however, its point has been blunted by the decline of the genre that it helped to dislodge. As a result, while its name is still well known, I doubt whether it is now widely read. Certainly, many of its finer points will be lost on modern readers, and some of its implications need to be spelled out in detail. One point should be emphasized at once: only the excesses of the genre are seriously affected by Gibbons's parody. It would be absurd to suggest that *Cold Comfort Farm* 'killed' the regional novel. All it was capable of killing was the last gasp of a genre that was inevitably coming to the end of its strength and was beginning to look particularly obsolete during the depressing political and economic crises of the 1930s.

A reading of Webb's work, for example, need not be spoilt by a prior reading of Gibbons's book. Glen Cavaliero has noted that members of the Darke family in *The House in Dormer Forest* 'are clearly the chief inspiration for the

Starkadder family in *Cold Comfort Farm*.'[6] This may be so, but we must acknowledge at the same time that Webb did not present the Darke family with anything approaching total solemnity. There is a great deal of humour – some of it worthy of Gibbons herself – in the early chapters of the novel; indeed, Webb goes to considerable lengths to 'place' the Darkes. The point leads, via Grandmother Velindre (whom Webb presents as a grotesque), to a more crucial matter. Gibbons pokes fun at both the recurrent conventions (e.g., 'the Dominant Grandmother Theme, which was found in all typical novels of agricultural life' [ch. 5]) and the 'close-to-the-soil' realism that was supposed to characterize regional fiction. But in concentrating on the excesses, Gibbons's parody seemed to be attacking the very novelists who were trying to move beyond a merely documentary fidelity. If her attacks damaged the reception of writers like Webb and the Powyses rather than Phillpotts and Kaye-Smith, then the result was both unfortunate and undeserved.

Moreover, our attitude to *Cold Comfort Farm*, from the critical perspective of a later generation, is likely to be complicated by responses not visible at the time of its first appearance. The fact that the novel was set 'in the near future' accentuates this since its datedness is now all the more evident. Thus it is now easier to notice that the basic structure of the novel – the arrival of Flora Poste at the farm, her disruption of its set ways, and her subsequent departure – is itself based firmly on the genre she is parodying (compare, for example, the structure of Phillpotts's *Widecombe Fair*). More serious, perhaps, is our recognition of the strong sense of cultural superiority assumed by Flora – and, one suspects, accepted by the author, since nothing in the narrative qualifies it to any significant extent. Author and reader are presumed to share certain basic assumptions – that rural ways are likely to be outdated and ridiculous, that the up-to-date ideas from London must necessarily be an improvement. Raymond Williams's phrases, 'a suburban uneasiness,' 'a kind of evasion of caricature,' seem to me wholly apt.[7] In many ways, *Cold Comfort Farm* is as much an upper-class romp as a literary satire. At the end, Flora is supposed to have brought the farm back to sanity, but one wonders. Ironically, the whole ethos of her London world has now been swept away as completely as that of the Starkadders.

That the book contains many passages of delightful wit and humour, that its satirical sallies are often both shrewd and justified, may be taken for granted, but it should not be interpreted as a dismissive indictment of a whole tradition of fiction. On the other hand, it would be as absurd as it would be pointless to lament the passing of Phyllis Bentley's 'golden age' of the regional novel. My purpose has been to demonstrate that, for over a century, it provided a form within which some of the finest novelists in the language could express their creative visions as well as their response to the rural landscape around them. In its time it was neither a limited nor a peripheral genre, nor were regionalists confined to the realistic mode. Contemporary regions of the imagination may seem very different, but they share more than is generally realized with the writers from Scott to Lawrence and Powys who explored the interconnections of individual and society with their local spirit of place. 'What does life consist in,' asked Lawrence, 'save a vivid relatedness between the man and the living universe that surrounds him?'[8] While that link still held, regional fiction had much to offer.

NOTES

1 / INTRODUCTION

1 The geographer E.W. Gilbert, however, maintains that 'the word "regionalism" first appeared in 1874 and since about 1890 it has been in common use.' See 'The Idea of a Region,' *Geography*, 40 (1960), 169.

2 Thomas Hardy, *The Life and Work of Thomas Hardy*, ed. Michael Millgate (Athens: University of Georgia Press, 1985), p. 126.

3 William Barnes, *A Glossary of the Dorset Dialect* [1886] (Guernsey: Toucan Press, 1970), p. vi.

4 Sheila Kaye-Smith, *Three Ways Home: An Experiment in Autobiography* (New York: Harper, 1937), p. 256.

5 F.W. Morgan, 'Three Aspects of Regional Consciousness,' *Sociological Review*, 31 (1939), 68.

6 Ibid., p. 74

7 Ibid., p. 85

8 H.J. Massingham, *Remembrance: An Autobiography* (London: Batsford, 1942), p. 81.

9 Gilbert, pp. 158, 168.

10 Ibid., p. 160

11 Phyllis Bentley, *The English Regional Novel* (P.E.N. Books. London: Allen and Unwin, 1941), p. 13. Subsequent page references in text.

12 Morgan, pp. 84–5.

13 John Cowper Powys, 'Dostoievsky,' in his *Visions and Revisions* [1915] (London: Macdonald, 1955), p. 191.

14 Glen Cavaliero, *The Rural Tradition in the English Novel, 1900–1939* (London: Macmillan, 1977), p. 100.

15 Samuel Johnson, *Rambler* 37 (24 July 1756), in W.J. Bate and Albrecht B. Strauss, eds, *The Rambler* (*The Works of Samuel Johnson*, volume III) (New Haven: Yale University Press, 1969), p. 203.

16 Raymond Williams, *The Country and the City* (London: Chatto and Windus, 1973), p. 253.

17 Morgan, p. 86

18 W.L. Renwick, *English Literature, 1789–1815* (Oxford History of

English Literature, volume IX.
Oxford: Clarendon Press, 1963),
p. 90.
19 Quoted in B.C. Southam, ed., *Jane
Austen: The Critical Heritage*
(London: Routledge and Kegan
Paul, 1968), p. 267.
20 Quoted in John Geoffrey Sharps,
*Mrs Gaskell's Observation and
Invention* (Fontwell, Sussex: Linden
Press, 1970), p. 127. On the other
hand, compare the following:
'Some years ago the writer gave a
copy of *Cranford* to a friend who
was on a visit to a small town in
Somersetshire, and the latter wrote
saying: "I believe this is the original
of *Cranford*; it is just such an old-
world place as Mrs Gaskell describes.
I suppose you knew the place and
thought I should be interested
in reading *Cranford* in its original
home".' Mrs. Ellis H. Chadwick,
*Mrs. Gaskell: Haunts, Homes, and
Stories* (London: Pitman, 1910),
p. 45.
21 See Waldo Hilary Dunn, *R.D.
Blackmore, The Author of 'Lorna
Doone'* (London: Hale, 1956), pp.
106, 239–40.
22 Q.D. Leavis, 'Regional Novels,'
Scrutiny, 4 (May 1936), 442.
23 Northrop Frye, *Anatomy of Criticism* (Princeton: Princeton University Press, 1957), p. 307.
24 William Hazlitt, *The Spirit of the
Age*, in John O. Hayden, ed., *Scott:
The Critical Heritage* (London:
Routledge and Kegan Paul, 1970),
p. 284.
25 Tom Winnifrith, *The Brontës* (New

York: Macmillan, 1977), p. 156.
26 Hardy, *The Life and Work of
Thomas Hardy*, p. 516. See also
R.L. Purdy and Michael Millgate,
eds, *The Collected Letters of Thomas
Hardy*, volume I (Oxford: Clarendon Press, 1980), pp. 195, 196.
27 George Watson, introduction to
Maria Edgeworth, *Castle Rackrent*
(London: Oxford University Press,
1964), p. vii.
28 Ibid., p. 97.
29 Ibid., p. xviii.
30 Ibid., p. vii.

2 / SIR WALTER SCOTT

1 Sidney Colvin, ed., *The Works of
Robert Louis Stevenson* (Vailima
edition. New York: Scribner's,
1923), XXII, 426.
2 Edgar Johnson, *Sir Walter Scott:
The Great Unknown* (2 vols.
[continuous pagination], New York:
Macmillan, 1970), p. 9.
3 Ibid., p. 10.
4 *Specimens of the Table-Talk of the
Late S.T. Coleridge* (London and
New York: Routledge, n.d.), p. 225
(entry for 4 August 1833).
5 H.J.C. Grierson, ed., *The Letters of
Sir Walter Scott* (12 vols. London: Constable, 1932–7), I, 146.
6 Scott in J.G. Lockhart, *Memoirs of
the Life of Sir Walter Scott* (5
vols. Toronto: Macmillan, 1900), I,
30–1).
7 Francis R. Hart, *Scott's Novels: The
Plotting of Historic Survival*
(Charlottesville: University Press of
Virginia, 1966), p. 263.

8 Lockhart, I, 167.
9 A.O.J. Cockshut, *The Achievement of Walter Scott* (London: Collins, 1968), p. 22.
10 *Minstrelsy of the Scottish Border* (4 vols. London: Adam and Charles Black, n.d.), I, 222, 224, 238.
11 John Buchan, *Homilies and Recreations* (London: Nelson, 1926), p. 22.
12 Quoted in John O. Hayden, ed., *Scott: The Critical Heritage* (London: Routledge and Kegan Paul, 1970), p. 69.
13 Quoted in John Lauber, *Sir Walter Scott* (New York: Twayne, 1966), p. 50.
14 Quoted in Johnson, p. 50.
15 Hayden, p. 117. Much of this review was written by Scott himself.
16 An even more ambitious project, R. Warner's three-volume *Illustrations, Critical, Historical, Biographical, and Miscellaneous, of Novels by the Author of Waverley*, was also appearing between 1821 and 1824.
17 Johnson, pp. 573, 1185−7.
18 F.A. Pottle, 'The Power of Memory in Boswell and Scott,' in A. Norman Jeffares, ed., *Scott's Mind and Art* (Edinburgh: Oliver and Boyd, 1969), pp. 250, 251.
19 Marcia Allentuck, 'Scott and the Picturesque,' in Alan Bell, ed., *Scott Bicentenary Essays* (Edinburgh and London: Scottish Academic Press, 1973), p. 191.
20 Jane Millgate, *Walter Scott: The Making of the Novelist* (Toronto: University of Toronto Press, 1984), p. 71.

21 James Reed, *Sir Walter: Landscape and Locality* (London: Athlone Press, 1980), p. 10.
22 I am referring here to the original intention. Jane Millgate, *Walter Scott*, p. 172, has recently clarified the vexed question of the time-setting of this novel: 'The truth of the matter is that while the manuscript of the novel, the first edition of 1819, and all subsequent editions for the next ten years set its events two or three years *before* the Union, the 1830 *magnum opus* edition transposes the action to two or three years *after* the Union.'
23 W.S. Crockett, *The Scott Originals* (London and Edinburgh: Foulis Press, 1912), p. 251.
24 Hart, p. 328.
25 Jane Millgate, 'Two Versions of Regional Romance: Scott's *The Bride of Lammermoor* and Hardy's *Tess of the d'Urbervilles*,' *Studies in English Literature*, 17 (1977), 730.
26 Alexander M. Ross's excellent monograph, *The Impact of the Picturesque on Nineteenth-Century British Fiction* (Waterloo, Ont.: Wilfrid Laurier University Press, 1986), appeared after my own work had been completed. It contains a valuable chapter on Scott and the picturesque, and other chapters on Charlotte Brontë, Eliot, and Hardy. It is not, of course, directly concerned with regionalism, but as a perceptive examination of the pictorial influence on landscape description in fiction it provides a

stimulating complement to the present volume.

3 / EMILY BRONTË

1 Winifred Gérin, *Emily Brontë: A Biography* (Oxford: Clarendon Press, 1971), pp. 21, 27.
2 John Hewish, *Emily Brontë: A Critical Biographical Study* (London: Macmillan, 1969), p. 120.
3 Gérin, pp. 29, 49.
4 Q.D. Leavis, 'A Fresh Approach to "Wuthering Heights",' in F.R. and Q.D. Leavis, *Lectures in America* (London: Chatto and Windus, 1969), p. 150. See also the whole of appendix D, ' "Wuthering Heights" and "The Bride of Lammermoor".'
5 Florence Swithin Day, *The Sources of 'Wuthering Heights'* (Cambridge: Heffer, 1937), p. 3.
6 Ian Jack, introduction to *Wuthering Heights* (World's Classics edition. Oxford: Oxford University Press, 1981), pp. viii–ix.
7 Northrop Frye, *Anatomy of Criticism* (Princeton: Princeton University Press, 1957), p. 304; Arnold Kettle, *An Introduction to the English Novel* (2 vols. London: Hutchinson, 1951–3), I, 140.
8 Leavis, pp. 149–50; Kettle, I, 139.
9 Barbara Hardy, *Wuthering Heights* (Oxford: Blackwell, 1963), p. 4; Terry Eagleton, *Myths of Power: A Marxist Study of the Brontës* (London: Macmillan, 1975), pp. 101, 102.
10 Elizabeth Gaskell, *The Life of Charlotte Brontë* [1857] (Everyman edi-

tion. London: Dent, 1966), p. 129.
11 Quoted in Miram Allott, ed., *The Brontës: The Critical Heritage* (London: Routledge and Kegan Paul, 1974), pp. 220, 221.
12 Quoted in ibid., p. 435n.
13 Kettle, I, 139; V.S. Pritchett, in Richard Lettis and William E. Morris, eds, *A Wuthering Heights Handbook* (New York: Odyssey Press, 1961), p. 71.
14 Ernest A. Baker, *The History of the English Novel* (10 vols. London: Witherby, 1937), VIII, 70.
15 An exception is Herbert Dingle, *The Mind of Emily Brontë* (London: Allen and Unwin, 1941), p. 17.
16 David Cecil, *Early Victorian Novelists* [1934] (Harmondsworth: Pelican Books, 1948), p. 116.
17 Phyllis Bentley, *The English Regional Novel* (P.E.N. Books. London: Allen and Unwin, 1941), p. 17.
18 John Cowper Powys, 'Emily Brontë,' in his *Suspended Judgments* [1916] (London: Village Press, 1975), p. 324.
19 See Edward Thomas, *The Country* (London: Batsford, 1913), p. 31.
20 Quoted in Allott, p. 246.
21 Leavis, p. 106.
22 See especially James Hafley, 'The Villain in *Wuthering Heights*,' *Nineteenth-Century Fiction*, 13 (December 1958), 199–215, and Leavis's comment, p. 86. For a more perceptive but ultimately (I think) extreme critique of Nellie, see Brian Crick, 'On Valuing *Wuthering Heights*,' *Compass* (University

of Alberta), no. 6 (Spring 1979),
23–36, and no. 7 (Autumn 1979),
23–45.

23 Mark Schorer, 'Fiction and the
"Matrix of Analogy",' *Kenyon Review*, 11 (Autumn 1949), 549.

24 The phrases are, respectively, from
W.A. Craik, *The Brontë Novels*
(London: Methuen, 1968), p. 40,
and Derek Traversi, 'The Brontë
Sisters and "Wuthering Heights",'
in Boris Ford, ed., *From Dickens
to Hardy* (Pelican Guide to English
Literature, vol. VI. Harmondsworth: Pelican Books, 1966), p. 265.

25 Walter E. Anderson, 'The Lyrical
Form of *Wuthering Heights*,'
University of Toronto Quarterly, 47
(Winter 1977/8), 113.

26 Kettle, I, 154.

27 Anderson, pp. 114, 115.

28 Ibid., p. 112.

29 Tom Winnifrith, *The Brontës* (New
York: Macmillan, 1977), p. 63.

4 / URBANISM, REALISM,
AND REGION

1 Kathleen Tillotson, *Novels of the
Eighteen-Forties* (London: Oxford University Press, 1961), p. 90.
Terry Eagleton, in *Myths of
Power: A Marxist Study of the
Brontës* (London: Macmillan,
1975), has objected to what he calls
the 'facetious indulgence of those
fanciful compound epithets' (p. 48),
but I can see nothing fanciful about
them. On the contrary, they insist
upon a regional differentiation
that is specific and particular.

2 Q.D. Leavis, 'A Fresh Approach to
"Wuthering Heights",' in F.R. and
Q.D. Leavis, *Lectures in America*
(London: Chatto & Windus, 1969),
p. 99.

3 John Geoffrey Sharps, *Mrs Gaskell's Observation and Invention*
(Fontwell, Sussex: Linden Press,
1970), p. 187.

4 *The Letters of Mrs Gaskell*, ed.,
J.A.V. Chapple and Arthur Pollard (Manchester: Manchester University Press, 1965), p. 508.

5 'The Last Generation in England,'
Sartain's Magazine, 5 (July
1849), 45.

6 Ibid., p. 47.

7 *Letters*, p. 537; Arthur Pollard, *Mrs
Gaskell: Novelist and Biographer*
(Manchester: Manchester Univer-
sity Press, 1965), p. 62.

8 Humphrey Repton, *The Art of
Landscape Painting*, ed. John Nolen
(Boston: Houghton Mifflin, 1907),
p. 51.

9 Angus Easson, who asserts in
general that 'the Knutsford background of her work has been exaggerated,' similarly argues that
'Hollingford is not Knutsford' and
offers valid evidence that, towards
the end of *Wives and Daughters*,
Gaskell 'had Warwickshire in
mind' *(Elizabeth Gaskell* [London:
Routledge and Kegan Paul, 1979],
pp. 3, 187). He ignores, however,
the specific connections with
Knutsford noted by Winifred Gérin
(Elizabeth Gaskell: A Biography
[Oxford: Clarendon Press, 1975],
p. 289).

10 Edgar Wright, *Mrs Gaskell: The Basis for Reassessment* (London: Oxford University Press, 1965), pp. 14, 116, 133. The name of Helstone, it seems worth noting here, may derive from Charlotte Brontë's *Shirley.*

11 Sharps, pp. 175–7, 183–4.

12 *The George Eliot Letters,* ed. Gordon S. Haight (7 vols. New Haven: Yale University Press, 1954–5), II, 86.

13 Wright, p. 191.

14 See especially *Letters,* p. 494

15 Harriet Kravitz Morris, 'Authorial Control of Sympathy for the Social Offender in Selected Novels by Elizabeth Gaskell and George Eliot,' unpublished PH D. dissertation, University of Toronto, 1979, p. 290.

16 Gordon S. Haight, *George Eliot: A Biography* (Oxford: Clarendon Press, 1968), pp. 15, 21, 34.

17 Henry Auster, *Local Habitations: Regionalism in the Early Novels of George Eliot* (Cambridge, Mass.: Harvard University Press, 1970), p. 25.

5 / R.D. BLACKMORE

1 Quoted in Waldo Hilary Dunn, *R.D. Blackmore, The Author of 'Lorna Doone'* (London: Robert Hale, 1956), p. 180.

2 Max Keith Sutton, *R.D. Blackmore* (Boston: Twayne, 1979), p. 24.

3 Quoted in William E. Buckler, 'Blackmore's Novels before "Lorna Doone",' *Nineteenth-Century Fiction,* 10 (December 1955), 179.

4 Sutton reveals that Blackmore is on record in a letter as describing Bulwer-Lytton as 'the greatest writer of the century' (p. 37).

5 See Sutton's study for the most detailed and original discussion of these mythic patterns in Blackmore.

6 Quoted in Buckler, p. 170.

7 See Dunn, pp. 139, 274; Kenneth Budd, *The Last Victorian: R.D. Blackmore and His Novels* (London: Centaur Press, 1960), pp. 57–8; and Sally Jones, 'A Lost Leader: R.D. Blackmore and *The Maid of Sker,*' *Anglo-Welsh Review,* 25 (Autumn 1975), 32.

8 Blackmore uses the spelling 'Bagworthy' throughout *Lorna Doone.* Other writers sometimes write 'Badgeworthy,' sometimes 'Badgworthy.' In the interests of consistency I follow the practice of modern Ordnance Survey maps and use 'Badgworthy.' The traditional local pronunciation is 'Badgery.'

9 'Wanderings on Exmoor,' *Fraser's Magazine,* 56 (October 1857), 492.

10 For Blackmore's specific acknowledgement of being aware of this version, see J. Charles Cox, 'The Doones of Exmoor,' *Athenaeum* (26 August 1905), 274.

11 For a judicious examination of the whole subject of Blackmore and the Doones, see S.H. Burton, 'Exmoor of the Doones,' in John Coleman-Cooke, ed., *Exmoor* (National Parks Guide, no. 8. London: Her Majesty's Stationery Office, 1970), pp. 59–67.

12 See F.J. Snell, *The Blackmore Country* (London: Black, 1906), p. 225.

13 John Buchan, 'Literature and Topography,' in his *Homilies and Recreations* (London: Nelson, 1926), p. 198.

14 Robert C. Gordon, *Under Which King? A Study of the Scottish Waverly Novels* (Edinburgh: Oliver and Boyd, 1969), p. 10.

15 Hugh Walpole, 'Scott and the Historical Novel,' in H.J.C. Grierson, ed., *Sir Walter Scott Today: Some Retrospective Essays and Studies* (London: Constable, 1932), p. 175.

16 Dunn, p. 21.

17 An older study of Blackmore still worth consulting, in addition to the books and articles referred to above, is Q.G. Burris, *Richard Doddridge Blackmore* (Urbana: University of Illinois Studies in Language and Literature, 1930).

6 / THOMAS HARDY

1 Thomas Hardy, *The Life and Work of Thomas Hardy*, ed. Michael Millgate (Athens: University of Georgia Press, 1985), p. 192. Subsequent references as *Life* in text.

2 F.W. Morgan, 'Three Aspects of Regional Consciousness,' *Sociological Review*, 31 (1939), 84.

3 William Archer, 'Conversation II. With Mr. Thomas Hardy,' in his *Real Conversations* (London: Heinemann, 1904), p. 31.

4 Robert Gittings, *Young Thomas Hardy* (London: Heinemann, 1975), p. 3.

5 W.M. Conacher, 'Thomas Hardy – Regional Novelist,' *Queen's Quarterly*, 35 (February 1928), 276.

6 See Archer, pp. 33–4, and *Life*, pp. 32–3.

7 Richard H. Taylor, ed., *The Personal Notebooks of Thomas Hardy* (London: Macmillan, 1978), p. 60.

8 Raymond Williams, *The Country and the City* (London: Chatto and Windus, 1973), p. 253. While I differ from Williams on his narrow, negative definition of regionalism, many of his insights into regional writers are extremely valuable.

9 This 'General Preface' appeared in the first volume of the Wessex edition (1912). It is conveniently reprinted in Harold Orel, ed., *Thomas Hardy's Personal Writings* (Lawrence: University Press of Kansas, 1966), pp. 44–50.

10 'The Rev. William Barnes, B.D.,' reprinted in Orel, pp. 105–5.

11 Ian Gregor, *The Great Web: The Form of Hardy's Major Fiction* (Totowa, NJ: Rowman and Littlefield, 1974), p. 47.

12 For a more detailed examination of this topic, see my 'Thomas Hardy and the Name "Wessex",' *English Language Notes*, 6 (September 1968), 42–4.

13 Morgan, p. 89.

14 John Holloway, *The Victorian Sage* (London: Macmillan, 1953), p. 259.

15 This map is reproduced in the *Countryman*, 13 (July 1936), 488–9.

16 Waveney Girvan, introduction to his edition, *Eden Phillpotts: An*

Assessment and a Tribute (London: Hutchinson, 1953), p. 20.

17 Orel, pp. 118–19.

18 Denys Kaye-Robinson, *Hardy's Wessex Re-appraised* (New York: St Martin's Press, 1971), p. 57.

19 I am indebted to Dr Ila Goody for first drawing my attention to these aspects of *The Mayor of Casterbridge;* see her study of the novel in 'Image, Symbol and Motif in Six Novels of Thomas Hardy,' unpublished PH D dissertation, University of Toronto, 1974.

20 Thom Gunn, 'Hardy and the Ballads,' *Agenda,* 10 (Thomas Hardy Special Issue, Spring/Summer 1972), 33.

21 Albert J. Guerard, *Thomas Hardy* [1949] (New York: New Directions, 1964), p. 31.

22 David Cecil, *Hardy the Novelist* [1943] (London: Constable, 1960), p. 42.

23 Lennart A. Björk, ed., *The Literary Notes of Thomas Hardy, Volume 1: Notes* (Göteborg, Sweden: Acta Universitatis Gothoburgensis, 1974), p. 357.

24 See Jane Millgate, 'Two Versions of Regional Romance: Scott's *The Bride of Lammermoor* and Hardy's *Tess of the d'Urbervilles,'* *Studies in English Literature,* 17 (1977), 729–38.

25 See Frank Chapman, 'Hardy the Novelist,' *Scrutiny,* 3 (June 1934), 29.

26 See Michael Millgate, *Thomas Hardy: A Biography* (New York: Random House, 1982), p. 508.

27 See Richard L. Purdy and Michael Millgate, eds, *The Collected Letters of Thomas Hardy,* volume II (Oxford: Clarendon Press, 1980), p. 54.

28 Ibid., p. 142.

29 Taylor, p. 24.

30 Because of the rearrangement of these stories in the Wessex Edition, this preface does not appear in modern editions of *Life's Little Ironies.* It may be found in Orel, p. 30.

31 See J.M. Barrie, 'Thomas Hardy, Historian of Wessex,' *Contemporary Review,* 56 (July 1889), 57–66.

32 Richard L. Purdy and Michael Millgate, eds, *The Collected Letters of Thomas Hardy,* volume I (Oxford: Clarendon Press, 1978), p. 237.

33 Kristin Brady, *The Short Stories of Thomas Hardy: Tales of Past and Present* (London: Macmillan, 1982), p. 143.

34 David Lodge, *Language of Fiction* (London: Routledge and Kegan Paul; New York: Columbia University Press, 1966), p. 170.

35 Morgan, p. 79.

36 Chapman, p. 31.

37 Joseph Warren Beach, *The Technique of Thomas Hardy* (Chicago: University of Chicago Press, 1922), p. 98; John Paterson, *The Making of 'The Return of the Native'* (Berkley and Los Angeles: University of California Press, 1960), p. 122.

38 See Simon Gatrell, 'Hardy the Creator: *Far from the Madding*

Crowd,' in Dale Kramer, ed., *Critical Approaches to the Fiction of Thomas Hardy* (London: Macmillan, 1979), p. 84.

39 See Arnold Kettle, *An Introduction to the English Novel* (2 vols. London: Hutchinson, 1951-3), II, 49-62, and Douglas Brown, *Thomas Hardy* (London: Longmans, 1954).

40 Gregor, p. 38.

7 / REGIONAL REALISM

1 Arnold Bennett, 'The Novels of Eden Phillpotts,' in Samuel Hynes, ed., *The Author's Craft and Other Critical Writings of Arnold Bennett* (Lawrence: University of Nebraska Press, 1968), p. 167.

2 The Dartmoor series comprises the following: *Children of the Mist* (1898), *Sons of the Morning* (1900), *The River* (1902), *The Secret Woman* (1905), *The Portreeve* (1906), *The Whirlwind* (1907), *The Mother* (1908), *The Virgin in Judgment* (1908), *The Three Brothers* (1909), *The Thief of Virtue* (1910), *Demeter's Daughter* (1911), *The Beacon* (1911), *The Forest on the Hill* (1912, reprinted as *The Forest*), *Widecombe Fair* (1913), *Brunel's Tower* (1915), *Miser's Money* (1920), *Orphan Dinah* (1920), *Children of Men* (1923), *Fun of the Fair* (1928, short stories), *Brother Man* (1928, short stories). The last two volumes, while part of their contents consisted of short stories from earlier collections, were first pub-

lished in the Widecombe Edition (London: Macmillan, 1927-8), which reprinted the eighteen novels in a uniform series with revised and often abridged texts. Here novels originally divided into separate books were given continuous chapter numbers, while some chapters were either omitted or run together. To avoid confusion, I shall therefore in this instance cite edition and page reference for quotations.

3 Newman Flower, ed., *The Journals of Arnold Bennett* (3 vols. London: Cassell, 1932), I, 96-7.

4 F.J. Snell, *The Blackmore Country* (London: Black, 1906), p. vii.

5 *Journals*, I, 96-7. For the opposing view, see Waveney Girvan, ed., *Eden Phillpotts: An Assessment and a Tribute* (London: Hutchinson, 1953), p. 19. The point was first cleared up by Lucien Leclaire in *Le Roman régionaliste dans les Iles Britanniques, 1800-1950* (Paris: Société d'édition 'Les Belles Lettres,' 1954), pp. 133-4.

6 *Sons of the Morning* (London: Methuen, 1900), p. 61.

7 *Children of the Mist* (London: Methuen, 1903), pp. 100-1, 147. The first passage quoted here is omitted from some later editions.

8 For useful maps illustrating this, see the end-papers of Girvan's collection, and Kenneth F. Day, *Eden Phillpotts on Dartmoor* (Newton Abbot: David and Charles, 1981), p. 55.

9 *The Virgin in Judgment* (New York:

Moffat, Yard, 1908), p. 5.

10 *The Portreeve* (London: Methuen, 1906), p. 108.

11 *The Secret Woman* (London: Collins, n.d.), p. 10; *The Whirlwind* (London: Macmillan, 1928), p. 292; *The Beacon* (London: Newnes, 1915), p. 6.

12 *Children of the Mist*, p. 154. For the comment about romantic conventions and Scott, see Bennett, *Journals*, I, 96. However, Phillpotts was later to write 'romances,' though he was careful to separate them from his novels. *The Lovers*, for instance, a romance of Dartmoor set in the eighteenth century, was not included in the Dartmoor series.

13 *From the Angle of 88* (London: Hutchinson, 1959), p. 127.

14 *The Three Brothers* (London: Hutchinson, 1909), p. 305.

15 For a good discussion of Phillpotts, see chapter 4 of Glen Cavaliero's *The Rural Tradition in the English Novel, 1900–1939* (London: Macmillan, 1977).

16 *Three Ways Home: An Experiment in Autobiography* (New York: Harper, 1937), pp. 4–5.

17 Ibid., p. 65.

18 Cavaliero, p. 80.

19 *Three Ways Home*, p. 103.

20 Ibid., pp. 122–3.

21 Ibid., p. 249.

22 Ibid., p. 248.

23 Ibid., p. 252.

24 See *All the Books of My Life: A Bibliography* (London: Cassell, 1956), p. 51.

25 *Three Ways Home*, p. 142.

26 Ibid., p. 29.

27 R. Thurston Hopkins, *Sheila Kaye-Smith and the Weald Country* (London: Cecil Palmer, 1925), p. 186.

28 For another treatment of Kaye-Smith, see Dorothea Walker, *Sheila Kaye-Smith* (Boston: Twayne, 1980).

8 / REGIONAL ROMANCE

1 Phyllis Bentley, *The English Regional Novel* (P.E.N. Books. London: Allen and Unwin, 1941), p. 37.

2 The 'later books' are *Beautiful End* (1918), *The Splendid Fairing* (1919), *Trumpet in the Dust* (1921), *The Things Which Belong—* (1925), *He-Who-Came?* (1930), and a collection of short stories, *The Wisdom of the Simple* (1937).

3 The only literary study of Holme's work that is of any consequence – and it is excellent – is 'A Land of One's Own: Constance Holme,' the tenth chapter of Glen Cavaliero's *The Rural Tradition in the English Novel, 1900–1939* (London: Macmillan, 1977).

4 Cavaliero, p. 145.

5 Ibid., pp. 145–6.

6 There has been some confusion on this point. Keith Sagar's *D.H. Lawrence Handbook* (Manchester: Manchester University Press; New York: Barnes and Noble, 1982) contains an article by Bridget Pugh, 'Location in Lawrence's fiction and travel writings,' in which the Devil's Chair is identified

as an outcrop on the Wrekin: '[Lawrence] renamed Hell Gate (the Devil's Chair) and Heaven Gate (the Angel's Chair) but retained the name Needle's Eye for local landmarks' (p. 260; and see map on p. 278). But the Devil's Chair is itself a real location on the Stiperstones which fits better in terms of distance and geographical detail. Besides, Lawrence is known to have visited the Devil's Chair while staying with Frederick Carter at Pontesbury (see Edward Nehls, *D.H. Lawrence: A Composite Biography* [3 vols. Madison: University of Wisconsin Press, 1957–9], II, 317–18). Lawrence may have telescoped the two locations for imaginative purposes, but the main inspiration is from the Devil's Chair itself. In *St Mawr and Other Stories*, edited by Brian Finney (Cambridge: Cambridge University Press, 1983), the correct identification is made, and in addition Aldecar Chapel is tentatively identified with the chapel of Lordshill, Mary Webb's God's Little Mountain in *Gone to Earth*. But Finney makes no comment on either the Angel's Chair or the Needle's Eye. To complicate matters still further, 'Aldecar' is a name transferred from Lawrence's Nottinghamshire countryside (see G.H. Neville, *A Memoir of D.H. Lawrence (The Betrayal)*, ed., Carl Baron [Cambrige University Press, 1981], p. 4).

7 E.T. [Jessie Chambers], *D.H. Law-*

rence: A Personal Record* [1935] (London: Frank Cass, 1965), p. 103.

8 Gladys Mary Coles, *The Flower of Light: A Biography of Mary Webb* (London: Duckworth, 1978), pp. 23, 25.

9 Thomas Moult, *Mary Webb: Her Life and Work* (London: Cape, 1932), pp. 164–5.

10 See Coles, pp. 42, 67–8, and Bernard Steff, *My Dearest Acquaintance: A Biographical Sketch of Mary and Henry Webb* (Ludlow: King's Bookshop, 1977), p. 17.

11 See Moult, pp. 16, 20.

12 Quoted in Coles, p. 234.

13 Charlotte S. Burne, ed., *Shropshire Folk Lore: A Sheaf of Gleanings from the collections of Georgina F. Jackson* (2 vols [continuous pagination], London: Trübner, 1883), p. 167.

14 Coles, p. 265.

15 In addition to the studies alluded to in this section, other work on Mary Webb includes Dorothy P.H. Wrenn, *Goodbye to Morning: A Biographical Study of Mary Webb* (Shrewsbury: Wilding and Son, 1964); Gordon Dickins, *Mary Webb: A Narrative Bibliography of Her Life and Works* (Shrewsbury: Shropshire Libraries, 1981); and John Studley, 'The Novels of Mary Webb: A Reading and Interpretation,' unpublished PH D dissertation, University of Toronto, 1977. A feminist study of Webb, Michèle Aina Barale's *Daughters and Lovers: The Life and Writing of Mary Webb* (Middle-

town, Conn.: Wesleyan University Press, 1986), appeared after the present chapter was completed.

9 / D.H. LAWRENCE

1 'Nottingham and the Mining Countryside,' in Edward D. McDonald, ed., *Phoenix: The Posthumous Papers of D.H. Lawrence* (London: Heinemann, 1936), p. 135.
2 Emily Lawrence, in Edward Nehls, *D.H. Lawrence: A Composite Biography* (3 vols. Madison: University of Wisconsin Press, 1957–9), I, 14.
3 Ibid.
4 Ada Lawrence, in ibid.
5 Ibid., I, 52,
6 E.T. [Jessie Chambers], *D.H. Lawrence: A Personal Record* [1935] (London: Frank Cass, 1965), p. 38.
7 Harry T. Moore, ed., *The Collected Letters of D.H. Lawrence* (2 vols [continuous pagination]. New York: Viking, 1962), pp. 952, 953.
8 For a useful and fair discussion of this subject, see A.P. and C.P. Griffin, 'A social and economic history of Eastwood and the Nottinghamshire mining country,' in Keith Sagar, ed., *A D.H. Lawrence Handbook* (Manchester: Manchester University Press; New York: Barnes and Noble, 1982), pp. 127–63.
9 'Nottingham and the Mining Countryside,' *Phoenix*, p. 135.
10 Ibid.
11 See 'Study of Thomas Hardy,' *Phoenix*, p. 411.

12 'Autobiographical Fragment,' in Warren Roberts and Harry T. Moore, eds, *Phoenix II* (London: Heinemann, 1968), p, 595.
13 Raymond Williams, *The English Novel from Dickens to Lawrence* (London: Chatto and Windus, 1970), pp. 170–1.
14 E.T. [Jessie Chambers], p. 94.
15 For *Cranford* and *Lorna Doone*, see ibid., pp. 96, 102; for Prior and Phillpotts, see *Letters*, pp. 87, 91, 205.
16 E.T. [Jessie Chambers], p. 103.
17 Ibid., p. 91.
18 See ibid., p. 110, and Sagar, p. 73.
19 'Study of Thomas Hardy,' *Phoenix*, pp. 410, 411, 419.
20 Ibid., p. 439.
21 F.R. Leavis, *Thought, Words and Creativity* (London: Chatto and Windus, 1976), p. 139.
22 E.D. Mackerness, ed., *Journals of George Sturt, 1890–1927* (2 vols [continuous pagination]. Cambridge: Cambridge University Press, 1967), p. 551.
23 Stephen Miko, *Toward 'Women in Love': The Emergence of a Lawrentian Aesthetic* (New Haven: Yale University Press, 1971), p. 180.
24 See John Worthen, *D.H. Lawrence and the Idea of the Novel* (London: Macmillan, 1979), pp. 105–7, and his introduction to *The Lost Girl* (Cambridge: Cambridge University Press, 1981).
25 See Michael Squires's discussion in *The Pastoral Novel: Studies in George Eliot, Thomas Hardy, and D.H. Lawrence* (Charlottesville:

University Press of Virginia, 1974).

10 / JOHN COWPER POWYS

1 Richard Perceval Graves, *The Powys Brothers* (London: Routledge and Kegan Paul, 1983), p. 9.
2 See Raymond Garlick, 'Powys in Gwynedd: The Last Years,' in Belinda Humfrey, ed., *Essays on John Cowper Powys* (Cardiff: University of Wales Press, 1972), p. 305.
3 G. Wilson Knight, 'Sadism and the Seraphic,' in Belinda Humfrey, ed., *Recollections of the Powys Brothers* (London: Peter Owen, 1980), p. 226.
4 Angus Wilson, 'John Cowper Powys as a Novelist,' *Powys Review*, 1 (Spring 1977), 23.
5 Glen Cavaliero, 'Recollections of John Cowper Powys,' in Humfrey, *Recollections*, p. 253.
6 *Letters from John Cowper Powys to C. Benson Roberts* (London: Village Press, 1975), p. 15.
7 Bernard Jones, 'Style and the Man,' in Humfrey, *Essays*, pp. 153–4.
8 '"Preface" or anything you like to *Porius*,' *Powys Newsletter*, no. 4. (1974–5), 8.
9 In *John Cowper Powys in Search of a Landscape* (London: Macmillan, 1982), p. 13, C.A. Coates quotes this passage and compares it with an earlier scene in *Wood and Stone*.
10 See the essay on Hardy in *Enjoyment of Literature* (New York: Simon and Schuster, 1938), p. 439.
11 Compare also Powys's description of

the cottages at King's Barton a few paragraphs earlier with the immediately preceding account of Casterbridge in Hardy's novel.
12 *Weymouth Sands* was first published in England with fictional names under the title of *Jobber Skald*. This does not constitute an exception to my argument, however, since the alterations were only made because Powys feared similar accusations of libel to those he had already suffered when he published *A Glastonbury Romance*.
13 H.P. Collins, *John Cowper Powys: Old Earth Man* (London: Barrie and Rockcliff, 1966), p. 17.
14 Knight, *Saturnian Quest: A Study of the Prose Works of John Cowper Powys* (London: Methuen, 1964), p. 51; Coates, pp. x, 119,
15 'My Welsh Home,' in *Obstinate Cymric* [1947] (London: Village Press, 1973), p. 81.
16 Quoted in *Powys Newsletter*, no. 4 [*Porious* issue] (1974–5), 6. This issue also contains Joseph Slater's 'Porius Restauratus,' an invaluable account of the original, unabridged manuscript, with summaries of the omitted sections.
17 George Eliot, '[Three Novels],' in Thomas Pinney, ed., *Essays of George Eliot* (London: Routledge and Kegan Paul, 1963), p. 326.
18 Malcolm Elwin, ed., *Letters of John Cowper Powys to his Brother Llewelyn, Vol II, 1925–1939* (London: Village Press, 1975 [so dated, but in fact published much later]),

p. 189.

19 *Rabelais* (London: Bodley Head, 1948), pp. 96–7.

20 'My Welsh Home,' *Obstinate Cymric*, p. 79.

21 *Rabelais*, p. 294.

11 / CONCLUSION

1 V.S. Pritchett, *The Living Novel* (London: Chatto and Windus, 1946), p. 43.

2 For an excellent discussion of this subject, see Jeremy Hooker, *Poetry of Place: Essays and Reviews, 1970–1981* (Manchester: Carcanet Press, 1982).

3 Northrop Frye, *The Secular Scripture: A Study of the Structure of Romance* (Cambridge, Mass.: Harvard University Press, 1976),

p. 15.

4 See Gladys Mary Coles, *The Flower of Light: A Biography of Mary Webb* (London: Duckworth, 1978), p. 326.

5 See Tom Winnifrith, *The Brontës* (New York: Macmillan, 1977), p. 54, and Glen Cavaliero, *The Rural Tradition in the English Novel, 1900–1939* (London: Macmillan, 1977), p. 27.

6 Cavaliero, p. 139.

7 Raymond Williams, *The Country and the City* (London: Chatto and Windus, 1973), p. 253.

8 D.H. Lawrence, 'Pan in America,' in *Phoenix: The Posthumous Papers of D.H. Lawrence*, ed. Edward D. McDonald (London: Heinemann, 1936), p. 27.

INDEX